DENMARK

PRUSSIA

•Berlin
•Potsdam

•Hanover

HOLLAND

•Antwerp
Terneuzen
•end
•Brussels

BELGIUM

•Dusseldorf
Cologne
•Bonn

Rhine

Aix-la-
Chapelle

Coblenz

LUX

1914

G
E
R
M
A
N
Y

Eisenach• •Gotha

•Meiningen

•Coburg

Kronberg
Hochheim •Frankfurt
Bingen•   Main
Mayence •Aschaffenburg •Wurzburg
Darmstadt

•Baden-Baden

•Munich

AUSTRIA

•Innsbruck

Lucerne

SWITZERLAND

C E

•Baveno

Aix-les-Bains •

Grande Chartreuse •

•Milan

I
T
A
L
Y

•Florence

Menton
Grasse •   •Nice
•Cannes

Hyères

All her life, from the time of her earliest
childhood in Kensington Palace to her long
years of widowhood, Queen Victoria drew
and painted. She was a passionate recorder of
everything around her.

   Queen Victoria's Sketchbook is entirely
illustrated with her own work, chosen with the
permission of Her Majesty The Queen from the
many albums in her possession. It presents an
important and wholly delightful dimension of
one of history's most famous characters.
Victoria shows us her rapturous pleasure in the
ballet and opera, her coronation and wedding,
the ever-increasing family, and her trips
abroad. We see the heather purples and mauves
of the 'dear Highland hills' around Balmoral;
the trees of Windsor Great Park; the golden
haze over the Solent from the Alcove at
Osborne where the Queen liked to work in
summer.

   Marina Warner's narrative draws on
contemporary accounts and Queen Victoria's
own journals to describe her private life and the
part her painting and her subjects played in it.
From the pictures and the text, the direct and
charmingly naive force of Queen Victoria's
character emerges, showing her as gayer,
lighter and much less severe than the usual
image of the redoubtable creator of the
Victorian Age.

The illustration on the following page shows Queen Victoria reviewing troops at Cobham in 1847, and was painted by Count D'Orsay

Victoria Travels

*Journeys of Queen Victoria between 1830
and 1900, with Extracts from Her
Journal*

by

DAVID DUFF

Illustrated with Photographs from the
Private Albums of the Queen's Constant
Companions—H.R.H. Princess Beatrice and
John Brown, her Personal Attendant, and
contemporary drawings, paintings and
photographs from a variety of collections.

TAPLINGER PUBLISHING COMPANY
NEW YORK

First published in the United States in 1971
by Taplinger Publishing Co., Inc., New York, New York

Copyright © 1970 David Duff

International Standard Book Number 0-8008-7972-4

Library of Congress Catalog Card Number 70-133434

Printed in Great Britain

Acknowledgments

THE extracts from the Journal of Queen Victoria, and the letter from the Queen to her eldest daughter, the Crown Princess of Prussia, are reproduced by gracious permission of Her Majesty the Queen. My thanks are due to Macmillan & Co. Ltd. for permission to reproduce an extract from *Henry Ponsonby: His Life and Times* by Arthur Ponsonby; and to Mrs George Bainbridge for the extract from "The Absent Minded Beggar" from Rudyard Kipling's *Definitive Verse*.

I am indebted to many people and organisations for providing me with information and illustrations concerning Queen Victoria's visits and travels. Firstly to Her Majesty the Queen for gracious permission to reproduce four works of art from the Royal Collection; to Mr G. F. Collie, of Aberdeen, for placing at my disposal the photograph album of John Brown, the Queen's personal attendant; to Sir Richard Williams-Bulkeley for information concerning the Bulkeley Arms, Beaumaris; to Baron Franz Recum, of New York, for providing me with details about the life of Madame de Kolémine, Baroness de Bacheracht; to the Marquess of Anglesey for the hitherto unpublished picture of Plas Newydd; to Mr F. J. Cridlan for information about the Queen's visit to the Regent Hotel, Royal Leamington Spa, and for providing a contemporary print; to Mr Robert Walker, of the *Eastern Daily Press*, for notes about the Queen's first visit to Norfolk; to Mrs O. M. Bent for permission to reproduce the letter of her great-grandmother dealing with the Queen's visit to Plymouth; to Mr John Lewis, author of *Printed Ephemera*, and Mr F. G. King, of W. S. Cowell Ltd., for providing me with the sailing certificate of the steam packet *Columbine*; to Mr B. E. Fruer, of Deinhard & Co. Ltd., London, and Messrs J. Neuss, of Ingelheim, for information and illustrations relevant to the visit of the Queen to the vineyard of Herr G. M. Pabstmann at Hochheim; to Mr Anthony Terry, Central European Correspondent of *The Sunday Times*, for information and anecdotes regarding royal visits to Germany; to Mr Tony Standish, for the loan of the rare four volume work *The Life and Times of Queen Victoria*; to the National Portrait Gallery for the frontispiece; to the National Maritime Museum for "*Victory* and *Favourite* at Margate"; to Institut Belge, Brussels, for the photograph of Laeken Palace; to M. Georges Sirot for the photograph of Queen Victoria at Biarritz; to Country Life Ltd. for the view of Powis Castle; to the Irish Tourist Board for the picture of Ladies' View, Killarney; to the National Gallery of Ireland for the painting by Jonathan Fisher; to Evans Brothers Ltd. for illustrations from *My Memories of Six Reigns*, by Princess Marie Louise and *The Shy Princess* by David Duff; to the *Office Thermal et Touristique*, Aix-les-Bains, for their co-operation and for the picture of the statue of Queen Victoria; to The Royal Company of Archers for the painting by W. S. Cumming; and to Illustrated London News and the Radio Times Hulton Library for various illustrations from their collections.

The photographs from the album of H.R.H. Princess Beatrice (Princess Henry of Battenberg) are reproduced with the approval of her late Majesty, Queen Victoria Eugenia of Spain. The cartoons appearing on pages 57 and 123 are taken from the collection of George, Duke of Cambridge, part of which is in the possession of the author. (The then Prince George began the collection of cartoons lampooning the Queen and Prince Albert at the time of the scandal over his supposed affair with Lady Augusta Somerset, and of his liaison with Miss Louisa Fairbrother, who became Mrs FitzGeorge on her marriage to the Prince. For some years the relationship between the Queen and the Cambridges was most strained. Twenty years later, when the Prince had succeeded his father as Duke and been promoted to Commander-in-Chief, his affections began to wander. Mrs FitzGeorge threatened that, if his philandering did not cease, she would inform the Queen about the cartoons.) The Commemorative China and other pieces have been selected from the author's collection.

My thanks are due to my wife and to Major and Mrs T. B. Ellis for assistance in checking the manuscript, and to Mrs J. M. Rochester for typing it with care and patience.

DAVID DUFF

Weybread, October 1968–May, 1970

Contents

Introduction

TRAVEL was an essential part of life to Queen Victoria. First as an only child and later as a lonely widow, journeys were a substitute for the lack of close companions. There was always excitement at departure and thrill at arrival. She was tireless. In her mid seventies, on reaching her destination in Italy after a forty hour journey from Windsor, she immediately set out on an evening drive. She was impervious to wind, cold and rain and considered it somewhat of a joke to find herself in a puddle on the carriage seat. In the south of France she drove out when the mistral was blowing and returned looking like a miller, and quite undisturbed. Her only enemy was heat, when she wilted quickly and used ice buckets as an antidote. Ladies and gentlemen in attendance upon her, even when half her age, often suffered fatigue and acute physical discomfort, but she appeared not to notice this. On the other hand, she studied most carefully the welfare of horses and engine drivers.

Carriages remained her favourite form of locomotion and, as a young married woman, she made journeys of more than a hundred miles in a day. Special roomy vehicles, representing perambulating nurseries, were constructed to accommodate her young family and the nurses, and these were used for the visit to the Duke of Wellington at Walmer Castle in 1842. While she appreciated the convenience of trains, she imposed strict speed limits and stops were made so that she could dress and undress and take her meals. Largely as a consequence of the death of Dr Baly, the royal physician, in a derailment between Wimbledon and Malden in 1861, the doctor falling through the carriage floor and being mangled by the wheels, she was terrified of railway accidents. On a journey north, she despatched John Brown to the superintendent with a message that the speed of the train should be reduced. The message, as delivered, was: 'The Queen says the carriage was shaking like the very devil.'

As a child, she was a good sailor and recorded that she ate a mutton chop in a swell. However, on her way to Scotland in 1842, her yacht, *Royal George*, ran into a storm off the Yorkshire coast and she was very ill indeed. The memory of that experience lived on. She received little moral support from her husband, who assumed a pallid hue on approaching a vessel and did not return to normal complexion until he was well clear of it. In later life she paid strict attention to weather forecasts and would delay leaving

The Royal George, c. *1842*

for the Continent if rough conditions were expected. She would never put to sea on a Friday.

This mistrust of the sea was one of the reasons why she did not extend her travels beyond Europe. After the bitterness resulting from certain incidents in the American Civil War had died away, the suggestion was made that she should cross the Atlantic, but she declined on the grounds of age. Thoughts of Australia were limited to the threat that she would emigrate there if the rude remarks about her appearing in the newspapers of 1870, did not cease. Only the call of the East tempted her to leave Osborne and Balmoral. When the Indian servants, headed by the Munshi Abdul Karim, took over the mantle of John Brown, she was consumed with a longing to see India. Her chance came in the autumn of 1888. The children of the Duke and Duchess of Connaught were to rejoin their parents in Bombay and the Queen planned to take them herself. However the Empress Frederick, broken-hearted at the death of her husband, had arranged to visit Windsor for a rest and a change, and her mother did not like to disappoint her.

Considering the length of her reign, Queen Victoria saw comparatively little of England. Some counties she never visited at all and in these she was known as 'The Great Unseen'. Her knowledge of Wales was restricted to the north and the Irish did not see her between the year of the Prince

Consort's death and 1900. Yet the total mileage that she covered in the British Isles was high, owing to her set habit of making the bi-annual circuit of Osborne, Windsor and Balmoral. One hundred thousand is an approximation of the miles that she travelled on her trips to and from Scotland where, in all, she spent the equivalent of seven years of her life. Matters were so arranged that official visits to cities and towns in the Midlands and North were accomplished by making detours on the Scottish journey. The majority of her sight-seeing expeditions and visits to private houses took place in Scotland,[1] and many of the beauty-spots of England were neglected. Holidays, to her, meant the Continent.

In this area of travel the Queen made a clean break with tradition. Of her three immediate predecessors only one, George IV, had left British shores, and he only to visit his own principality of Hanover. After 1843 the royal yacht ferried the Sovereign back and forth across the Channel once, and sometimes twice, during the years when international conditions permitted. She broke with established custom by departing without first appointing a regent and, when travelling under an assumed and inferior title, took no responsible minister with her. At the time of her death plans were well advanced for her to take a spring holiday at Nice.

The Queen's first trips overseas were, primarily, visits to her relations. In France the family of King Louis Philippe had become intertwined with the Coburgs by marriage. 'Dear Uncle Leopold' reigned in Belgium. Her mother's and her husband's relatives were in force in Germany. Understandably, Prince Albert was anxious to show her the beauties of Coburg and she recorded that, as she approached the town, she felt that she was coming home. In the event, she had but narrowly escaped being born in Germany. The Duchess of Kent had spent much of her pregnancy at her former husband's castle at Amorbach in Lower Franconia. There the Duke, whose capacity for controlling financial matters was non-existent, spent all his money on interior decoration of the castle and lavish entertaining. Determined that his child should be born in England, he applied to his family for a loan to cover the expenses of the journey home. However each and everyone of them had suffered previously in this direction and no help was forthcoming. Time was running very short when, at last, a small sum arrived from Walter Allen, his trustee. At once a coach, piled high with luggage, left Amorbach for Dover. The Duke was on the box as the shortage of funds precluded engaging the services of a driver. One of the passengers was Charlotte von Siebold, midwife and qualified doctor, a precaution against the lurching of the coach inducing a premature birth.

[1] The life and journeys of Queen Victoria in Scotland were described in two volumes of extracts from her diary—*Leaves from the Journal of Our Life in the Highlands,* published in 1868, and *More Leaves,* in 1884. *Victoria in the Highlands,* a condensation of the two volumes, introduced and edited by David Duff, was published in 1968.

However Kensington Palace was reached without mishap. With such parents, it is readily understandable why Queen Victoria became such a hardened traveller.

As the years passed the call of Germany became less enticing. Three wars —the death of her daughter, Alice, Grand Duchess of Hesse—the bullyings of Bismarck—the antics of her Prussian grandson, William—the tragic end of the Emperor Frederick—the amorous and financial adventures of her brother-in-law, Duke Ernest of Coburg, added together, did not allow of her enjoying the peaceful recuperative periods that she found essential as a break from her arduous State duties. She therefore substituted holidays for family visits. She went to Baden-Baden, Lucerne, Baveno, Biarritz, Aix-les-Bains and Florence, and finally settled for the south of France.

Queen Victoria preferred to be mistress of her own household rather than a guest when on the Continent. She spent endless care over the hiring of villas and hotels, planning for a spring holiday beginning the previous summer. With her she took her bed and desk, her couch and mirror, and a gallery of family pictures. She drove out only in her own carriage, drawn by her own horses and, latterly, the donkey always went with her. The saloon carriages in which she travelled were her own property and the passengers on the royal train numbered between sixty and one hundred. Her slow progress along the Continental lines was a spectacle.

In only two periods of her life did travel lose its attraction for her. From the time of her accession until the birth of her second child, her days were filled with the novel duties of Queenship, her Coronation, the coming of Albert and her marriage, and nursery matters. The second period was immediately after the death of the Prince Consort.

The ever changing scenes which unrolled throughout a journey were a constant source of interest and delight to the Queen. She had her mother to thank for that. On her travels as a child, she was taught to observe, and make note of, the people and the countryside over which one day she would rule. When she was thirteen the Duchess of Kent gave her a diary so that she might keep a record of their tour of Wales. That diary was continued, with only minor interruptions, until the dawn of 1901.

The spelling of place names as practised by the Queen has been retained throughout. On occasion this is at variance with common usage today.

Journey One
1832

Early Days and a Holiday in Wales

THE education of Princess Victoria of Kent began when she was four. Her tutor was George Davys, a gentle clergyman who took the services in Kensington Palace chapel. Faced with plump, pink cheeks and steady, rebellious eyes, Davys decided that, if his life was to remain peaceful and unpunctuated by screams, tactful methods were preferable to those of coercion. He produced a box of letters and some coloured cards. On the cards he wrote simple words and placed them about the room. He then called out a word and it was the task of the Princess to find it with the aid of the letters. Davys proved a success and he stayed on as the Princess's preceptor until 1830, when he was appointed Dean of Chester. His place was taken by the Duchess of Northumberland, of whom the Queen was later to say that she 'drew a large salary for doing nothing'.

In 1825 Victoria passed from the care of her nurse, Mrs Brock, into that of Louise Lehzen, governess to Princess Feodore of Leiningen, daughter of the Duchess of Kent by her first marriage. Fräulein Lehzen was the daughter of a German Lutheran pastor. She was plain, highly strung and a victim of many pains, some real and some imagined. She was an exile and never allowed to forget it by many with whom she came into contact. Her table manners fell far short of the standard demanded by the code of the stately homes and it was pointed out to her that the habit of sprinkling caraway seeds over her food was looked upon with disfavour. Yet, buried deep in her, was a fount of understanding and affection. Convinced that her charge was destined to be a great Queen, she devoted all her thoughts and efforts to that end. She was successful. When she died in 1870, Queen Victoria said of her: 'She knew me from six months old and from my fifth to my eighteenth years devoted all her care and energies to me with most wonderful abnegation of self, never even taking one day's holiday. I adored her, though I was greatly in awe of her.'

In the days of Fräulein Lehzen education was forced into children in stronger and larger doses than it is today. Adult responsibilities came earlier

–midshipmen of twelve took part in the battle of Trafalgar. There were few holidays except for Saints' days and family anniversaries and lessons continued during visits to the seaside or to friends. The result was that those who could not absorb knowledge at the prescribed rate became either rebellious or ill. Victoria went through both phases. In the following generation of the Royal Family the same fate overtook 'Bertie', Prince of Wales, and, strangely enough, his mother did not seem to understand.

When the pressure was turned on, the Princess was quick to rebel. She later admitted that, when in a temper, she had 'set pretty well *all* at defiance'. The climax was a piercing shriek. She was then shepherded, by superior forces, to her bedroom where she was left to simmer down. At this stage there was only one person who could make her do that which she did not want to do without back answer or complaint. That was Stillman, an old soldier who had served her father. His task was to lead her donkey about the gardens of Kensington. Forty years later, when the Queen was a lonely widow, the voice of Stillman echoed back to her in the words of John Brown. The role of the gillie was easy to understand.

The progress achieved under the guidance of Lehzen can be seen in letters written by the Princess in 1825 and 1826. The first was to the house-keeper at Claremont, Prince Leopold's home, and the second to her uncle, the Duke of Sussex:

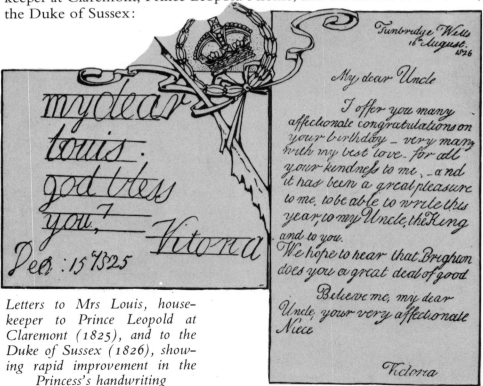

Letters to Mrs Louis, house-keeper to Prince Leopold at Claremont (1825), and to the Duke of Sussex (1826), showing rapid improvement in the Princess's handwriting

As the years passed the grip tightened. A twig of holly was pinned to the front of her dress to ensure that she kept her head up. While being dressed, Lehzen told tales of history, thus preventing her charge from chatting with the maids. Germanic theories throttled the common touch. When the Duchess of Clarence, who became Queen Adelaide, asked her niece what treat she would like on her birthday, Victoria answered that she would like to wash the windows.

Except for the dark interludes when she was confined in her bedroom for punishment, she was never alone for a moment of the day or night. She slept in her mother's room and Lehzen sat beside her until the Duchess retired. She never played alone with the few children who were asked to tea. She never came down stairs unless her hand was held.

Daily, now, a band of tutors reported at the Palace. Thomas Steward, writing master at Westminster school, taught writing and arithmetic, and John Bernard Sale, organist at St. Margaret's, singing. Monsieur Barez instructed in German, the first language to be introduced into the curriculum. Contrary to then current belief, German was not spoken outside the schoolroom and it was not until Queen Victoria became engaged to Prince Albert that her mother's native tongue was used in private conversation. The French teacher was Monsieur Grandineau and his success was such that his pupil came to speak it more grammatically than she did English. As her writings show, she never really mastered English grammar and her punctuation was an haphazard affair. Italian she did not study until later, when she became fascinated by opera. The love was fostered by Luigi Lablache, the great tenor who took over the training of the Princess's voice. Madame Bourdin and, later, Mlle. Marie Taglioni, taught dancing, and these were the lessons that Victoria liked best of all. She had exceptional grace and great stamina, but she was handicapped by a point of measurement—her body was too long for her legs. Another favourite subject was drawing, her instructor being academician Richard Westall.

Apart from the professionals, amateur educationalists weighed in with advice. Her mother's brother, Uncle Leopold, and his amanuensis, Baron Stockmar, hovered around, always ready with suggestions to ensure that the Coburg line prospered. The Duke of Sussex, perhaps the most cultured of the sons of George III, added scraps of Hebrew to the mental diet. Often a group of spectators would gather round to watch the Princess at her lessons, a custom which she found most disconcerting.

When her daughter was ten, the Duchess of Kent decided that it was time that the country was made aware of the state of her education. She accordingly invited the Bishops of Lincoln and London to attend at Kensington Palace and conduct a *viva voce* examination. Questions were put on 'a great variety of subjects', among them being chronology, scripture, history, arithmetic and Latin. Victoria survived the ordeal and the Duchess was

Princess Victoria on the sands at Broadstairs

puffed up with pride. Yet there was a price to pay. The plump, pink cheeks, from which once had come the piercing shrieks of rebellion, now became dull and pallid from the long concentration in the schoolroom. The Princess tossed sleepless in her bed at nights and, for no apparent reason, would dissolve into floods of tears. It was not until she began her travels and found mental relaxation and a changing scene that her vitality returned.

The Princess's childhood companions were her half-sister Feodore (a), who was twelve years her senior, and Victoire Conroy, who was the same age as herself. Her half-brother, Charles, born in 1807, spent most of his time in Germany and she did not meet him until 1826 when he visited England with the Princess's maternal grandmother, the Dowager Duchess of Saxe-Coburg-Saalfeld.

Victoire was the daughter of Sir John Conroy, the Comptroller of the Duchess of Kent's Household. An Irish adventurer, he was for ever scheming to promote his own ends by furthering those of the Duchess. His aim was that she should become Regent. His familiarity with her was the cause of scandal and, if in truth he was not her lover, he did little to deny the impression which he gave. He was sarcastic to Victoria and attempted to bully her. He teased her, saying that she had inherited the meanness of old Queen Charlotte. The Princess hated him and his influence in her home tainted her childhood, but at least he provided her with a girl, in the person of his daughter, with whom she could romp in the nursery. It was not until she grew old enough to sense the intrigues of Conroy that she realised that she must be careful in her conversation with Victoire.

Feodore was the only true confidante of the Princess and she missed her sorely when she turned to Germany to be married in 1828. Feodore was not happy in England. She described her period at Kensington Palace as 'the years of trial', and thanked God when they were over. Years afterwards she wrote to Queen Victoria: 'Not to have enjoyed the pleasures of youth is nothing, but to have been deprived of all intercourse, and not one cheerful thought in that dismal existence of ours was very hard. My only happy time was going out or driving with you and Lehzen; then I could speak and look as I liked. I escaped some years of imprisonment, which you, my poor darling sister, had to endure after I was married.'

Many of those who had short acquaintance with Queen Victoria when she was young later took advantage of this experience to write their impressions of her. These were rose-tinted, to say the least. They wrote of a laughing, happy girl romping in the haycocks, watering the flowers, gurgling at bishops, and building sand castles on the shore of Kent. They described her display of the love of truth, her thoughtfulness for others less fortunate than herself and her adherence to duty in terms so glowing that the Princess was set apart from other children. When Queen Victoria bluntly announced that her childhood had been unhappy, some treated her words with disbelief and others considered that it would have been better if they had been left unsaid.

The contributors who filled the columns of the home magazines of the second half of the nineteenth century with stories of the infallibility and faultlessness of the Queen-Empress, insisted on perfection as a guide to the standard expected to be maintained by the full range of middle class homes. Her marriage was painted as an example of marital bliss (which it was not), her attitude towards her children always adoring and patient (which, on occasion, it most certainly was not) and her childhood free of such blemishes as fibs, tantrums and refusal to devour stewed rhubarb and rice pudding. There was thus created, for the benefit of hard pressed parents and their recalcitrant offspring, a second woman who walked for ever by the Queen's side. Queen Victoria did not really appreciate this shadow of perfection. She often tried, by blunt comment, to put matters in their right perspective, but to no avail. Many people still believe her to have been the shadow that walked beside her and not the woman that she really was.

The Regent Hotel, Royal Leamington Spa, the first public building in which Queen Victoria slept on her Royal Progresses. Built in 1819, and then the largest hotel in Europe, it was so named by permission of the Heir to the Throne who visited Leamington shortly after the opening. The Prince, who four months later became George IV, also granted the hotel the honour of bearing his coat of arms. The then Princess Victoria of Kent stayed at the Regent in August 1830, while on her way to spend a holiday at Malvern. Leamington was en fête to receive the royal visitors and the Princess acknowledged the cheers of the crowd from a first floor window. Her last appearance was at ten o'clock at night. She stood on a stool, one hand in her mother's, Sir John Conroy holding up wax candles behind them

A point about her childhood, which ties in with the words of Princess Feodore, is that, once she became Queen, she cut away the years behind her as if with a knife. She detached herself from the people with whom she had previously mixed. She did not go back to Kensington Palace until she was an old woman and she allowed it to fall into a state of dilapidation. With the exception of the Isle of Wight, she showed little interest in returning to the places which she had known as a child. She never travelled with her mother in a carriage for twenty years. That which she did not wish to remember she cast completely out of her mind. Victoire Conroy was forbidden the presence and the Queen appeared surprised when a message of condolence on her mother's death reached her through a third person.

Princess Feodore had, however, admitted that, unpleasant as their training had been, it had at least been of benefit to them both. Probably the most rewarding of the Duchess of Kent's measures was her insistence that her daughter should see as much of the country as possible. It might well be said that it would have been preferable if she had seen more of the terrace houses and farms, and less of the stately homes. She could have learned much then that was prohibited to her once she became Queen. In the event she never became familiar with the way of life of the majority of her subjects. Yet it was essential that she should meet the big families on their own ground and she forged personal links which were of great value to her in later life.

Because she was the Kents' only child, the powers of observation were more easily developed. There were none of the distractions – the squabbles and the laughter, the games and the chatter – that would have come if she had been in the company of children of her own age. When, in the days of William IV, she travelled as far afield as Bristol and York, Anglesey and the Norfolk coast, she was alone with grown-ups. A lonely, often sad little

Broadstairs, 1829

person, she sat by the carriage window from dawn to twilight, as a hundred miles went by. In 1839 she told Lord Melbourne that she had lived so much with adults that she often forgot that she was young. Her diary became a conversation piece with herself. She noted how the fields and the churches changed with a county boundary, how the black smoke plumed from a distant factory, how white and pinched were the faces of the children in the industrial areas.

The King referred to the tours of his niece as 'Royal Progresses' and took strong exception to the loyal addresses and gun salutes which Conroy

Victory and Favourite, *steamers engaged on the London-Margate run*

organised for the reception of the Heir to the Throne. On his seventy-first birthday at Windsor, he stood up after supper and lambasted the Duchess in such terms that she could scarce be restrained from leaving the Castle immediately. His dearest wish was that he would live to see his niece reach the vital age of eighteen, and this he did, by one month.

As a young child, Princess Victoria was taken to resorts such as Broadstairs, Ramsgate, Tunbridge Wells and Dover for her holidays. Her first long tour came in the summer of 1830, when she spent two months at Malvern. The outward journey was through Oxford, Blenheim, Stratford-on-Avon, Leamington, Kenilworth and Birmingham. From Malvern she was taken on expeditions to Hereford, Bristol and Worcester and saw the statelier side of English country life at Madresfield and Eastnor. The return journey to London was made by Gloucester, Badminton, Bath, Stonehenge, Salisbury and Portsmouth.

In 1832 the Duchess of Kent and Sir John Conroy planned an even more ambitious programme. It was so that she might chronicle this 'Royal Progress' that the Duchess gave her daughter a diary and Victoria's impressions open this story of her seventy years of travel. The route lay through Wolverhampton and Shrewsbury to Powis Castle, one time home of the

Duchess of Northumberland, and then over the Menai Bridge to the Bulke-ley Arms at Beaumaris, which had been taken over for a month. An outbreak of cholera cut short the stay here and the Duchess decided to move on to Plas Newydd, placed at her disposal by the Marquis of Anglesey. On 15th October the royal party arrived at Eaton Hall, travelling via Conway, and from there drove to Chester where the new bridge over the Dee was opened and named 'Victoria'. Lord Grosvenor handed over to the Duke of Devonshire, who received the Duchess and her daughter at Chatsworth. Expeditions were made to Haddon and Hardwicke and, in contrast, to Mr Strutt's cotton mills at Belper. Victoria saw more stately homes on this trip than she did in the rest of her life. Lord Lichfield entertained at Shugborough, Lord Shrewsbury at Alton Towers and Lord Liverpool at Pitchford. The Princess was shown to the people of Lichfield and Stafford and to the boys of Shrewsbury school. Before she arrived at Oxford, she had seen Church Stretton, Ludlow, Tenbury, Bromsgrove, Shipston-on-Stour and Woodstock. She was the guest of Mr Clive at Oakley Court, Lord Plymouth at Hewell Grange and the Earl of Abingdon

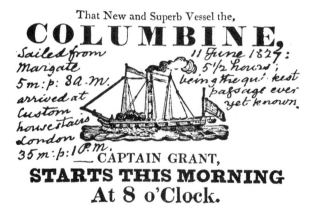

When she was a small girl, in the reign of George IV, Princess Victoria spent her summer holidays at Kentish seaside resorts. She and her mother were escorted by her Uncle Leopold, who lived at Claremont prior to becoming King of the Belgians in 1831. To the great excitement of them all they travelled 'by steam'. Above is a Sailing Notice of one of these steam packets, announcing the departure of the Columbine *from Margate. A contemporary hand, presumably that of a passenger, has written on the Notice: 'Sailed from Margate 5m:p:8a.m. arrived at Custom house stairs London 35m:p:1p.m. 11 June 1827: 5½ hours; being the quickest passage ever yet known.'*
(Reproduced from Printed Ephemera *by John Lewis)*

at Wytham Abbey. On 9th November she returned to Kensington via High Wycombe and Uxbridge. Behind her she left many beds which were later to be pointed out with pride as the one time resting place of the Queen, and many people who had seen a little girl waving a podgy hand from the carriage, little guessing that she would still be reigning when the century changed.

No editorial comments have been appended to the extracts from the Princess's diary for the years 1832–36. Her reactions and observations were straightforward and her companions were the same. There emerges a clear

Jug commemorating the death of George IV, and a
mug issued for the accession of William IV

picture of a girl growing up. To begin with, the importance of times of arrival and departure predominate, as if the diary is a new friend and must be told everything. The interest is on ponies, sailors and hours set aside for play. As the years pass, the interest shifts. Boys and young men become an obvious attraction, the outpouring of affection for relations points to the loneliness at fifteen, and ambition shows in her musical endeavour. At sixteen signs of weariness begin to appear. Three years before, she had been able to doze off in the carriage as the conversation of the grown ups droned on and on. Now there were crowds awaiting her at every town and village. After the long haul from York to East Anglia, she was so tired on arrival at Holkham that she found difficulty in keeping her eyes open during dinner. When the call at Euston was over and she was heading for London once more, she wrote: 'Here is an end to our journey, I am glad to say.' At seventeen an impatience with delays on the road becomes apparent and, where earlier it had been an excitement to stay at a roadside inn, now it was an inconvenience that disturbed her toilette.

★

Kensington Palace was early astir on the morning of the first of August 1832. A carriage waited in the courtyard. A little girl, thirteen years old came down the stairs, one hand in her mother's, the other holding a diary in which all the pages were clean.

Wednesday, August 1.—We left K.P.[1] at 6 minutes past 7 and went through the Lower-field gate to the right. We went on, & turned to the left by the new road to Regent's Park. The road & scenery is beautiful. 20 minutes to 9. We have just changed horses at Barnet, a very pretty little town. 5 minutes past $\frac{1}{2}$ past 9. We have just changed horses at St. Albans. The situation is very pretty & there is a beautiful old abbey there. 5 minutes past 10. The country is beautiful here: they have began to cut the corn; it is so golden & fine that I think they will have a very good harvest . . .

A $\frac{1}{4}$ to 11. We have just changed horses at Dunstable; there was a fair there; the booths filled with fruit, ribbons, &c. looked very pretty. The town seems old & there is a fine abbey before it . . . About $\frac{1}{2}$ past 1 o'clock we arrived at Towcester & lunched there. At 14 minutes past two we left it. A $\frac{1}{4}$ past 3. We have just changed horses at Daventry. The road continues to be very dusty. 1 minute past $\frac{1}{2}$ past 3. We have just passed through Braunston where there is a curious spire. The Oxford canal is close to the town. 1 minute to 4. We have just changed horses at Dunchurch & it is raining.

For some time past already, and now, our road is entirely up an avenue of trees going on and on, it is quite delightful but it still rains. Just now we go at a *tremendous* rate. 4 minutes to 5. We have just changed horses at Coventry, a large town where there is a very old church (in appearance at least). At $\frac{1}{2}$ past 5 we arrived at Meridon; and we are now going to dress for dinner. $\frac{1}{2}$ past 8. I am undressing to go to bed. Mamma is not well and is lying on the sofa in the next room. I was asleep in a minute in my own little bed which travels always with me.

Thursday, August 2.—I got up after a very good night at 5 o'clock this morning. Mamma is much better I am happy to say, and I am now dressing to go to breakfast. 6 minutes to $\frac{1}{2}$ past 7. We have just left Meridon,

[1] Kensington Palace.

a very clean inn. It is a very bad day. 10 minutes to 9. We have just changed horses at Birmingham where I was two years ago and we visited the manufactories which are very curious. It rains very hard.

We just passed through a town where all coal mines are and you see the fire glimmer at a distance in the engines in many places. The men, women, children, country and houses are all black. But I can not by any description give an idea of its strange and extraordinary appearance. The country is very desolate every where; there are coals about, and the grass is quite blasted and black. I just now see an extraordinary building flaming with fire. The country continues black, engines flaming, coals, in abundance, everywhere, smoking and burning coal heaps, intermingled with wretched huts and carts and little ragged children . . .

I received from the mayor an oaken box with a silver top and filled with the famous Shrewsbury cakes. We lunched there. We left it at a $\frac{1}{4}$ to 3. As we passed along the streets a poor unhappy hen, frightened by the noise flew on the carriage but she was taken off. We had our horses watered half way. When we arrived at the outskirts of Welshpool we were met by a troop of Yeomanry who escorted us for a long time and the little town was ornamented with arches, flowers, branches, flags, ribbons, &c., &c. The guns fired as we came up the park and the band played before Powis Castle; Lord Powis[2] and Mr Clive met us at the door of his beautiful old Castle and Lady Lucy and Lady Harriet Clive were in the gallery. The Castle is very old and beautiful; the little old windows jutting in and out and a fine gallery with a dry-rubbed floor and some beautiful busts. I am now dressing for dinner . . .

Thursday, August 9.—At $\frac{1}{2}$ past 10 Mamma received an address from the Mayor and Corporation of Beaumaris,[3] and another from the gentlemen inhabitants, and visitors of the town. At $\frac{1}{2}$ past 11 we got into our carriages with my Cousins on the box of ours. In passing the Menai-bridge,[4] we received a salute, and on entering the town of Carnarvon, we were met, not only by an immense crowd, who were extremely kind, and pleased, but by the Corporation also, who walked before the carriage, while a salute was firing. We then arrived at the inn, where Mamma received an address. The address being over we took luncheon, and after that was over, we went to see the ruins of the Castle, which are beautiful, while a salute was fired, from the rampart. We then got into the *Emerald*,[5] where we were several times saluted, at the last being nearly

[2] Edward, 1st Earl of Powis (1754–1839), the eldest son of the famous Lord Clive.
[3] It was at Beaumaris that the Princess carried out one of her first public duties—the presentation of prizes at the National Eisteddfod.
[4] Opened in 1826.
[5] The cutter *Emerald* and the steamers *Palmerston, Llewellyn* and *Paul Pry*, all mounting guns, awaited the royal party. The *Palmerston* had brought four carriages and fifteen horses from Bristol.

Powis Castle

becalmed, we were towed by a steam packet, called *Paul Pry*, which saluted us 4 times in the day. We arrived at home at $\frac{1}{4}$ to 7, and dined at $\frac{1}{2}$ past 7. We drank Uncle Leopold's[6] health in honour of his marriage that day. I stayed up till $\frac{1}{2}$ past 9. I went to bed soon after, and was soon asleep . . .

Wednesday, August 29. – At $\frac{1}{2}$ past 3 went to Baron Hill, Sir R. Bulkeley's[7] place. We arrived there at a little after 4. We were received at the door by Sir Richard & farther on by Lady Bulkeley whose dress I shall describe. It was a white satin trimmed with blonde, short sleeves & a necklace, ear-rings and sévigné of perridos & diamonds with a wreath of orange-flowers in her hair.

We then went upon the terrace & the band of the Anglesea Militia played "God save the King". We then presented all the bards & poets

[6] King of the Belgians. Married to Louise Marie, daughter of King Louis Philippe.
[7] 10th Baronet, M.P. for Anglesey.

with medals. We then [went] into the drawing-room and remained there till dinner. In the drawing-room there were a great many other people. At 5 we went to dinner, which was in a temporary building which was lined in the inside with pink and white linen. The dinner was splendidly served & the china was rich and beautiful. The fruit was magnificent.

After dessert was over Sir Richard made a speech and brought out a toast in honor of Mamma & me. We then left the room & went into the drawing-room. We went upstairs into Lady Bulkeley's pretty little dressing-room. Her toilet table was pink with white muslin over it trimmed with beautiful lace & her things on the toilet table were gold. We then went downstairs and took coffee and the famous dog of Lady Williams[8] Cabriolle, played tricks. At about 7 we left Baron Hill & proceeded homewards . . .

Monday, September 17. – We breakfasted at 9 downstairs. I then played and did other things. At 1 we lunched. I then played on the piano, & at a little before 3 played at billiards downstairs, with Victoire[9] & then went out walking. When I came home I first worked & then we blew soap-bubbles.

[8] Wife of Sir John Williams of Bodelwyddan, 1st Baronet.
[9] Daughter of Sir John Conroy, Comptroller to the Duchess of Kent.

Plas Newydd, Anglesey, c. 1820–30
(by permission of the Marquess of Anglesey)

Sunday, October 14.–I awoke at 7 and got up at $\frac{1}{2}$ past 7. At $\frac{1}{2}$ past 8 we breakfasted. I then wrote my Journal and some music and at 11 we went to chapel for the last time and the sailors likewise for the last time. The service was performed as usual by Mr W. Jones. It was over at $\frac{1}{4}$ past 12. I then walked out with Lehzen[10] and Victoire. At 1 we lunched. At 3 we went out riding, and as we passed through the Park gate the old woman at the lodge came out as usual, to open the gate and she thanked Mamma for what she had given her. We galloped over a green field which we had already done several times. Rosa went an enormous rate; she literally *flew*. We then went on towards the Menai bridge but turned back under the hill. We cantered a great deal and Rosa went the whole time beautifully. It was a delightful ride. When we came home Mamma got on Rosa and I got on Thomas and cantered him. We came in at $\frac{1}{2}$ past 4. Alas! it was our last ride at *dear* Plas Newydd.[11]

Monday, October 15.–I awoke at $\frac{1}{2}$ past 5 and got up at 6. At 7 we breakfasted with all the family; and a most beautiful falcon which Sir John Williams[12] sent me was brought in that I might see it. The sailors were so busy and so useful for I saw Kew and Sparks going to and fro. At a $\frac{1}{4}$ to 8 we got into our carriages and drove out amidst the shouts of the sailors of the *Emerald*, who were standing on the rigging two by two on the rope-ladders, till the last man was at the very top of all. I looked out of the carriage window that I might get a last look of the *dear Emerald* and her *excellent crew* . . .

10 minutes to 4.–We have just passed through Northop. At about $\frac{1}{2}$ past 4 we went through the Park of Mr Granville up to his castle. Lord Grosvenor met us there at the head of his Cavalry. And Lord Westminster[13] sent his own fine horses, which were put to our carriage. At about $\frac{1}{2}$ past 5 we arrived at Eaton Hall. We were received at the door by Lord and Lady Westminster, Lady Grosvenor and Lady Wilton. The house is magnificent. You drive up to the door under a lofty vaulted

[10] Louise Lehzen became Governess to Princess Victoria in 1825. In 1827 George IV created her a Hanoverian Baroness. When in 1830 the Duchess of Northumberland was made the Princess's Governess, her "faithful Lehzen" remained on as Lady in Waiting. She stayed at Court till 1842, when she returned to Germany.

[11] An outbreak of cholera had broken out at Beaumaris and the Duchess of Kent considered it advisable to leave the Bulkeley Arms there. She gratefully accepted the offer of the Marquess of Anglesey to stay at his nearby home, Plas Newydd. Henry William, 2nd Earl of Uxbridge, had been created Marquess of Anglesey in 1815. A brilliant soldier and one of the most picturesque men of his time, the Marquess had lost a leg at Waterloo. But he managed to ride a pony round his estate and shot from the saddle. Queen Victoria's affection for the Pagets began during her time at Plas Newydd, and continued until the end of her reign.

[12] Afterwards Sir John Williams-Hay, 2nd Baronet, of Bodelwyddan.

[13] Robert, Earl Grosvenor (1767–1845), had in 1831 been created Marquess of Westminster.

portico with a flight of steps under it, and it takes you to the hall, which is beautiful. The floor is inlaid with various marbles, and arches spring from the sides. Then you enter a beautiful drawing-room; the ceiling joins in a round gilt, with great taste and richness, while the sides arch towards the top. An organ on the right as you enter the room and a large fireplace on the left with stained glass windows. Then Lady Westminster, after we had been downstairs a little, showed us our apartments, which are indeed beautiful. I was in bed at $\frac{1}{2}$ past 8.

Tuesday, October 16. – I awoke at 6 and got up at 7. I then dressed and took some tea. At $\frac{1}{2}$ past 9 we breakfasted. The breakfast-room is magnificent. There are 4 fireplaces; and the windows are of stained glass very beautifully done. A massive lustre of gold with an eagle likewise in gold hangs from the ceiling in the middle of the room. Pillars arching to the top and gilt in parts rise from the sides. Several tables of oak and elm stand in the windows, and the breakfast was served in handsome silver tea and coffee pots; a crown of gold with precious stones contained the bread . . .

At 12 Mamma went into the great saloon where all the ladies were and an address from the mayor and corporation of Chester arrived and then another from the gentlemen and inhabitants of Chester, presented by Lord Robert.[14] After this we looked about the room which is indeed beautiful. The ceiling is done in the same splendid manner and a magnificent lustre of gold and glass with a coronet of velvet and pearls hung from the ceiling in the room. Two windows of stained glass, very handsomely done, are on different sides. A superb chimney-place with beautiful furniture and rich carpets, complete the room. 4 beautiful pictures painted by different artists are likewise in the room.

We then walked out with most of the people; I walking in front with the eldest and third little girl, the second not being well. We walked about the garden and looked at an aloe which flowers only once in 100 years. We came in at $\frac{1}{2}$ past 1, and lunched at 2. At $\frac{1}{2}$ past 2 we went out driving; Lady Westminster and little Elinor,[15] the eldest child, were in our carriage; she is a delightful child. Lady Catherine and Lehzen followed in another carriage. We drove about the park which is beautiful. When we came home we walked in the kitchen gardens which are indeed very pretty.

At $\frac{1}{2}$ past 4 we came home and I worked. At 7 we dined. The dining-room is a fine room beautifully worked at the ceiling. Four large statues of Maltese stone occupy 4 corners, very beautifully executed; one with

[14] Third son of Lord Westminster, at this time M.P. for Chester and afterwards for Middlesex. He was created Lord Ebury in 1857.

[15] Afterwards Duchess of Northumberland.

a helmet is Sir Gilbert le Grosvenor,[16] and the lady [17] next by him is the heiress of Eaton; on the opposite side the man is Sir Robert le Grosvenor, distinguished in the battle of Cressy; the lady near him is a Miss Davis who by intermarrying brought the possessions in town, as Grosvenor Square, Belgrave Square, etc., etc.[18] The window is stained glass with the figure of Hugh Lupus on it. The dinner was served on plate, and the plateau was very handsome with gilt cups on it. The side table was covered with gold plate. After dinner we played at a game of letters and then I sang . . .

Thursday, October 18. – When we went out after luncheon we went in the garden first and saw a Roman altar which had been dug up near Chester. At 7 we dined. The breakfast-room had been arranged for this purpose. A temporary floor had been arranged at the top of the room, for our table (for all the company who had come to the bow-meeting dined here), and the other four were lower. After the dinner (we being still at table) was over some glee-singers from Chester came and sang the grace in Latin . . .

Friday, October 19. – $\frac{1}{2}$ past 4. We have just changed horses at Buxton, which is a pretty place. The houses are well built and form a crescent. The country about here is very pretty, high rocks covered with trees. There are all about here little rivulets and fountains, rippling over stones. At $\frac{1}{2}$ past 6 we arrived at Chatsworth, which is a beautiful house. It was quite dark. It is built in the shape of a square joined by an arch under which one must drive. We were met at the door by the Duke of Devonshire[19] who conducted us up the staircase, which is made of wood, to our apartments which are indeed beautiful . . .

Saturday, October 20. – I awoke at $\frac{1}{2}$ past 7 and got up at 8. At a little past 9 we breakfasted, us 5 by ourselves in a lovely room giving on the park and garden where one could see a cascade which ran all the way down. The room is small; the ceiling is painted and represents some mythology, with books round the room and a splendid carpet. At about 11 we went over the house with the company . . . It would take me days, were I to describe minutely the whole. We went all over the house, and the carving of the framework of some looking-glasses was quite beautiful; they are carved in the shape of birds, the plumage being so exquisite that if it was not of the colour of wood one might take them for feathers. It not only surrounds the mirrors but the ceilings of some of the rooms. We saw Lady Cavendish's little boy who is 10 months old,

[16] Gilbert le Grosvenor, nephew of Hugh Lupus, Earl of Chester.

[17] Joan (*temp.* Henry VI), only daughter and heiress of John Eton of Eton (now Eaton), married Raufe le Grosvenor, Lord of Hulme.

[18] Sir Thomas Grosvenor, 3rd Baronet, M.P. for Chester, married Mary, only daughter and heiress of Alexander Davis, of Ebury, Middlesex. She died in 1730.

[19] William Spencer, 6th Duke.

a beautiful child. We likewise saw the kitchen which is superb for its size and cleanliness; and the confectionary which is as pretty and neat.

The Duke's own apartments contain some superb statues of Canova and others; likewise a beautiful collection of minerals. We saw the library and dining-room which are all beautiful. The library's ceiling is painted in figures; and the carpet is beautiful. The conservatory which leads from the dining-room is very pretty.

Chatsworth

We then walked out in the garden, I went into another conservatory which contains a rockery with water falling from it. There are some curious plants there, amongst others two which are worthy of remark; the one is called the pitcher-plant because at the end of each leaf hangs a little bag or pitcher which fills with the dew and supplies the plant when it wants water; the other is called the fly-catcher plant, because whenever a fly touches it, it closes. From the conservatory we went and looked at a monkey which is in the garden, chained. We then went to the cascade and saw some other fountains very curious and pretty. When we had come on the terrace the Duke wished us to plant two trees down under the terrace. So we did, I planted an oak and Mamma a Spanish chestnut.

After that we went upon the terrace again and went up a platform which had been arranged with carpets, to view the cricket-match below; the Buxton band playing "God save the King" and the people hurraying and others under tents looked very pretty. From there we went to the stables where we saw some pretty ponies and a Russian coachman in his full dress, and the only Russian horse which remained reared at his command; there were three other horses, English ones, but trained like the other. At about $\frac{1}{2}$ past 1 we came home and lunched with the whole party.

At $\frac{1}{2}$ past 2 we went in a carriage and 6 with the Duke and Mrs Cavendish, to Haddon Hall, a very old and singular place. The old tapestry still remaining and iron hooks to keep it back. We then went to the Rookery, a small cottage belonging to the Duke on the banks of the river Wye, very pretty and cool. From there we walked to the Marble Mills and saw how they sawed and polished the marble. There was a little cottage where they sold Derbyshire spar in different little shapes and forms, and some pieces of marble too.

We then drove home after having bought a good many things. We came in at 5. At 7 we dined and after dinner at about $\frac{1}{2}$ past 9 we looked at the cascade illuminated, which looked very pretty, and the fountains, blue lights, red lights, rockets, etc. At about 10 the charade began in 3 syllables and 4 scenes . . . When it was over, which was at $\frac{1}{4}$ to 12, I went to bed . . .

Wednesday, October 24.–. . . At 1 we arrived at Alton Towers, the seat

Alton Towers

of Lord Shrewsbury.[20] This is an extraordinary house. On arriving one goes into a sort of gallery filled with armour, guns, swords, pistols, models, flags, etc., etc., then into a conservatory with birds. We lunched there and the luncheon was served on splendid gold plate. We then walked in the gardens. At ½ past 2 we left it . . .

Wednesday, October 31.[21] – I awoke at 7 and got up at ½ past 7. At ½ past 9 we breakfasted in the drawing-room, for the gentlemen who were going to hunt breakfasted in the other room, all the ladies and Sir John breakfasting with us. After breakfast at about ½ past 10 we went into the room where they were, and they gave us a toast with many cheers. After that we walked out to see the hunt. We saw them set off.

It was an immense field of horsemen, who in their red jackets and black hats looked lively and gave an animating appearance to the whole. They had a large pack of hounds and three huntsmen or Whippers-in. They drew a covert near here in hopes of finding a fox, but as they did not they returned and we got into the carriage with Lady Selina[22] and Lehzen while all the huntsmen and the hounds followed.

When we came to a field, they drew another covert and succeeded; we saw the fox dash past and all the people and hounds after him, the hounds in full cry. The hounds killed him in a wood quite close by. The huntsman then brought him out and cutting off the brush Sir Edward Smith (to whom the hounds belong) brought it to me. Then the huntsmen cut off for themselves the ears and 4 paws, and lastly they threw it to the dogs, who tore it from side to side till there was nothing left. We then went home.

At 1 we lunched, and at 2, I, Lady Selina, Lady Louisa[23] and dear Lehzen went out walking, towards a farm of Lord Liverpool's, and when we had passed the farm and were going to return by the village, we heard the blast of a horn and we looked and saw the hounds and hunters going full gallop along a field which was below the field in which we were walking. They came and crossed the field in which we were and we saw all the riders leap over a ditch. We went back the same way that we might see them. When we came near home we saw them go home by the house. At ½ past 3 we came home. At ½ past 6 we dined, and I received my brush which had been fixed on a stick by the huntsman; it is a beautiful one . . .

Wednesday, November 7. – ¼ to 4. We have just changed horses at Woodstock, and another detachment of Yeomanry commanded by Lord Churchill[24] ride with us now. We passed through Oxford on our way. At about a little past 5 we arrived at Wytham Abbey, the seat of Lord

[20] John, 16th Earl.
[21] Staying with the 3rd Earl of Liverpool at Pitchford Hall, Shropshire.
[22] Lord Liverpool's second daughter.
[23] Third daughter of Lord Liverpool.
[24] Francis, 1st Lord Churchill, third son of 4th Duke of Marlborough.

Blenheim Palace

Abingdon.[25] We were received at the door by Lord and Lady Abingdon, Lady Charlotte Bertie and Lady Emily Bathurst, their daughters. The house is very comfortable; in the drawing-room there is a lovely picture by Angelica Kauffman, Penelope . . .

Thursday, November 8.—I awoke at a little to 8 and got up at 8. At a little past 9 we breakfasted with the whole party. At 10 o'clock we set out for Oxford in a close carriage and 4 with Lord Abingdon and Lady Charlotte Bertie; the other ladies going in carriages before us.

We got out first at the Divinity College, and walked from thence to the theatre, which was built by Sir Christopher Wren. The ceiling is painted with allegorical figures. The galleries are ornamented with carving enriched with gold. It was filled to excess. We were most WARMLY and ENTHUSIASTICALLY received. They hurrayed and applauded us immensely for there were all the students there; all in their gowns and caps. Mamma received an address which was presented by the Vice-Chancellor, Dr Rowly, and Mamma answered it as usual. Then Sir John[26] was made a Doctor of Civil Law.

After that was over, we returned through Divinity College and proceeded in our carriages to the Council Chamber where Mamma received an address there, from the corporation of Oxford, and Sir John the

[25] 5th Earl of.
[26] Sir John Conroy.

freedom of the City of Oxford. We then went to Christ Church, which is very fine, viewed the hall and chapel and library. Dr Gaisford[27] is the Dean of Christ Church and is at the head of that college. From there we went to the Bodleian library which is immense. Amongst other curiosities there is Queen Elizabeth's Latin exercise book when she was of my age (13). We went through Mr Sneed's house to our carriages. From there to All Souls' College where Mr Sneed is the warden. It is not a college for education, but after they have taken their degree. We saw the library and chapel which is very beautiful.

We then went to University College of which the Vice-chancellor is the head. We lunched there and saw the chapel which is very fine. From there we went to New College of which Dr Shuttleworth[28] is the head. We saw the chapel and hall. From there to the Clarendon printing-press which is very amusing but would take up too much space and time to describe . . .[29]

Friday, November 9.—. . . At about $\frac{1}{2}$ past 5 we arrived at Kensington Palace. My aunt Sophia[30] came after dinner . . .

[27] Thomas Gaisford, Dean from 1831–55.
[28] Philip Nicholas Shuttleworth, afterwards Bishop of Chichester.
[29] The Princess was presented with a Bible, printed at the University Press, and the story of her visit printed on white satin.
[30] Princess Sophia (1777–1848), daughter of George III.

Journey Two
1833

Portsmouth to Plymouth

Monday, July 1.–I awoke at $\frac{1}{2}$ past 4 and got up at $\frac{1}{4}$ past 5. At a $\frac{1}{4}$ past 6 we all breakfasted. At 7 o'clock we left Kensington Palace, Sir John going in a post-chaise before us, then our post-chaise, then Lehzen's landau, then my Cousins'[1] carriage, then Charles's,[2] then Lady Conroy's, and then our maids'. It is a lovely morning . . . POOR DEAR LITTLE Dashy[3] could not go with us as he was not quite well, so he is gone with Mason with the horses. 4 minutes past 1; we have just left Liphook where we took our luncheon. 5 minutes to 2, we have just changed horses at Petersfield. 5 minutes to 3, we have just changed horses at Horndean.

At 4 we arrived at Portsmouth. The streets were lined with soldiers, and Sir Colin Campbell[4] rode by the carriage. Sir Thomas Williams, the Admiral, took us in his barge, on board the *dear Emerald*. The Admiral presented some of the officers to us. We stayed about $\frac{1}{2}$ an hour waiting for the baggage to be put on board the steamer, which was to tow us. We then set off and arrived at Cowes at about 7. We were most civilly received. Cowes Castle, the yacht-club, yachts, &c., &c., saluting us . . . We drove up in a fly to Norris Castle, where we lodged two years ago, and where we are again living. My cousins and my brother were *delighted* with it.

Monday, July 8.–At about 10 we went on board the *Emerald* . . . We were towed up to Southampton by the *Medina* steampacket. It rained several times very hard, and we were obliged to go down into the cabin very often. When we arrived at Southampton, Mamma received an address on board from the Corporation. We then got into the barge and rowed up to the new pier. The crowd was tremendous. We went into a tent erected on the pier, and I was very much frightened for fear my cousins and the rest of our party should get knocked about; however

[1] Princes Alexander and Ernst of Würtemberg, sons of the Duchess of Kent's sister Antoinette.
[2] Prince of Leiningen, Princess Victoria's half-brother.
[3] A King Charles's spaniel.
[4] Afterwards F.-M. Lord Clyde, Commander-in-Chief in India (1792–1863).

Princess Victoria rescued from a falling mast

they at last got in. We then got into our barge and went on board the *Emerald* where we took our luncheon. We stayed a little while to see the regatta, which was going on, and then sailed home . . .

Friday, July 12.—I awoke at 6 and got up at $\frac{1}{2}$ past 6. At 7 we breakfasted. It was a *sad* breakfast, for us indeed, as my dear cousins were going so soon. At about a $\frac{1}{4}$ to 8 we walked down our pier with them and there took leave of them, which made us both VERY UNHAPPY. We saw them get into the barge, and watched them sailing away for some time on the beach. They were so amiable and so pleasant to have in the house; they were *always satisfied, always good humoured;* Alexander took such care of me in getting out of the boat, and rode next to me; so did Ernst. They talked about *such interesting things*, about their Turkish Campaign, about Russia, &c., &c.. We shall miss them at *breakfast*, at *luncheon*, at *dinner, riding, sailing, driving, walking,* in *fact everywhere* . . .

Thursday, July 18.—At a $\frac{1}{4}$ to 10 we went on board the *Emerald* . . . and were towed by the *Messenger* steam-packet up to Portsmouth. We then got into the Admiral's barge, and landed in the docks. We then saw from an elevation, the launch of the *Racer*, a sloop of war. We then re-entered the Admiral's barge and went to the *Victory*, his flag-ship. We there received the salute on board. We saw the spot where Nelson fell, and which is covered up with a brazen plate and his motto is inscribed on it, "Every Englishman is expected to do his duty". We went down as low as the tanks, and there tasted the water which had been in there for two years, and which was excellent. We also saw the place where Nelson died. The whole ship is remarkable for its neatness and order. We tasted some of the men's beef and potatoes, which were excellent, and likewise some grog.

Friday, August 2.—I awoke at about a $\frac{1}{4}$ to 6 and got up at $\frac{1}{2}$ past 7. At $\frac{1}{2}$ past 8 we all breakfasted. We then saw several ladies and gentlemen. At about $\frac{1}{2}$ past 9 we went on board the *dear little Emerald*. We were to be towed up to Plymouth. Mamma and Lehzen were very sick, and I was sick for about $\frac{1}{2}$ an hour. At 1 I had a hot mutton chop on deck. We passed Dartmouth. At about 4 we approached Plymouth Harbour. It is a magnificent place and the breakwater is wonderful indeed. You pass Mount Edgecumbe, the seat of Lord Mount Edgecumbe.[5] It is beautifully situated . . .

As we entered the harbour, our dear little *Emerald* ran foul of a hulk, her mast broke and we were in the *greatest danger*. Thank God! the mast did not fall and no one was hurt. But I was *dreadfully* frightened for *Mamma* and for *all*. The poor dear *Emerald* is very much hurt I fear. Saunders[6] was not at all in fault; he saved us by pulling the rope which

[5] Richard (1764–1839), 2nd Earl, Lord-Lieutenant of Cornwall.
[6] The pilot. He was promoted to Master. On his death Queen Victoria made financial provision for his widow and daughter.

fixed us to the steamer. We arrived at Plymouth at 5. It is a beautiful town and we were very well received. *Sweet Dash* was under Saunders's arm the whole time, but he never let him drop in all the danger. At 7 we dined. The hotel is very fine indeed. After dinner Sir John saw Saunders, who said that the mast of the *Emerald* was broken in two places, and that we had had the *narrowest escape possible;* but that she would be repaired and ready for us to go back in her on Tuesday.

Saturday, August 3.—At ½ past 11 Mamma received an address from the Mayor and Corporation of Plymouth, downstairs in a large room full of people. At 12 we went with all our own party to a review of the 89th, the 22nd, and the 84th regiments. Mamma made a speech, and I then gave the colours to the 89th regiment. The names of the two Ensigns to whom I gave the colours are Miles and Egerton. We then saw them march by in line.

We then went to the Admiral's house where we had our luncheon, and then proceeded to the docks. We went in the Admiral's barge on board the Admiral's flag-ship, the *St. Joseph*, taken by Lord Nelson from the Spanish, in the battle of St. Vincent. We received a salute on board. She is a magnificent vessel of 120 guns. We saw her lower decks and cabins, which are extremely light, airy, roomy and clean. We then returned in the Admiral's barge, rowed round the *Caledonia* 120 guns, and the *Revenge* 76 guns. We landed at the Dockyard and went home. At 7 we dined . . .

Journey Three
1834

Hastings and St. Leonards

ST. LEONARDS, *Wednesday, November 4.*—I said in my last journal book that I would describe in this book all what passed yesterday. We reached Battle Abbey at about a $\frac{1}{4}$ to 1. We were received at the door by Lady Webster.[1]

Battle Abbey was built by King William the Conqueror and stands on the site where the famous battle of Hastings was fought. The place is still preserved where Harold fell. She showed us first into a large hall supposed to be the highest in England. There are portraits of King Charles the 2nd, King William the 3rd, and Queen Anne in it, &c. &c.

[1] Charlotte, wife of Sir Godfrey Vassal Webster, of Battle Abbey, formerly M.P. for Sussex.

The Duchess of Kent and Princess Victoria leaving Tunbridge Wells, 1834

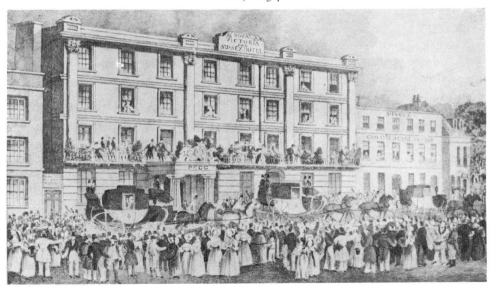

There is also a very large picture of the battle of Hastings. Some old suits of armour are also in the hall. We saw also what were the cloisters now turned into a room. We saw the Beggar's Hall, a curious walk of the monks, and the garden. We lastly partook of some refreshment in a very pretty room in which there was a picture of the Emperor Napoleon, not full length, only to the waist; which is said to be very like.

The outside of the abbey is very fine too. We left it again at $\frac{1}{2}$ past 1. The tenants again accompanied us till Broadeslowe. There some gentlemen from Hastings met us and accompanied us to St. Leonards. We passed under an arch formed of laurels and decorated with flowers and inscriptions. As soon as we passed the 2nd arch the Mayor got out of his carriage and came to our door asking leave to precede us in his carriage. An immense concourse of people walking with the carriage. The mayor and aldermen preceding us in carriages as also a band of music.

Throughout Hastings the houses were decorated with flowers, ribands and inscriptions, and arches of flowers and laurels. Ladies and children waving handkerchiefs and laurels on the balconies and at the windows. Cries of "Welcome, welcome, Royal visitors", were constantly heard. We reached Hastings at $\frac{1}{2}$ past 2, and it was 4 o'clock before we arrived at our house at St. Leonards. It was indeed a most splendid reception. We stepped out on the balcony and were loudly cheered.

One sight was extremely pretty. Six fishermen in rough blue jackets, red caps and coarse white aprons, preceded by a band, bore a basket ornamented with flowers, full of fish as a present for us. We found *dear* Dashy in perfect health. Our house is very comfortable . . . After 8 the fireworks began and lasted till 9. They were very fine.

Thursday, November 5.—I awoke this morning at 7 and got up at $\frac{1}{2}$ past 7. At 9 we breakfasted. At 12 Mamma received an address from the Mayor, Corporation, and Inhabitants of Hastings and St. Leonards.

Tuesday, November 11.—. . . At $\frac{1}{2}$ past 11 we went out driving in the barouche with Lady Flora[2] and Lehzen. We got out and walked and sent the barouche home. We afterwards got into the close landau with a postilion and horse in hand.

As we came to the commencement of the town where a seminary is to be built, the hand-horse kicked up and getting entangled in the traces fell down, pulling the other with it; the horse with the postilion however instantly recovered itself but the other remained on the ground kicking and struggling most violently. Two gentlemen very civilly came and held the horse's head down while we all got out as fast as possible. I called for poor dear little Dashy who was in the rumble; Wood (our footman) took him down and I ran on with him in my arms calling Mamma to follow, Lehzen and Lady Flora followed us also. They then

[2] Lady Flora Hastings, Lady of the Bedchamber to the Duchess of Kent.

cut the traces, the horse still struggling violently. The other horse which had been quite quiet, being frightened by the other's kicking, backed and fell over into a foundation pit, while Wood held him, and he (Wood) with difficulty prevented himself from falling; the horse recovering himself ran after us and we instantly ran behind a low stone wall; but the horse went along the road, and a workman took him and gave him to Wood. The other horse had ceased kicking and got up.

We ought to be *most grateful* to Almighty God for His merciful providence in thus preserving us, for it was a *very narrow escape*. Both Wood and Bacleberry behaved very well indeed. The names of the two gentlemen who held the horse's head are Rev Mr Gould and Mr Peckham Micklethwaite[3] The latter I am sorry to say was hurt, but not very materially. The poor horse is cut from head to foot; but the other is not at all hurt only very much frightened. We walked home . . .

[3] He was made a baronet in 1838 for this act.

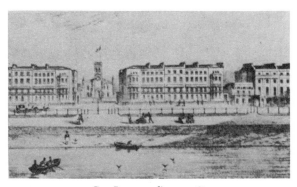

St. Leonard's-on-Sea

*Queen Victoria, from a miniature by Sir W. Ross, 1837
(centre); The Duchess of Saxe-Coburg Saalfeld, from a
miniature by W. Schmidt, 1831 (below); The Duchess of Kent,
from a miniature by Sir W. Ross (above); Charles, Prince of
Leiningen, from a miniature by Arland, 1821; Feodore,
Princess of Leiningen, from a miniature by Stewart*

Journey Four
1835

Music at York

Friday, September 4. – At $\frac{1}{2}$ past 9 we left Wansford.[1] It is a very nice clean Inn. We passed through Stamford, a large and populous town, after having changed horses at Witham Common. We changed horses 2ndly at Grantham, also a large town. These 3 are in Lincolnshire. 3rdly at Newark, also a large town, and lastly at Scarthing Moor.[2] The country from Wansford to Scarthing Moor was like yesterday, extremely flat and ugly. From Scarthing Moor to Barnby Moor, where we arrived at 5 o'clock, the country is rich and wooded, but very flat. This Inn (Barnby Moor) is extremely clean and pretty. Newark, Scarthing Moor and Barnby Moor are all in Nottinghamshire. I am struck by the number of small villages in the counties which we passed through today, each with their church. And what is likewise peculiar is, that the churches have all steeples of a spiral shape.

I read in the *Alhambra* again in the carriage. Finished the 1st vol. and began the 2nd. We all walked in the little garden behind the house for a short time. When we came in I wrote my journal. At a $\frac{1}{4}$ to 7 we all dined. After dinner Lady Catherine[3] played on the piano, for there was one in the Inn. She played a variation of Herz's, one of Hünten's, and the Polacca; and she accompanied us while we sang "Il rival".

Saturday, September 5. – I awoke at $\frac{1}{2}$ past 6 and got up at 7. Read in the *Exposition of St. Matt.'s Gospel* while my hair was doing, and also in the Venetian History. Last night I also read in the Gospel and in Mme. de Sévigné. At a $\frac{1}{4}$ to 8 we all breakfasted. At a $\frac{1}{4}$ to 9 we left Barnby Moor. It is a remarkably nice and clean Inn. We changed horses 1st at Doncaster, a very pretty town, 2ndly at Ferry bridge, where there is a fine bridge, and lastly at Tadcaster. All these towns are in Yorkshire. We reached Bishopthorpe (the Archbishop of York's Palace) at 2. It is 2

[1] On the journey from London a visit had been paid to Hatfield House, the home of the Cecils.
[2] At the inn there, between Weston and Tuxford.
[3] Lady Catherine Jenkinson. She later married Colonel Francis Vernon Harcourt, son of the Archbishop of York and Equerry to the Duchess of Kent.

miles and a half from York. It is a very large house and part of it is very old. Besides the Archbishop[4] and Miss Harcourt (his daughter), the Duchess of Northumberland, Lady Norreys,[5] Sir John and Lady Johnstone[6] (Lady Johnstone is the Archbishop's daughter), Mr and Mrs and Miss Granville Harcourt,[7] Colonel Francis Harcourt, Mr Vernon, are staying in the house. After half an hour we lunched in a large dining-room. We then went to our rooms which are very nice. I finished the *Alhambra*. It is a most entertaining book and has amused me very much. I wrote my journal when I came into my room. Wrote a letter to Feodore and read in the Venetian History.

Ye Olde Bell, *Barnby Moor*

The country through which we travelled today is very flat and ugly, but extremely rich. I find the air in Yorkshire cooler than in Kent and the South of England. I read in Mrs Butler's journal which amuses me. There are some very fine feelings in it. At a $\frac{1}{4}$ to 7 we dined . . . After dinner Lady Norreys and her cousin Miss Vernon sang a duet from *Le Gazza Ladra* beautifully, and also "Suoni la tromba". They are both extremely pretty. They are pupils of Tamburini. We sang something then. I like Miss Vernon's voice the best of the two. We then went to prayers. After that I sang the Barcarola from *Faliero*, frightened to death . . .

[4] Edward Vernon-Harcourt (1757–1847).
[5] Wife of Montagu, Lord Norreys, M.P. for Oxfordshire, afterwards 6th Earl of Abingdon.
[6] 2nd Baronet (1799–1869).
[7] George Granville Harcourt, M.P. for Oxfordshire and eldest son of the Archbishop.

BISHOPTHORPE, *Wednesday, September 9.*—. . . At a $\frac{1}{4}$ past 11 we went to the York Minster . . . The Minster was fuller than on the preceding day. It was Handel's Oratorio of *The Messiah*. It is considered very fine, but I must say that, with the exception of a few Choruses and one or two songs, it is very heavy and tiresome. It is in 3 parts. In the 1st part Grisi[8] sang "Rejoice greatly" *most beautifully*. She pronounces the English so *very well*, and sang the whole in such excellent style . . . The Hallelujah Chorus at the end of the 2nd part and another at the end of the 3rd act are the finest things besides "Rejoice greatly". But I am not at all fond of Handel's music, I like the present Italian school such as Rossini, Bellini, Donizetti &c., *much better* . . .

Friday, September 11.—. . . Lablache[9] and Rubini sang only once each. Alas! it will be a long time before I shall hear their two fine voices again. But time passes away quickly and April and the dear Opera will soon return. I am to learn to sing next year. Mamma promised I should; and I hope to learn of Lablache. What a delightful master he would be to learn of! Grisi sang "Laudate Dominum", by Mozart, accompanied by Dr Camidge[10] on the organ. She executed the delicate passages in it *beautifully*. Between the two parts we lunched at the Deanery with our party and many others.

Grisi came in with her uncle while we were at luncheon. She is extremely handsome, near-by, by day-light. Her features are not small, but extremely fine, and her eyes are beautiful as are also her teeth. She has such a sweet amiable expression when she smiles, and has pleasing quiet manners. She had an ugly dingy foulard dress on, with a large coloured handkerchief under a large muslin collar. And she had a frightful little pink bonnet on, but in spite of all her ugly attire she looked very handsome. She is a most fascinating little creature . . . Grisi sang the last air "Sing ye to the Lord". Never did I hear anything so beautiful. It was a complete triumph! and was quite electrifying! Though a very little bit and with very little accompaniment, the manner, the power with which she sang it, and the emphasis which she put into it, was truly splendid. I shall just write down the lines:

Sing ye to the Lord, for He hath triumphed gloriously:
The horse and his rider hath He thrown into the sea.

She pronounced it beautifully. When she had sung "The horse and his rider hath He thrown" she paused a moment, and then came out most emphatically with "into the sea"! . . .

[8] Giulia Grisi (1811–69).
[9] Luigi Lablache (1794–1858). He became the Princess's favourite teacher.
[10] Organist at York Minster 1799–1842. For five generations the family of Camidge supplied organists in the county of York.

Saturday, September 12.– . . . At 11 we left Bishopthorpe, but not without regret. They are a very amiable family. Miss Harcourt is a very nice
person. She ought by rights to be called Miss Georgiana Harcourt, the
Archbishop's eldest daughter being unmarried, but as she never goes out
and does not make the *honneurs* in the house, Miss Georgiana is always
called Miss Harcourt.[11] The Archbishop has *10* sons, 5 of whom were at
Bishopthorpe . . . We passed a pleasant time at Bishopthorpe in spite of
fatigues which were *not slight* and which I begin to *feel* . . .

Although the Princess was feeling the strain and anxious not to annoy
her uncle, the King, by overdoing the 'royal' in her progresses, the Duchess
insisted on a long and circuitous journey south, so that her daughter might
see as much of the country as possible, and be seen by as many of the people
as possible, particularly important people. A call was made at Harewood
House, one day in the long ahead to be the home of Queen Victoria's great-
granddaughter, Mary, Princess Royal. Then on wound the cavalcade,
through Leeds, Wakefield and Barnsley, to rest with the Earl of Fitzwilliam
at Wentworth. It was the time of the Doncaster races. When the Princess
arrived by carriage at the Moor next day, the crowds were immense, there
being a competition in interest between finding the winner of the St. Leger
and catching a glimpse of the Heir to the Throne.

The next stop was at Belvoir, near Grantham, the home of the Duke of
Rutland. Here the entertainment programme was in contrast, the Princess's
sight-seeing itinerary of the Castle including a detailed examination of the
family mausoleum.

A short stage along the Great North Road took the party to Burleigh
House, where the Marquess of Exeter had made great preparation. Diarist
Charles Greville was there, on his way south after watching his horse run
nowhere in the St. Leger. He wrote:

> They arrived from Belvoir at three o'clock in a heavy rain, the civic author-
> ities having turned out at Stamford to escort them, and a procession of different
> people all very loyal. When they had lunched, and the Mayor and his brethren
> had got dry, the Duchess received the address, which was read by Lord Exeter
> as Recorder. It talked of the Princess as 'destined to mount the throne of these
> realms'. Conroy handed the answer, just as the Prime Minister does to the King.

This was a typical example of the behaviour of the Duchess and Sir John.
Very understandably, William IV found it infuriating.

Three hundred people attended a ball at Burleigh House that night. The
Princess danced but once with her host and then retired to bed. She had an
arduous journey ahead of her–the long haul to Holkham in Norfolk. It
was late in the afternoon when King's Lynn was reached, and here awaited

[11] She afterwards married Major-General G. A. Malcolm.

her one of the most enthusiastic receptions that she had yet received. The inhabitants insisted that the horses be taken from the carriage and themselves pulled it through the streets to the Duke's Head inn. The next relay of horses was sent on towards Gaywood and took over from manpower at the eastern boundary. Encouraging as the reception was, it added an hour and a quarter to the day's journey and resulted in one of the helpers being run over. It was dark as the fresh horses trotted by the policies of Sandringham, a quarter of a century later to become the beloved home of the Queen's eldest son.

Meantime the host stood at the door of Holkham Hall, frenzied with worry as he speculated on the cause of the delay in the arrival of his guests. His tenants were massed about the drive and the Preventive men formed a guard of honour, allowing the smugglers an undisturbed night to run in their brandy.

The host was Thomas William Coke, for many years Member of Parliament for Norfolk, a great character who was known throughout East Anglia as 'Mr Coke, of Holkham'. In 1837 he was created Earl of Leicester. At last his anxiety was brought to an end by the sound of carriage wheels. He hurried out into the darkness and pouring rain. Two female figures appeared before him. He bowed low. When he looked up, the figures had disappeared. It turned out that they were dressers. At dinner the eyes of the Princess kept closing, so overcome was she with the wish to sleep.

On 23rd September the Princess drove into Wells to receive a loyal address, and the next day moved on to Euston Hall. At Swaffham the races were being held, the programme being held up so that the crowds could see her. After she had said goodbye to the Duke of Grafton and was on her way back from Thetford to Kensington, she confided to her diary that she was absolutely tired out.

Princess Victoria and her mother, 1834, by Sir George Hayter

Journey Five
1835

On Ramsgate Pier

CANTERBURY, *Thursday, September 29.* – I awoke at 6 and got up at $\frac{1}{2}$ past 7. At $\frac{1}{2}$ past 8 we all breakfasted. At $\frac{1}{2}$ past 9 Mamma received an address from the Mayor and Corporation here. We then saw some officers. After this we left Canterbury. It is a very clean nice Inn. It was a fine day.

We reached Ramsgate at $\frac{1}{2}$ past 12. The people received us in a most friendly and kind way. The whole was very well conducted, and the people were very orderly. The streets were ornamented with arches of flowers and flags. The open, free, boundless (to the eye) ocean looked very refreshing. There is nothing between us and France but the sea, here. We have got a small but very nice house, overlooking the sea. At a $\frac{1}{4}$ past 2 we walked down to the Albion Hotel to see the preparations made for dear Uncle Leopold and dear Aunt Louisa.[1]

At a little past 4 we went down to the Hotel with Lady Flora, Lehzen and Lady Conroy, as the steamer was in sight. With beating hearts and longing eyes we sat at the window, anxiously watching the steamer's progress. There was an immense concourse of people on the pier to see them arrive. After about half an hour's time, the steamer entered the Harbour, amidst loud cheering and the salute of guns from the pier, with the Belgian flag on its mast. My *dearest* Uncle Leopold, King of the Belgians, and *dearest* Aunt Louisa were very warmly received. It was but the people's duty to do so, as dear Uncle has lived for so long in England and was so much beloved. After another $\frac{1}{4}$ of an hour of anxious suspense, the waiter told us that "Their Majesties were coming". We hastened downstairs to receive them. There was an immense crowd before the door. At length Uncle appeared, having Aunt Louisa at his arm. What a happiness was it for me to throw myself in the arms of that *dearest* of Uncles, who has always been to me like a father, and whom I love so *very dearly!*

[1] Daughter of Louis Philippe, King of the French, she had married the King of the Belgians in 1832.

Wednesday; December 2.—. . . We walked on the Pier which was very amusing. There are a number of foreign ships in the harbour; Portugese, Finland, and a number of French fishingboats. The dress of the French fishermen is very picturesque. There were some Spanish sailors playing on the pier, who looked very singular. Amongst others there was a little French fisherboy playing with another boy with a pulley. He had a funny round rosy face, and was dressed in a loose blue woven whoolen jacket, with huge boots which reached to his knees, and a red cap. Mamma asked him what he was doing, upon which he answered with naïveté, "Nous sommes à jouer un peu". She asked him where he came from; "De Dunkirk", was his reply. He said this all, and some other things, in such a funny naif way, and with such a sly arch smile, that it was quite amusing. He asked for a "sou", and we gave him 6 pence, which pleased him very much . . .

On Ramsgate sands, by W. F. Frith

Journey Six
1836

A Canterbury Tale

Tuesday, November 29.– . . . At 8 we left poor West Cliff House[1] . . . We reached Canterbury in safety in spite of the rain and some wind, but not very long after we left it, it began to blow so dreadfully, accompanied by floods of rain at intervals, that our carriage swung and the post-boys could scarcely keep on their horses. As we approched Sittingbourne, the *hurricane,* for I cannot call it by any other name, became quite frightful and even alarming; corn stacks were flying about, trees torn up by their roots, and chimneys blown to atoms.

[1] Ramsgate.

West Gate, Canterbury

We got out, or rather were *blown* out, at Sittingbourne. After staying there for a short while we got into the carriage where Lady Theresa[2] and Lehzen were, with them, which being larger and heavier than our post-chaise, would not shake so much. For the first 4 or 5 miles all went on more smoothly and I began to hope our difficulties were at an end. Alas! far from it. The wind blew worse than before and in going down the hill just before Chatham, the hurricane was so tremendous that the horses stopped for a minute, and I thought that we were undone, but by dint of whipping and very good management of the post-boys we reached Rochester in safety. Here we got out, and here it was determined that we must pass the night. Here we are therefore, and here we must remain, greatly to my annoyance, for I am totally unprepared, Lehzen's and my wardrobe maid are gone on to Claremont, and I hate sleeping at an Inn. I had been so glad at the thought of not doing so this time, mais "l'homme propose et Dieu dispose", and it would have been temerity to proceed, for a coach had been upset on the bridge just before we arrived, and the battlements of the bridge itself were totally blown in . . .

[2] Lady Theresa Fox-Strangways.

Pierremont House, where Princess Victoria stayed at Broadstairs

Princess Victoria, 1836, by H. Collen
(reproduced by gracious permission of H.M. The Queen)

Milestones

1837–40

Tuesday, June 20 1837.—I was awoke at 6 o'clock by Mamma, who told me that the Archbishop of Canterbury and Lord Conyngham were here, and wished to see me. I got out of bed and went into my sitting-room (only in my dressing-gown), and *alone*, and saw them. Lord Conyngham (the Lord Chamberlain) then acquainted me that my poor Uncle, the King, was no more, and had expired at 12 minutes p. 2 this morning, and consequently that I am *Queen*.

Thursday, June 28 1838.—I reached the Abbey amid deafening cheers at a little after $\frac{1}{2}$ p. 11; I first went into a robing-room quite close to the entrance, where I found my eight Train-bearers: . . . all dressed alike and beautifully, in white satin and silver tissue, with wreaths of silver corn-ears in front, and a small one of pink roses round the plait behind, and pink roses in the trimming of the dresses. After putting on my Mantle, and the young ladies having properly got hold of it, and Lord Conyngham holding the end of it, I left the robing-room and the Procession began. The sight was splendid; the bank of Peeresses quite beautiful, all in their robes, and the Peers on the other side. My young Train-bearers were always near me, and helped me whenever I wanted anything. The Bishop of Durham[3] stood on one side near me. At the beginning of the Anthem where I've made a mark, I retired to St. Edward's Chapel, a small dark place immediately behind the Altar, with my Ladies and Train-bearers; took off my crimson robe and kirtle and put on the Supertunica of Cloth of Gold, also in the shape of a kirtle, which was put over a singular sort of little gown of linen trimmed with lace; I also took off my circlet of diamonds, and then proceeded bare-headed into the Abbey; I was then seated upon St. Edward's chair where the Dalmatic robe was clasped round me by the Lord Great Chamberlain. Then followed all the various things; and last (of those things) the Crown being

[3]Edward Maltby (1770–1859), Bishop of Durham, to which he had been recently translated from Chichester.

placed on my head;—which was, I must own, a most beautiful impressive moment . . .

Tuesday, October 15 1839.—Saw my dear Cousins come home quite safe from the Hunt, and charge up the hill at an immense pace . . . At. about ½ p. 12 I sent for Albert; he came to the Closet where I was alone, and after a few minutes I said to him, that I thought he must be aware *why* I wished them to come here,—and that it would make me *too happy* if he would consent to what I wished (to marry me). We embraced each other, and he was *so* kind, *so* affectionate. I told him I was quite unworthy of him,—he said he would be very happy "das Leben mit dir zu zubringen", and was so kind, and seemed so happy, that I really felt it was the happiest brightest moment in my life.

Counting the Chickens

Monday, February 10 1840. – The Ceremony was very imposing, and fine and simple, and I think OUGHT to make an everlasting impression on every one who promises at the Altar to *keep* what he or she promises. Dearest Albert repeated everything very distinctly. I felt so happy when the ring was put on, and by Albert.

★

Maiden Voyage to France

THE launching of the new royal yacht, *Victoria and Albert*, in the spring of 1843, presented the Queen with the chance to travel in greater comfort and convenience than had been the case with previous vessels provided for her use. It was also hoped that the horrors of *mal de mer* would be lessened, as she had been violently sick when travelling in the *Royal George* to Scotland the previous year. Anxious to test their latest acquisition, the Queen and Prince Albert decided to spend part of their summer holiday aboard *Victoria and Albert*. Accordingly, when Parliament had risen and the rigours of the London Season were over, the captain, Lord Adolphus Fitzclarence, a natural son of William IV, was ordered to Southampton. On 28th August the royal party embarked.

There were two objectives behind this maiden cruise. The first was of a domestic character—the finding of a site where the Queen and her husband could build a private residence—'a place of one's own, quiet and retired', as the Queen said. This was soon settled, the choice falling on Osborne, by the shore of the Isle of Wight. The second was of a very different nature, of importance both politically and historically. It was a visit to France.

This was to be Queen Victoria's baptism in foreign travel. Historic interest was attached to it as no English Sovereign had visited a French equivalent since Henry VIII appeared on the Field of the Cloth of Gold at the invitation of Francis I in 1520. There was a break with tradition as the Queen was leaving the shores of Britain without a Regent having been appointed. The Crown lawyers had decided, to the Queen's delight, that such a safeguard could be dispensed with on this occasion.

From the political angle, the visit had importance as it marked the end of the period of bad feelings between Great Britain and France engendered by the incident referred to by the Queen as 'the Turko-Egypto affair'. In 1840 Egypt, under her Viceroy, Mohammed Ali, had attempted to break away from her allegiance to the Sultan of Turkey, and found a friend in France. But Britain's Foreign Minister, Lord Palmerston, gave energetic support to the Sultan. For a time it seemed as if France and Britain were drifting towards war, and the views of the Queen and Prince Albert clashed with those of the Foreign Minister. Then the French King wavered, and Mohammed Ali yielded to British coercion. The danger of war was over, but relations remained strained.

In 1843 Louis Philippe, 'King of the French, by the grace of God and the will of the people', was seventy years old. So closely was he linked, by friendship and family ties, to Queen Victoria and Prince Albert, that war between his country and their's would have led to the tragedy of divided loyalties. It was these ties that were being used to re-cement the *entente* between Great Britain and France.

The friendship went back nearly half a century. In 1796 Louis Philippe, then Duc d'Orléans, was forced to leave France. Near destitute, he took ship for Halifax, Nova Scotia, where he had a friend with influence. The friend was none other than Madame Julie de St. Laurent, the mistress of Prince Edward, Duke of Kent, Commander of the British troops in Nova Scotia and one day to be father of Queen Victoria. The Duke of Kent became close friends with the Frenchman and lent him £200, which, considering the financial morass in which he continually struggled, was exceedingly generous. This loan enabled Orléans to proceed to Philadelphia, where he made his living as a teacher. He never forgot the Duke of Kent's kindness, and on becoming King, immediately repaid the £200 to the Duke's daughter.

On his return to Europe the Duc d'Orléans became friends with the Prince Regent and, later, with his daughter, Princess Charlotte[1] and her husband, Prince Leopold of Coburg. The Duc d'Orléans became King of the French in 1830, and Prince Leopold, King of the Belgians in 1831. The following year Leopold of the Belgians married Louise, daughter of Louis Philippe. Thereafter followed no less than three marriages between the children of King Louis Philippe and the House of Coburg. The soil of France was therefore strewn with the cousins of Victoria and Albert.

It was the Queen of the Belgians who first urged that Queen Victoria should visit the French King. Careful of procedure and the international atmosphere, Victoria let it be known to one of her cousins that she thought that it was time that she met *all* the French family. When Louis Philippe heard that the Queen and her husband would be cruising in the English Channel in their new yacht, the Comte de Saint Aulaire was instructed to tell Lord Aberdeen, 'in a natural manner', that a visit to the Château d'Eu would be highly gratifying to the King and Queen of the French. The invitation was accepted.

There then arrived in London a very large order for plain cheese and bottled beer, this apparently being the Citizen King's notion of the fare which the royal visitors would enjoy. This caused Sir Robert Peel, who

[1] Died in 1817.

was not going on the cruise, to write to Lord Aberdeen, who was, expressing the hope that the weather would be calm so that he could do justice to all the delicacies.

The Château d'Eu had been bequeathed to Louis Philippe by his mother in 1821. A magnificent mansion, with a frontage of over three hundred feet, the building was begun in 1578 by the Duc de Guise. It was completed by Madamoiselle de Montpensier in the latter half of the seventeenth century. The Château was largely destroyed by fire in 1902.

In sunshine and on calm waters the royal yacht made her leisurely way along the coastline of Dorset and Devon. Calls were made at resorts, and at each landfall mayoral parties were waiting to greet the Queen and her husband. One Mayor excused himself from taking off his hat because he was a Quaker. Another, in his excitement, fell from the jetty into the water. When fished out, he was too wet 'to present either himself or the address'.

In Plymouth the interest in seeing the Queen for the first time since her marriage was intense. The following letter was written by Mrs E. Morris, wife of the agent of the Bank of England. The family lived at the Bank in George Place, but Mrs Morris was on holiday at nearby Knacker's Knowle[2] with three of her daughters. She was writing to another who was away from home:

1843   Knacker's Knowle
September 1st, Friday.

    . . . I must give you some details of the week which is closing, as it has been rather a more bustling one for Plymouth than usual.

There was for some days a report that the Queen was to visit Plymouth, and you can easily imagine the bustle such an event would cause in *such* a place, Wednesday, August 30th was the day named for her arrival, and after breakfast Papa kindly drove out to fetch us all in to see her majesty.

We found *everybody* on the Hoe looking out eagerly for the Royal "Steamer", and the Sound presented a magnificent sight. So many large ships, and a *lovely day* (a wonder when there is any public sight!). We dined early with Papa, and then proceeded to the Hoe like the rest of the world. . . .

To proceed with my queenly history – we waited gazing until past five, and no queen came, so hearing that the visit was postponed until the next day, and finding I had caught quite sufficient cold in the brilliant east wind, we returned (to George Place) and begged Papa to drive us all back to our rural abode here (Knacker's Knowle).

As we went down Mutley Lane, we heard a grand salute and saw much smoke. Of course this was the Queen and we had just missed seeing the arrival. We did not care much as Agnes *detests* a crowd (and I am not *over* loyal!). So we were easily reconciled to our loss on *that* occasion, but the next day I own to being a little disappointed, when Papa came out in the evening full of all the gay sights and doings, and we the only people away. Even *this* proved the

²Now called Crownhill.

deserted village, on the extraordinary occasion, as every creature that could posted in to the town.

We thought surely if anything were going on Papa would let us know, but it seems he was completely engaged on all hands—our drawing room was filled— he regaled all comers with biscuits and wine, and the queen passed twice under our windows with prince Albert, two maids of honour, and all the *mobility* including the Mayor and Corporation!

Now as it will be many years before I introduce my daughters at *Court*, I do rather lament that they did not get a peep of her little majesty from their own *drawing-room* instead of hers—but we have got well over our disappoint- ment and were quite content with hearing the booming of the great guns last night, and seeing the reflection of a tremendous bonfire on the Hoe, the good natured easterly wind giving us all it could of distant bells ringing and guns firing for hours. . . .

The girls belong to our landlady were present, and I asked how the queen looked. I was answered, "She seems to have a very chuff countenance—very plain, and wore a pale straw coloured bonnet with crimson wreath and red flowers under"! Very French.

This is all my news on this subject—she is gone, but no one can tell whether to Falmouth or France.

On 2nd September the royal yacht headed for Le Tréport, the port but two miles from Eu. No movement upset the Queen's equanimity. She planted her camp-stool in a sheltered spot on deck, and instructed her ladies in the art of plaiting paper to make bonnets. Unfortunately she had taken up position in front of the door to the storeroom where the rum was kept. This upset the crew considerably. She only agreed to move on condition she was allowed to sample the grog. She pronounced that it was not strong enough.

Victoria and Albert showed an unexpected turn of speed and soon out- distanced the warships which formed her escort. Soon she was alone in the Channel. She arrived off Le Tréport at half past five, instead of the schedul- ed hour of seven o'clock. Fortunately the King had taken the precaution of sending out his son, the Prince de Joinville, in his yacht *Pluton*, and a signal from her gave warning.

The King, who was engaged in a Cabinet Council at the Château, headed the rush for the waiting wagonettes. Then the Queen, the Princesses and their ladies clambered aboard. As there was no time for their maids to fix their poke bonnets, they had to arrange one another's side feathers and tie the bonnet-strings in bows as they were rushed towards the jetty. The nurse of the King's grandson, the Comte de Paris, threw him a new hat and collar as he hurried towards his carriage.

Waiting at the jetty steps was the King's barge. Made for Napoleon and Marie Louise, it was manned by twenty-two sailors wearing white sum- mer uniforms and scarlet sashes. It took the King swiftly towards the royal yacht. The Queen, as she watched the barge approach, was quick to note the excitement in the air, but remained ignorant of the fuss which her early arrival had caused.

I felt, as it came nearer and nearer, more and more agitated. At length it came close, and contained the King, Aumale, Montpensier,[3] Augustus,[4] M. Guizot,[5] Lord Cowley, and various officers and ministers. The good kind King was standing on the boat, and so impatient to get out that it was very difficult to prevent him, and to get him to wait till the boat was close enough. He got out and came up as quickly as possible, and embraced me warmly. It was a fine and really affecting sight, and the

Landing at Le Tréport, 1843, by P. Skelton

emotion which it caused I shall never forget . . . The King expressed again and again how delighted he was to see me. His barge is a very fine one, with many oars, and the men in white, with red sashes, and red ribbons round their hats . . .

The landing was a fine sight, which the beauty of the evening, with

[3] Sons of the King.
[4] Prince Augustus of Saxe-Coburg and Gotha, first-cousin of the Queen and Prince, and married to the Princess Clémentine of Orleans.
[5] Foreign Minister.

Arrival at Château d'Eu

the setting sun, enhanced. Crowds of people (all so different from ours), numbers of troops (also so different from our troops), the whole Court, and all the authorities, were assembled on the shore. The King led me up a somewhat steepish staircase, where the Queen received me with the kindest welcome, accompanied by dearest Louise,[6] Hélène,[7] in deep mourning, Françoise,[8] and Madame Adélaide.[9] All this—the cheering of the people, and of the troops, crying "Vive la Reine! Vive le Roi!"— well nigh overcame me . . . The King repeated again and again to me how happy he was at the visit, and how attached he was to my father and to England.

Sunday, September 3.—Rose at half-past seven. I felt as though it were a dream that I was at Eu, and that my favourite air-castle of so many years was at length realised. But it is no dream—it is a pleasant reality . . . The morning was lovely, and the distant ringing of the church bells (much prettier than ours) was the only thing to remind me of Sunday; for the mill was going, and the people were sweeping and working in the garden. The Château is very pretty . . . At half-past two the King and Queen, &c. came to fetch us, and took us over the greater part of the

[6] Queen of the Belgians.
[7] Duchesse d'Orleans. Her husband had been killed in a carriage accident the previous year.
[8] Princess de Joinville.
[9] The King's sister.

Château. The number of family pictures is quite enormous. The little chapel is beautiful, and full of painted windows and statues of saints, &c.– quite a little *bijou*. It is the first Catholic chapel I have seen. There are numbers of pictures and reminiscences of Mademoiselle de Montpensier. She built part of the Château, and there are some interior decorations still of her time. The rooms of the Queen, including a little *cabinet de toilette*, are charming . . . We then set out on a drive . . . The people are very respectable-looking and very civil, crying, "Vive la Reine d'Angleterre!" The King is so pleased. The caps of the women are very picturesque, and they wear also coloured handkerchiefs and aprons, which look very pretty . . . It is the population, and not so much the country, which strikes me as so extremely different from England–their faces, dress, manners, everything.

Monday, September 4.–Up at half-past seven and breakfasted at eight. Good news from the children. The band of the 24th Regiment (*Infanterie légère*) played under my window, and extremely well. They are 55 in number . . . At half-past ten the King and family came and fetched us to their delightful, cheerful breakfast. I sat between the King and Aumale. I feel so gay and happy with these dear people . . . Later we saw M. Guizot, who came to express his great joy at our visit. It seems to have done the greatest good, and to have caused the greatest satisfaction to the French . . . I hear that I should have been most kindly received at Paris even. The French naval officers give this evening a banquet on board the "Pluton" to our naval officers, and I trust that the "*haine pour les perfides Anglais*" will cease . . . At dinner the King told me that the French officers had a dinner at which my health had been drunk with great enthusiasm: "*ce qui n'est pas mal pour des soldats Français*", he added; and he repeated again and again his wish to become more and more closely allied with the English, which would be the sure means of preventing war in Europe, and that his love for the English "*était dans le sang*". After dinner there was very fine music by the *artistes du Conservatoire*. They played beautifully, particularly the things from Beethoven's Symphonies.

Tuesday, September 5.–Albert got up at half-past six in order to go and see the *Carabiniers* with Aumale . . . At ten dear Hélène came to me with little Paris, and stayed till the King and Queen and family came to fetch us to breakfast. She is very clever and sensible, and shows great courage and strength of mind. She spoke with tears in her eyes of my sympathy in her joys and her griefs–poor, excellent Hélène . . . Before we went to our rooms the King took us downstairs, where he gave us two splendid pieces of Gobelins,[10] which have been thirty years in hand, and a beautiful box of Sèvres china.

Wednesday, September 6.–Albert off at seven to bathe. I up before

[10] The tapestries were hung in the room known as 'the Oak Room', at Windsor Castle.

eight . . . The band again played under my window, as yesterday and
the day before . . . At breakfast I sat between the King and Aumale. We
were so much amused at the King's ordering, at this late hour, everything
to be ready for a *Déjeuner dans la forêt*. The King told me that Joinville
would accompany us back to Brighton . . . I showed the Queen the
miniatures of Puss[11] and the Boy,[12] which she admired extremely, and
she said to us so dearly, so kindly, "*Que Dieu les bénisse, et qu'ils puissent
ne jamais vous donner du chagrin*". I then expressed a wish that they might
become like her children, and she said, in one thing she hoped they might,
viz., "*dans leur attachement pour leurs parents. Mais ils donnent aussi du
chagrin*". In saying this, she looked down, her eyes filled with tears, and
she added, "*Enfin, ce que Dieu veut*"!

At two we set off with the whole company in *char-à-bancs*, Albert
sitting in front with the King, then I with the Queen (for whom I feel
a filial affection), and behind us Louise and the other Princesses . . . We
arrived at St. Catherine, a *garde-chasse*. The day was beautiful, and the
endroit of the *forêt* charming. After walking about for some little time
in the garden, we all sat down to a *déjeuner* under the trees, I sitting
between the King and Queen. It was so pretty, so merry, so *champêtre*;
and it is quite wonderful the rapidity with which everything had been
arranged . . . We came home (the evening lovely), at half-past six . . .
After dinner, we remained in a little room near the dining-room, as the
Galerie, where we generally are, was fitted up as *un petit théâtre*. At a little
after nine we went in. The little stage and *orchestre* were perfectly
arranged, and we were all seated in rows of chairs one above the other.
The pieces were all admirably performed. The first was *Le Château de ma
Nièce*, in which Madame Mira acted delightfully; the second, *L'Humoriste*,
in which Arnal sent us into fits of laughter. The speech in which he read
out of a paper the following advertisement, "*Une Dame Espagnole désire
entrer dans une maison, où il y a des enfants, afin de pouvoir leur montrer sa
langue*", was enough to kill one . . .

Thursday, September 7.—At a quarter to six we got up, *le coeur gros*, at
the thought that we must leave this dear, admirable family. At half-past
six the King (who with all the Princes was in uniform), and the Queen
and all the family, came to fetch us to breakfast. Joinville was already
gone to Tréport. I felt so sad to go. At half-past seven we went in the
large state carriage, precisely as we came the day we arrived, with the
Princes riding, and the same escort, &c. It was a lovely morning, and
many people out. We embarked in the King's fine barge with great
facility. The King and Queen, and Louise, and all the Princesses, and
Admiral Mackau were with us in the barge. The Princes, our suite, and

[11] Victoria, Princess Royal, born 1840.
[12] Albert Edward, Prince of Wales (Bertie), born 1841.

the King's gentlemen and Ministers, &c., followed us on board . . . At last the *mauvais moment* arrived, and we were obliged to take leave, and with very great regret . . . It was a pleasure to keep Joinville, who is so amiable, and our great favourite. The dear Queen said, when she paid me that visit yesterday, in speaking of the children, "*Je vous les recommande, Madame, quand nous ne serons plus, ainsi qu'au Prince Albert; que vous les protégiez; ce sont des amis de coeur.*" . . . We stood on the side of the paddle-box, and waited to see them pass by in a small steamer, which they had all got into; and the King waved his hand and called out "Adieu! Adieu"! We set off before nine . . . At half-past three we got into the barge off Brighton, with Joinville, the ladies, Lord Aberdeen, and M. Touchard . . . When we arrived at the Pavilion, we took Joinville upstairs with us, and he was very much struck with the strangeness of the building.

The Pavilion, Brighton

Stately Visits, 1841–5

DURING the early years of her marriage the travel plans of Queen Victoria were hampered by the short intervals between the arrival of her children, but she nevertheless took every opportunity of showing her husband the big houses of England. She had certainly put the score straight by the time it came for him to show her the stately homes of Coburg.

On 26th July, 1841 the royal party set off to visit the Duke of Bedford at Woburn Abbey. The journey had its lighter moments. At Dunstable fifty farmers cantered beside the Queen's carriage and she was lost to sight in the dust. The ladies and gentlemen in the following carriage were entertained by the adventures of Lord Headfort, Irish peer and Lord-in-Waiting.

Woburn Abbey

Hatfield House

It had long been suspected that his hair was not all his own, and he wore his hat at a jaunty angle on the top of his head. A movement of passengers dislodged the hat and it bowled away down the road. Uttering 'Irish brogue screams', Lord Headfort got out to retrieve it. On his return he sat down in a basket full of currants intended for luncheon.

Woburn was not so entertaining. The musical evenings were dull and the meals, despite great effort, contrived to be *almost* as sumptuous as the daily dinners at Windsor. Lady Lyttelton, the royal governess commented: 'The pomp and glory of courts and nobles don't wear well; one need not think of their end or be at all philosophical . . .'

The Queen, who from childhood had been taught to take care of the pence, had ever a strong respect for the possessions and wealth of the British aristocracy, and Woburn impressed her. She seemed afraid to ask about pictures and treasures for fear of being thought ignorant. The part of the tour that she liked best was peeping into other people's rooms.

Outside she was more at ease. She saw the menageries and aviaries, dairy and farms, the garden, the tennis court and the riding school. Prince Albert thought that it was the most complete house he had ever seen.

Their next host was Lord Cowper at Panshanger, famed for its collection of Italian pictures, and from here the Queen and Prince drove over to see Lord Melbourne at Brocket. On the way home a call was made on Lord Salisbury at Hatfield House. Albert was most impressed by the link with Queen Elizabeth and the wonderful wood carving.

In November, 1842 the Queen and Prince absented themselves from the

Palaces for over three weeks, a unique occasion among their English visits. Their host was the Duke of Wellington—the place, Walmer Castle near Deal. As 'Bertie', Prince of Wales, and 'Pussy', Princess Royal, were included in the party, it was decided that the specially constructed, four-horse 'nursery' coach should be used. It was apparently not fully appreciated how great an attraction the children would prove to the mothers of Kent.

The journey of 103 miles was accomplished in eight and half hours running time, two stops for refreshment being made on the way. This excellent time was not achieved without risk and incident and it was a very tired cortège which followed the Queen and the Duke up the grand staircase at Walmer. Lady Lyttelton wrote to her family: 'It was . . . very fatiguing, owing to the immense crowds, the continual cheers, the fright lest we should smash hundreds at every turn, and all the excitement of wreaths and bonfires and triumphal arches, churchbells and cannons all the way along, while we kept flying and dashing, escort panting and horses foaming, and carriages swaying with speed. The children will grow up under the strangest delusions as to what travelling means, and the usual condition of the people in England!'

An incident which occurred at Rochester was long remembered. A very fat and smartly dressed lady, making full use of her weight, snatched the Prince of Wales from the arms of Nurse Sly and kissed him soundly. Furious at being taken by surprise, days passed before the temperament of Mrs Sly returned to normal.

The residence of the Lord Warden of the Cinque Ports, Walmer had been built for coastal defence. 'A big round tower, with odd additions stuck on. Immense thick walls and a heap of comical rooms . . . built close upon the shingly beach.' The draughts whistling through the ill fitting windows and under the doors made venturing outside to take the fresh air entirely unnecessary, yet on the first evening the Queen was seen upon the ramparts, silhouetted by a patch of watery moonlight.

Despite the gales and the draughts, those in attendance enjoyed their stay at Walmer. The reason for this was that the Queen was in a good temper. The reason for her good temper was that she was having a love affaire with Albert. The reason for the love affaire was that Albert was at last rid of the influences of Lord Melbourne and Baroness Lehzen, influences which had acted like a nettle in the connubial bed ever since the Princeling from Coburg had been installed at Windsor. But now the take-over bid of Uncle Leopold and Stockmar was complete and the last of the troublesome directors sent packing—Melbourne, suffering from a stroke, to Brocket, and the governess to Germany, so heart-broken that she could not bear to say goodbye to the girl whom she had nursed and cared for every day since childhood.

Albert could never understand the love of a Queen in her early twenties for a statesman in his late sixties. It simply was not German. He did not fully appreciate that the kind and brilliant man, who had suffered so long at the hands of Lady Caroline Lamb, had much to give to the lonely ruler whose training for the job had been plagued by the schemings and bickerings of her mother and John Conroy. More understandably, he could not tolerate the iron grip which Lehzen maintained over the daily life of his wife. It became a power struggle and youth won. There was little sympathy for the vanquished, though Melbourne and Lehzen had moulded Victoria into the woman she was. So Albert sat proud, king of Walmer Castle, king of a heart, king of a household. There was peace at last in his unfathomable eyes. He walked hand in hand with Victoria down to the sea, swopping pleasantries with the peasants on the way. He read to her Hallam's *Constitutional History of England*, while she purred over her cross-stitch. Albert the martyr loved to be right.

The idyll of Walmer came to an abrupt end with the journey home. It was a nightmare. Prince Albert had decided that, to shorten the carriage journey, the royal train should be used for the last leg from London to Windsor. The Queen had made her first journey by rail, over this same line, the previous June. She had found it most convenient, but the experience had upset some of her Household. The Master of the Horse inspected the engine, coaches and station several hours before the time of departure, while the coachman rode on the footplate and insisted on manipulating the controls, about which he knew nothing. But his scarlet livery was so dirty on arrival at Paddington that he was deterred from repeating the experiment. Prince Albert had restricted his comment to 'Not so fast next time, Mr Conductor'. By November the railway had become accepted as the most convenient means of travel between London and Windsor.

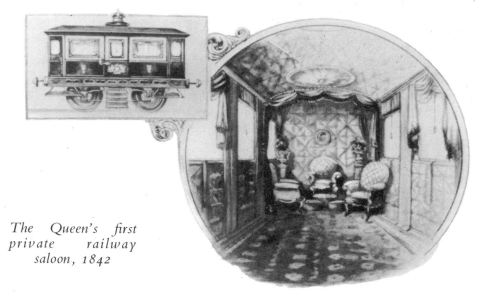

The Queen's first private railway saloon, 1842

It had been decided that the main body of the royal staff, including the maids of honour and the nursery maids, and all the luggage, should travel by train to London and rendez-vous with the travellers in the nursery coach at Paddington. But somebody blundered and, when the Queen and Prince boarded the royal special, there was no sign, or word, of the main rail party. On arrival at Windsor Nurse Sly retired to bed, prostrate after a surfeit of galloping, swaying and puffing. It was left to Lady Lyttelton to care for two squally, bad tempered, tired out children, crying out for toys and food and juvenile equipment which were far away in some baggage waggon. Victoria was not accustomed to such intimacies with her offspring and adopted a role of second fiddle without comment. Demurely she trotted about the Castle on errands and did an excellent job as understudy for a nursery maid.

A year later short stays were made at Drayton Manor, Chatsworth and Belvoir. Among Sir Robert Peel's guests at Drayton[13] were the Queen Dowager and a number of Ministers. Prince Albert thought that the royal descent would strengthen Peel's political position, but others, considering the Chartists, doubted this. The Queen wore a pink silk dress with three flounces at the banquet and afterwards, it was reported, 'completely unbent', going so far as to join in a game of patience with her ladies.

Chatsworth was fantastic. Charles Greville commented that 'there was never anything so grand'. The Hon. Matilda Paget, who was in waiting on the Queen, wrote on 1st December: 'The grandeur of this place far surpasses anything I could have imagined . . . This evening there have been lovely fireworks, the cascades and fountains all lighted up with red and green lights, which had a fairylike effect. I was so amused at the Duke of Devonshire coming up to me in the middle of it all, when every one was so amazed and excited, and saying, in an insinuating voice, "Do you like my little fireworks?" '

There was surprise, too, for the guests when they looked out of their bedroom windows the following morning. Not a trace was to be seen of the multitude of lamps, or the poles and platforms which supported them. Joseph Paxton, the superintendent of the Duke's gardens and the manager of his Derbyshire estates, had worked through the night with a gang of two hundred men. The Prince was most impressed by such efficiency. He was also impressed with the great conservatory which Paxton had recently completed. When the dream at the back of his mind for a Great International Exhibition became a plan, the summons went out for Paxton.

A little cloud of sadness put a shadow into the sunlight of the Chatsworth visit. Lord Melbourne was a guest there. He had been so excited at the thought of talking with his Queen again. He had looked forward to a

[13] The Queen so enjoyed the food at Drayton that she insisted on making a personal inspection of the kitchen range.

tête-à-tête, and even dreamed that one day she would call him back to power. But, in the event, she never talked with him alone and, when he was seated next to her at dinner, soon turned away to converse with her neighbour to the other side. Albert had chased away the past.

Next it was the turn of the Duke of Rutland. Matilda Paget wrote of the journey: 'At Chesterfield I helped the Queen to get up on a chair, that her Majesty might look out of a very high window. She took such very tight hold of my hand to prevent herself falling, that one said her Majesty is evidently not used to getting on chairs. The crowds at Derby and Notting-ham were perfectly astonishing, especially at the latter place, which was more like Edinburgh than anything else . . .'

Then on over the Trent river and the straight Fosse Way, which the Romans laid down to link Lincoln with Bath, into the vale of sleepy red villages where once the Cavaliers and Roundheads fought, and so to the hills and woods of Belvoir.

The Duke of Rutland had arranged that the Prince should have a day's hunting with the Belvoir hounds and the news of this aroused great interest throughout the Shires and in the London clubs. While it was known that the Prince was a master at slaughtering well conserved pheasants and hares, and driven deer, there was much doubt, and expectation, as to how he would fare over Rutland fences. The insular belief prevailed that only the English could ride. Even Victoria was a doubting wife.

The field was very large, very curious and very competitive. The first few fields would obviously be a cavalry charge.

George Anson, the Prince's Secretary, a keen rider to hounds, took station on Albert's left, and Colonel Bouverie, his Equerry, on the right. The party round the Prince soon thinned. Anson went, and then Bouverie. Victoria picked her husband out, 'skimming over the fences like a swallow on a summer evening', and well up with the hounds. And up he stayed throughout the day.

Albert's ride made the head lines. The Queen was greatly satisfied, but wrote to King Leopold: 'One can scarcely credit the absurdity of people, but Albert's riding so boldly has made such a sensation that it has been written all over the country, and they make much more of it than if he had done some great act!'

In November, 1844 the royal pair set out for Burghley, passing through Northampton (Radical but all cheers). The Queen had been guest of the Marquess of Exeter on a previous occasion – in 1835. She had good reason to remember it. During dinner a footman had upset a pail of ice into her mother's lap, 'which made a great bustle'. Victoria followed in the foot-steps of Queen Elizabeth, but in more comfort, the way of approach being so poor in the sixteenth century that H.M. had to travel pillion behind her Lord Steward. Elizabeth had planted a lime to commemorate her visit and

Burghley House

now Victoria did the same. Albert also had a task to perform. At a baptismal service in the chapel he stood as godfather to the Marquess's youngest daughter, who returned to her nursery as Lady Victoria Cecil. The Prince had brought with him a gold cup duly inscribed. Next day the people of Stamford presented him with a pair of Wellington boots.

In the middle of January, 1845 the Queen and Prince Albert descended upon Stowe. They saw the last blaze of sunlight before the twilight came down over the great house. Politically, the visit had some success, but financially it proved disastrous.

The Duke of Buckingham was a staunch protectionist. He was known as 'the Farmer's friend'. He had lately resigned from Peel's Government owing to the Prime Minister's views on Free Trade. But the Queen had had her say about the guest list and insisted that Peel and Lord Aberdeen, Minister for Foreign Affairs, should be on it. The Duke, although he was already in debt, decided that the visit would be one that was long remembered.

For the arrival, the park was packed with the carriages of neighbours and tenants, and waggons full of labourers. When darkness fell lights picked out the famous eighteenth century house and the garden buildings by Kent and Gibbs. The battue was fantastic. So well had the game been preserved in the plantations of Stowe that neither the pheasants nor the hares seemed to be aware of the role that they were supposed to play. The Prince's bag was enormous, but the sporting reputation which he had acquired at Belvoir was somewhat tarnished.

Around the dinner table there was an air of uneasy peace, for it was not only the host who had political differences with the statesmen who were his guests. Among those who had been invited were Benjamin Disraeli and his unconventional wife, twelve years older than himself. Impressed as he was by the ducal surroundings, the forty year old Jew was smarting at the Conservative leader's apparent indifference to his rare capabilities. His application for a place in Sir Robert's Government had been curtly refused and now he was planning a counter-attack. This was the Queen's first private meeting with Disraeli and he reported that she was very courteous to him. Many were the emotions that she was to feel for him, suspicion and distrust, curiosity and downright anger, before at last they came to smile at one another among the primroses at Hughenden.

So the party dispersed, the Queen and the Prince to taste of the hospitality of another stately home, the politicians to the stormiest of sessions, and the Duke of Buckingham to his sums.[14] Already deep in the red, the vast expense of the royal progress hurried on a crisis. In 1847, by when he owed a million pounds, his residences and estates were seized by his creditors.

On the afternoon of Monday, 20th January, the Duke of Wellington

[14] At Stowe the Queen was required to pay her footing. The Duke was too far indebted to his chef, who levied this time-honoured tax, to be able to dismiss him.

Strathfield Saye

awaited the arrival of the royal carriages in the hall of Stratfield Saye. He had long wished to entertain the Queen in his own home and at last she consented, on condition that the visit was informal so that the old man should not tire himself. And informal it certainly was. Meals were taken at small tables and the Duke helped his guests to big helpings of rich puddings as if they were children at a party. Every evening he sat beside Victoria on a sofa after dinner and each eleven o'clock he lit her to bed with a candle. He pleased her by making flattering remarks about her father, tact diverging somewhat from the truth as, in the years after Waterloo, Wellington had christened the Duke of Kent 'the corporal', had delighted in retailing the story that his sisters called him 'Joseph Surface', and was most sarcastic about the way in which Kent had dropped his mistress to marry the widow from Leiningen.

The Queen's visit to the country's hero aroused great public interest and a newspaper reporter applied for permission to observe, and make notes on, the royal activities. He received the following reply: 'F.M. the Duke of Wellington presents his compliments to Mr −−−−−, and begs to say he does not see what his house at Stratfieldsaye has to do with the public press.' Exasperated by the curiosity of sightseers, the Duke ordered a large notice to be erected in the grounds. This said that those who wished to see the house might drive up to the hall door and ring the bell, but they were to abstain from walking on the flagstones and looking in at the windows.

The Duke staged no German battues for Prince Albert. If he wanted a bird, he had to tramp the plough, in the way that the English did. When it rained, as it did most of the time, there was a most suitable royal game for the Prince to play, and the Queen to watch. When the gay cry went up, 'Any one for tennis?' the couple accompanied the Duke's younger son, Lord Charles Wellesley, a very keen player, and his friends to the covered court. Albert liked to try all English amusements at least once.

After visits to the Pavilion at Brighton, Arundel Castle and Buxted Park in February, the circular tours of the high level by the Queen and her husband slowed down and all but petered out. The curtain also fell on Brighton. So fast had the town grown that it was impossible to catch more than a glimpse of the sea, and that only from some of the upper windows, and the rude behaviour of the crowds which assembled each morning to watch the walk to the pier annoyed H.M. considerably. Osborne, in the Isle of Wight, now claimed all the weeks that could be spared from Windsor and London, and the dream of a home in the Highlands was not far away from fulfilment. No longer did Albert have but to admire the talents and work of builders of centuries past. Now he was free to plan the policies, level the terraces, modernise the dairies, build the towers, emblazon the arms of Coburg and dream up the vistas that the years ahead would show. His efforts proved most successful.

Journey Eight
1845

Up the Rhine to Coburg and Gotha

BEING free for a while of the handicaps and fatigues of bearing children, the Queen now decided that the moment had come for her to visit the scenes of her mother's and her husband's youth, and to meet her numerous German relations. On the way to Coburg and Gotha, a return visit was to be paid to King Frederick William IV of Prussia, godfather to the Prince of Wales, at his castles by the Rhine – Brühl and Stolzenfels. Although the Queen was to be away for a month, again no question of providing a regency was raised. However Lord Aberdeen, Minister for Foreign Affairs, joined the royal party.

Friday, August 8, 1845. – A very fine morning when we got up. Both Vicky and darling Alice were with me while I dressed. Poor, dear Puss would much have wished to go with us, – and often proposed how she might go, and said, "Why am I not going to Germany"? Most willingly would I have taken her, and I wished much to have taken one of dearest Albert's children with us to Coburg; but the journey is a serious undertaking, particularly the first time, and she is very young still. But what chiefly decided us is the visit to the King of Prussia, where I could not have looked after her. All four children[1] were with us at breakfast – after which I gave Lady Lyttelton[2] my last instructions, and then with a heavy heart we bade them all adieu in the Hall. Poor little Vicky seemed very sorry, but did not cry . . . It was a very painful moment to drive away with the three poor little things standing at the door. God bless them and protect them, which He will! And they are in excellent hands. Our dear Osborne is so lovely and so enjoyable, that we left it with the greatest regret . . . We reached Buckingham Palace at one. Everything so deserted and lonely here, and I miss the poor children so much.

[1] The newcomers were Alice, born in 1843, and Alfred, the following year. The nickname of Princess Victoria was in process of change from 'Puss' to 'Vicky'.
[2] Royal Governess.

The royal yacht arrived at Antwerp on the evening of the 10th, and at six o'clock next morning the Queen and Prince Albert began the arduous journey that was to take them to the eastern borders of Germany. At Malines they were met by the King and Queen of the Belgians and at Aix-la-Chapelle by the King of the Prussians. The narrow streets of Cologne were bedecked and crowded. Here the roadway had been sprinkled with eau-de-Cologne, and members of the British party were in doubt as to whether this was to disguise some failure of the sanitary department or to advertise the local product. A further fifteen minutes in a train brought the travellers to the King's castle of Brühl:

One drives into the Hall, where a truly magnificent marble staircase begins, which, like the rest of the Castle, is in rococo style. The Queen, Princess of Prussia, Archduke Frederick of Austria, the Duchess of Anhalt-Dessau with her daughter, and the whole Court in state received us and showed us upstairs . . . We went into one of the salons to hear the splendid *Zapfen-streich* (tattoo) performed before the Palace, by 500 musicians (military), the place illuminated with torches and lamps of coloured glass, which had a splendid effect. The evening was lovely, and the whole thing the finest of the kind I ever witnessed. They played "God save the Queen", and it was better played than I ever heard it. So, too, thought Lord Aberdeen.

August 12—We felt so strange to be in Germany at last, and at Brühl, which Albert said he used to go and visit from Bonn . . . Immediately after breakfast we drove to the railroad (Albert with the King), the Queen, the Archduke (who has been sent here to compliment me), and the Prince of Prussia with me, and went by rail to Bonn. From the station we drove to the house of Prince Fürstenburg, a very rich and influential man, where we were received by the Prince and his wife . . . Many gentlemen connected with the University, and who had known Albert were there, and were presented to me, which interested me much. They were greatly delighted to see Albert, and pleased to see me. Amongst them were Universitäts-Richter Salomon, Betthmann-Hollweg, Professor Walther. I felt as if I knew them all, from Albert having told me so much about them. We stepped on to the balcony to see the unveiling of Beethoven's Statue, in honour of which great festivities took place, concerts, &c. But, unfortunately, when the statue was uncovered, its back was turned to us.

The *Freischützen* fired a *feu de joie*, and a chorale was sung. The people cheered us, and dear Albert most particularly, who is beloved here; and the band played a 'Dusch' at the same time, which is a flourish of trumpets, and is always given in Germany, when healths are drunk, &c. From here we drove with the King and Queen,—only a few of our suite following—to Albert's former little house. It was such a pleasure for me to be able to see this house. We went all over it, and it is just as it was, in no way altered . . . We went into the little bower in the garden, from which you have a beautiful view of the Kreuzberg, a convent situated on the top of a hill. The *Sieben Gebirge* (Seven Mountains) you also see, but the view of them is a good deal built out.

At four that afternoon a banquet was staged at Brühl. To it were invited all the distinguished citizens of Bonn and Cologne, so that they might have the opportunity of meeting the royal visitors. Oratorically, the King excelled himself:

Gentlemen, fill your glasses! There is a word of inexpressible sweetness to British as well as to German hearts. Thirty years ago it echoed on the heights of Waterloo from British and German tongues, after days of hot and desperate fighting, to mark the glorious triumph of our brotherhood in arms. Now it resounds on the banks of our fair Rhine, amid the blessings of that peace which was the hallowed fruit of the great conflict. That word is, *Victoria!* Gentlemen, drink to the health of Her Majesty the Queen of the United Kingdom of Great Britain and Ireland (*bowing gracefully to the Queen*), and (*making his glass ring, according to German wont, against the glass of Prince Albert*) to that of her august Consort.

Later the guests were taken by train to the Rhine, where they embarked on a steamer so that they might see Cologne lit up as it had never been before. 'A constant blaze of coloured lights, rockets and salutes of every kind dazzled the eye and stunned the ear'. Overall loomed the cathedral, so red with light it seemed to be on fire. Although she was not in bed until the early hours, by ten o'clock next morning the indefatigable Queen was on her way to Bonn to listen to a concert which formed an important part of the Beethoven Festival:

Unfortunately, though very well executed, there was but very little of Beethoven;—only part of one of the Symphonies, brought into a Cantata by Liszt, and the Overture to Egmont directed by Spohr. From here we drove to the University, where were drawn up all the Professors, who were all presented to me, and many of whom had taught my beloved Albert, and spoke with pleasure and pride of my all in all—Professor Harrles, Professor Perthes (from Gotha), Professor Arndt, a most distinguished and amiable old man—Professor Breitenstein, who taught Albert thorough bass . . . Several of the students were there in the fine dress they wore at the Beethoven Festival, with the rapier in their hands; many fine young men, with loose hair, and beards and moustaches, and most with *Säbelhiebe* (sword-cuts) across their faces. It interested me exceedingly.

From Brühl the King escorted his guests to Schloss Stolzenfels, a few miles above Coblentz. The party on the Rhine steamer included two Kings, three Queens, an Archduke, a Prince Consort and a galaxy of ordinary Princes and Princesses. To the discomfort of Queen Victoria, the military, the villagers and the sightseers who lined the bank felt it incumbent upon themselves to open fire with every weapon available as the steamer drew level. At one point twenty thousand soldiers gave a display of their efficiency with muskets. This was said to be the reason why the journey began in brilliant sunshine and ended in teeming rain.

It was at Stolzenfels that the Queen first discerned something hard and cold beneath the velvet glove which the Prussians extended to her. Archduke Frederick of Austria, uncle of the Emperor of Austria, claimed precedence over Prince Albert. The King of Prussia upheld this claim. The Queen considered this a slight on her husband and it rankled for a long time in her memory. Thereafter she was notedly reluctant to accept offers of hospitality from the Prussian court.

The next stage of the journey was made in the Queen's own yacht, the *Fairy*, which carried the party as far as Mainz. Here another display of military might awaited them. There was a march past of 4,000 Prussian and Austrian soldiers, and military bands played by torchlight far into the night. But after a stay of one day at Mainz, the Queen and Prince Albert began the journey that was for them the *raison d'être* of the holiday—the long drive through the quiet countryside to Coburg, the Prince's birthplace, of which the Queen was to say: 'If I were not who I am—*this* would have been my real home, but I shall always consider it my *2nd* one'. There was for them something of a honeymoon about the journey.

Now they were very much alone, alone in their carriage from early in the morning until late at night. Although they started their day's drive as early as six o'clock, their suite had already gone ahead, and only one carriage followed. This contained Lord Aberdeen, Lord Liverpool (Lord Steward) and two ladies-in-waiting. On occasion an official from the local Post department rode ahead to insure that the road was clear. But the man ahead and the carriage behind might as well have been in another world as the travelling chaise bowled through the shadows of the deep woods and the sunshine of the harvest fields. Only the change of horses at country inns broke up the day.

Höchst, Frankfort, Offenbach, Seligenstadt to Aschaffenburg, and then through the woods of the Spessart to Wurzburg. Here a night was spent at the Royal Palace, so soon to echo with the dancing feet of Lola Montez. Then on to Bamberg, by way of Kissingen, Erbach and Windheim. The Queen was fascinated by the picturesque clothes of the women who worked in the corn fields—the quaint head-dresses, the green bodices, the brilliant coloured neckerchiefs. At mid-afternoon the last change of horses was made on Franconian territory, and the moment for which the Queen had been waiting came close.

I began to feel greatly moved, – agitated indeed in coming near the Coburg frontier. At length we saw flags and people drawn up in lines, and in a few minutes more we were welcomed by Ernest (the Duke of Coburg) in full uniform . . . We got into an open carriage of Ernest's with six horses, – Ernest sitting opposite to us. The good people were all dressed in their best, the women in pointed caps, with many petticoats, and the men in leather breeches. Many girls were there with wreaths of flowers. We came to a triumphal arch, where we were received by the Vice Land-Director (the Land-Director being ill), who said a few kind words of welcome, to which I replied, all those who accompanied him standing on either side, and the good people receiving us in such a warm and really hearty and friendly way.

We then drove to Ketschendorff, the pretty little house of our dear late grandmother, where we found uncle Leopold and Louise, who got into the carriage with us. Ernest mounted a horse and rode next to the carriage on my side, Alvensleben on the other. Then the procession was formed, which looked extremely pretty. At the entrance to the town, we came to another triumphal arch, where Herr Bergner, the Burgo-master, addressed us and was quite overcome. On the other side stood a number of young girls dressed in white, with green wreaths and scarfs, who presented us with bouquets and verses.

I cannot say how much I felt moved on entering this dear old place, and with difficulty I restrained my emotion. The beautifully ornamented town, all bright with wreaths and flowers, the numbers of good affection-ate people, the many recollections connected with the place, – all was so affecting. In the *Platz*, where the Rathhaus and Regierungshaus are, which are fine and curious old houses, the clergy were assembled, and Ober-Superintendent Genzler addressed us very kindly, – a very young-looking man for his age, for he married Mama to my father, and christened and confirmed Albert and Ernest.

The official reception was at Coburg Palace, where the Duchess of Kent was waiting to greet her daughter and 'the staircase was full of cousins'. Then the Queen and the Prince drove to the Rosenau, the favourite home of the late Duke and where Prince Albert had been born.

Wednesday, August 20. – How happy, how joyful, we were, on awak-ing, to feel ourselves here, at the dear Rosenau, my Albert's birthplace, the place he most loves . . . He was so, so happy to be here with me. It is like a beautiful dream . . . Before breakfast we went upstairs to where my dearest Albert and Ernest used to live. It is quite in the roof, with a tiny

The Castle, Coburg

little bedroom on each side, in one of which they both used to sleep with Florschutz their tutor. The view is beautiful, and the paper is still full of holes from their fencing; and the very same table is there on which they were dressed when little.

The 22nd August was the Feast of Saint Gregory, which the people of Coburg celebrated with a Children's Festival. From the balcony of the Palace, the Queen watched the procession of 1,300 schoolchildren.

All the children marched two and two into the courtyard, headed by their schoolmaster and a band, the boys first, and then the girls,—some in costume as shepherdesses, &c., and a little boy in court dress and powder—and the greater part of the girls in white with green. Three girls came upstairs and presented us with a very pretty poem to the tune of "God Save the Queen",—and which they sang extremely well . . . The children then marched off as they came.

After this we drove to the Anger, a meadow close to the town. Here were pitched two tents, decorated with flowers, and open at the sides, under which we were to dine. All the children were in front of us. We walked round among them, and then sat down to dinner. A band of music played the whole time . . . The children danced—and so nicely and so merrily—waltzes, polkas, &c.; and they played games, and were so truly happy,—the evening was so beautiful,—the whole scene so animated,—the good people so quiet, it was the prettiest thing I ever saw . . .

Sunday, August 24.—Another beautiful morning. We again breakfasted

out of doors. At half-past ten we drove with Ernest and Alexandrine—
our ladies and gentlemen following—to Coburg, to the St. Moritz
Kirche, a fine large church, in fact the cathedral of the town. The
clergy received us at the door, and Genzler addressed a few words to me,
expressive of his joy at receiving the great Christian Queen, who was
descended from the Saxon Dukes, who were the first Reformers, and
at the doors of the church where the Reformation was first preached.
The church was immensely full . . . The service is much like the Scotch,
only with more form—less prayer, and more singing. I think they sang
three or four times, besides a *Te Deum* not sung by the congregation. But
the singing of those beautiful Chorales by the whole congregation was
the most elevating, impressive thing imaginable . . . Genzler[3] preached
a fine sermon. He speaks so well and with such ease. The clergyman sings
the *Segen* (Benediction) and one or two other things, and three clergymen officiated. We drove home at half-past twelve. The peasants, in their
smart dress with its bright colours, looked remarkably well. The men,
when in their best clothes, wear jackets with steel buttons, leather
breeches and stockings, and a fur cap . . . I cannot think of going away
from here. I count the hours—for I have a feeling here which I cannot
describe—a feeling as if my childhood also had been spent here.

[3] General-Superintendent W. A. F. Genzler, theologian.

The Rosenau

On the 27th the royal party left Rosenau and made north towards Gotha, where they had been invited to stay by the seventy-four year old Dowager Duchess of Gotha. The night was to be spent at the lovely hunting lodge of Reinhardtsbrunn in the the Thuringian forest. The presence of the Duke and Duchess of Coburg beside the Queen ensured that each little town on the way was waiting with carefully rehearsed reception. This reception consisted of lines of peasants arrayed in their Sunday best, 'white and green young ladies' ready at a signal to bestow their wreaths and verses, and the clergyman armed with a speech. The first performance, at Rodach, was quite a novelty, but this soon wore off. At Hildburghausen the Queen noted that the clergyman's speech was 'very discursive and somewhat confused' and at Themar she had difficulty in keeping a straight face when she

Reinhardtsbrunn

was referred to a ' "*Die herrliche Britten Königin*" in such an extraordinary way'. At Meiningen they were given dinner by the reigning Duke, Queen Adelaide's brother, and at six in the evening reached Schmalkald.

Here there was an amazing crowd, and a very ridiculous postmaster. A little stream runs through the street, which has a very good effect. Soon after Schmalkald the most beautiful scenery begins,—fine mountains covered with spruce fir—like Scotland, but much more wooded, and then we have very little spruce fir;—valleys and meadows, with little houses, and smoke rising from where the charcoal-burners are; so solemn, wild, and impressive,—and such pure, cool, mountain air. At Klein

Schmalkald Ernest's territories begin. It was getting dark here, and still more a little farther on, where, on the top of the Thüringer-Wald, were a number of people. Herr von Stein made a very pretty speech. A number of peasant girls, prettily dressed and with caps, presented verses. There was a triumphal arch, and everything picturesquely arranged, and with great taste. From here we drove down a long but gradual descent, with noble wooded mountains on either side, and all the people running after us. It was quite dark by the time we came to Friedrichsroda, which was prettily illuminated, and where all the miners were drawn up. We drove at a foot's pace to Reinhardtsbrunn, which is quite near, and where a number of people were assembled . . . The fine trees, with their great branches sweeping to the ground, and their deep rich green, the luxuriant flowers, the wooded mountains that surround the house, the piece of water in front, make it one of the most beautiful spots imaginable.

At Gotha, which was reached the following afternoon, the Queen and her husband stayed at the Friedrichsthal Palace. A highlight of the visit was the *Schützenfest* arranged for the 29th.

We drove, quite in procession, to the *Vogelschiessen* (the Popinjay shooting) through the very pretty town of Gotha, in broiling heat. We went up to a fine room, a ball-room, just opposite the *Schützenhaus*, in front of which was a large platform, handsomely arrayed, where we all stood. In walking through the ball-room, a number of young (some pretty) ladies strewed flowers before us.

When we were established on the platform, the procession began— first came the *Schützen* (riflemen), with their chief, the *Schützen-König*, wearing innumerable medals given by the *Schützen-König* of each year. After these came all the public officials (*Beamten*); eight peasants from each place, on horseback; and the women, in their best and various pretty costumes, in waggons all decorated with flowers and branches. I am sure 2,000 passed. It was extremely pretty, and to see them file off in the fields was quite a picture. The crowd was immense, and all so orderly, so well behaved. Many of the women wear caps with feathers, such as the children have, only very high.

We then went to another platform, where a goblet I had won was brought me; and after this to the Schützenhaus, a small, hot room, and smelling strongly of tobacco, in front of which is the wooden bird on a pole. Uncle Leopold and all the Princes shot, and almost all hit it, but did not bring it down.

Whilst this Ruritanian idyll was being diarised amid the forests and harvest fields of Coburg and Gotha, a very different strain ran through the reports and comment appearing in the London papers and magazines. Satire and criticism grew sharper as the days passed and more news came through from the correspondents covering the tour, until by early September the storm against Prince Albert, and to a lesser extent the Queen, grew to proportions only to be rivalled by the tirade against the Royal Family which attended the Republican outburst of 1870.

There had been opposition to the visit to Germany from the moment of its first announcement. There were many reasons for its unpopularity, these varying with the state of life of the critic. But three main platforms emerged. They were connected with the Chartist Movement, English nationalism, and finance.

The Chartist Movement, though roundly condemned in conservative circles for its violence, had drawn attention to the terrible conditions under which low grade workers toiled in the mines and factories, and at the loom. There was no curb on the exploitation of labour, except for a single Act which limited the daily working hours of certain children to twelve. The housing and medical care available to these unfortunates were a disgrace, and this was widely appreciated. Although certain remedial measures, such as the Corn Law Repeal and Lord Shaftesbury's factory reforms, were in train, there was as yet little sign of alleviation. At such times of economic and political crisis and unrest, trips abroad in royal yachts were wide open to criticism.

The nationalism was essentially English. Victoria lived in England and was regarded as the Queen of England, the claims of Scotland, Ireland, and even Wales, being subsidiary. That was how the people saw it. She had not as yet trodden on Irish soil. There had even been criticism that she was deserting her post when she visited Scotland in 1842. But then it was only twenty-five years since the English troops of occupation had been withdrawn from north of the Border. The people there had not as yet fully accepted her, nor were they interested where she spent her holidays.

The Napoleonic wars had caused the English upper classes to become isolationist, and to keep within their own shores. The days of the Grand Tour were over, and the railway expresses had not yet opened up the Continental countries to a new era of holiday travel. After the London season was over, the English gentleman returned to his country estates and busied himself with the harvest and preparations for hunting. What was good enough for him, was good enough for his Sovereign. He wanted no foreign Prince involving England in the politics of Germany and France.

As to finance, this was a worry shared by all classes of society, for the aspirations of the House of Coburg in this direction were suspect. The drain of sterling eastward towards the Duchys of Coburg and Gotha had begun in 1816. Then Prince Leopold of Coburg had married the Prince Regent's only daughter, Charlotte, and been granted an annuity of £50,000 by Parliament. The death of his wife in childbirth the following year did not influence the Prince's income and by the time of the marriage of his niece, Victoria, he had drawn over £1,000,000 out of British funds. Added to this was the £6,000 a year allowed to his sister, the Duchess of Kent, which was raised to £16,000 on the death of George IV. When his nephew, Albert, became engaged to Queen Victoria, the thought of another £50,000 a year going to a Coburger was too much both for the public and for Parliament. The figure was cut to £30,000. The general opinion, not shared by the Queen or the Prince, was that even this sum was too generous.

When Prince Albert arrived in England there was a general suspicion that it was his aim to have as large a family as possible, in due season to claim a large allowance from Parliament for each of them, and then plant them, in matrimony, around the Grand Ducal palaces of Germany. To some extent the suspicion was to be proved correct. Such financial demands were to be made, the offspring were to be despatched to the Continent with healthy allowances, and the family would not have been limited to nine but for the doctors telling the Queen that she had done enough, a curtailment of her pleasures to which she took strong exception.

The Prince's behaviour immediately after marriage increased the fears of the public. His acumen was obvious. He pruned ruthlessly the costs of running Buckingham Palace, raised the income from the Duchy of Cornwall from £16,000 per year to nearly £60,000, objected to paying Poor Rates on the Windsor farms, and firmly planted in his pocket any small prizes that he picked up with cattle at agricultural shows. In the cartoons John Bull, in tattered coat, surveyed the splendid royal yacht and the fine new mansion at Osborne, and wondered where the spending would stop.

The mounting feeling against the German tour can be traced through successive issues of *Punch*, a magazine which crossed swords with the Prince until the Great Exhibition and the Crimean war proved that a Coburger could be an investment as well as an expense.

The attack opened comparatively mildly. There was a skit on the tragedy of the poor little orphans left all alone at Buckingham Palace, the barb here being that the Prince had applied for a large sum of public money to be spent on enlarging the nursery quarters, which were said to be cramped and pervaded by the smell of glue from the carpenter's shop. Next came a cry that London had been deserted both by the Queen and the political leaders:

The only man of any mark
In all the town remaining,
I sauntered in St. James's Park,
And watched the daylight waning.
"The Speaker's lips", I said, "are sealed,

They've shut up both the Houses;
Sir Robert's gone to Turnabout field,
Sir James to shoot the grouses.
The Queen and all the Court are out
In Germany and Flanders,
And, happy midst his native *kraut*,
My princely Albert wanders . . . . ."

The autocratic King of Prussia was most unpopular in England, and the visit to the castles on the Rhine did not escape comment. The Queen was criticised for assisting at the inauguration of a statue to 'an old, stone-deaf musitian, named Beethoven', it being suggested that she would be better employed in unveiling a statue to Shakespeare in England. She was also taken to task for bestowing an honour on the German philosopher, Baron Humbolt. This, in the event, proved to be well merited criticism, as it was later to be revealed that the author of *Kosmos* was meantime writing rude remarks about Albert in his diary.

The thought of peaceful summer days in Coburg seems to have riled the satirists:

Sleep, softly sleep, O royal pair! and be your slumbers cosy now;
Watch round their pillows, angels fair, and give their eyes repose enow;
And summer flowers and summer air breathe soft around Schloss Rosenau . . .
Then softly sleep, O royal pair, and pleasantly repose ye now,
In England there is state and care, and weariness and woes enow;
But summer wind and summer air breathe gently round Schloss Rosenau.

The correspondents on the spot appeared to have become wearied of following the Queen as Prince Albert led her on a conducted tour of all the scenes and possessions and memories of his childhood:

At Rosenau, where His Royal Highness Prince Albert first saw light, they show affectionately, not only the cradle in which the royal infant was laid, but *the silver spoon which he had in his mouth* when he was born. The Correspondent of the *Morning Herald* fainted when he saw this admirable relic. It is as large as a soup-ladle; handsomely embossed with the arms of England; and in the custody of Madame Eyerglück, His Royal Highness's excellent nurse . . .

The contrast between the way of life and outlook of the ordinary people of Coburg and of England was a subject of the greatest interest. Here is a letter from an imaginary lady-in-waiting, attending the Queen, to a friend in London:

Dearest Emily,
I must steal ten minutes to tell you how charmed we all are with everything here. Such an agreeable disappointment. The reigning Duke is really very comfortably off, and the palace is a well-appointed place, such as one might manage to live in very tolerably—*dans le cas*. But the people, my dear girl—the

people! You never saw anything half so picturesque and delightful,—more like the chorus at the Opera, than real living peasants, such as I've seen about Papa's place at home. And they are so well bred; the men take their hats off as one passes them, and the girls drop such graceful curtsies! It is the thing here to be very affable, and mix freely with everybody. Lord Stalk is very much distressed about the effect it may have upon the Q-E-N, who has not been used to that sort of thing. He says that it is terribly levelling and revolutionary; but we all find it charming. Of course, one couldn't think of doing anything of the kind at home, where the labourers are so dirty and disgusting, and wear nasty ginghams instead of the prettiest fancy costumes in the world . . .

The parade of the children before the Queen on the feast of St. Gregory proved too much for the correspondents who knew only too well the lot of boys and girls in the industrial areas at home:

We're happy German children;
You praise our glossy hair,
Our wreaths and pretty costumes,
Our cheeks so fat and fair;
Our little bodies never
Grew stunted at the loom;
Our infant eyes ne'er ached in
The pit-seam's choky gloom.
We never sobb'd to sleep, on straw
Close crouched for warmth, like vermin—
We are not English children;
No, *Gott sei dank*, we're German . . . . .

When you go back to England,
You'll think on what you've seen;
Then ask our English sisters
To dance upon the green.
Perhaps they'll look less savage,
With seemlier clothes and food;
Perhaps with kindly teaching
You'll change their sullen mood.
'Tis sad that they should go in rags,
And you, their QUEEN, in ermine—
We are not English children;
No, *Gott sei dank*, we're German!

Yet it was the events of 30th August that were to provide the critics with a quiver full of arrows. These were to find their mark on the Queen and Prince Albert many a time in the following months, causing wounds which made the previous attacks seem like pin pricks. The cause of the trouble was the staging of 'a drive of deer in the old style'.

Early that morning a long procession wound out from Coburg. It consisted of the British party, the court and dignitaries of Coburg, huntsmen and foresters, musicians and hangers-on. The Queen noted 'the bright blue sky, the heavenly air, the exquisite tints'. The procession halted for refreshment at Reinhardtsbrunn and then headed deep into the forest towards the isolated shooting lodge of Jägersruh—Hunter's Rest. The Queen noted:

"What is so beautiful is, that between the noble and solemn forest of silver and spruce firs you come to the greenest and most beautiful little vallies, overshadowed by these deep green firs, with here and there some beeches and oaks among them. These reminded us of Windsor—only the latter seems stiff and tame after this . . ."

From Jägersruh a track had been constructed by an army of peasants in the preceding two days. The track ended in a wide clearing in the forest. This was the place of slaughter.

All around the clearing, under the trees, had been erected a wall of thick canvas. It was a corral from which there could be no escape.

In the centre of the clearing a pavilion had been built. It was covered with branches cut from the fir trees, and was decorated with wreaths of flowers and of laurel. Into this pavilion trooped the elite. The ladies relaxed on chairs. The men looked to their guns.

At a signal, a piece of the canvas fence was drawn back to form a gateway. There was dead silence. Then echoed through the woods the strange, wild hunting cry of the Chasseurs of the Duke of Coburg. There came the thunder of hooves and the crash of branches, and fifty-five stags and hinds, wild with fear, were driven into the clearing.

As the guns began to fire, a band, hidden in the trees, struck up martial music. Two hours later thirty-one stags and twenty-four hinds lay dead, or dying, on the red grass. The Queen commented: 'As for the sport itself, none of the gentlemen liked this butchery.' But the memory was short lived. She completed her diary entry thus: 'The day had been, and the evening was, more beautiful than any I remember, and the soft blue haze over the hills, as we left Reinhardtsbrunn for Gotha, perfected the charm of the scene by the delicate veil which it threw over it'.'

The news of this day's slaughter sent a wave of anger and revulsion across the English counties. As Roger Fulford makes clear in *The Prince Consort*, at this stage of English history, shooting was a modest and gentlemanly pursuit, two or three guns, a loader and a couple of setters being considered sufficient for a satisfactory day's sport. 'The huge shooting-party with hordes of minions, the "slap-up" luncheon and the minimum of exercise, beloved by the best county families of Surrey, had not as yet made its expensive appearance'.

Court Pastimes

The newspapers did not spare their readers. From *The Times*:

The dead or dying deer were either dragged, or carried suspended from poles, across towards the pavilion, when the huntsman plunged his enormous *couteau de chasse* into their throats.

From the *Chronicle*:

The ladies passed along the line of dead on the way to their carriages. It was a wretched sight. The poor creatures arranged side by side – their dull, dim dead eyes looking as ghastly as the wounds from which the clotted blood came oozing in black drops down the yet warm carcass. I had as lief see a knacker's yard.

Punch opened up the attack with verses entitled 'The Gotha Huntsman's Chorus', of which this was the first verse:

What sportsman can view with the sportsman of Gotha?
For whom foams more brightly life's glass of champagne?
What butcher can boast him a handsomer quota
Of meat in the course of his life to have slain?
With rifle his hand in,
He takes his proud stand in
His shooting-box raised on a hillock's ascent;
And from that pavilion,
Deals 'Death to the Million'
Of deer down below him in fold snugly pent.

Next came a suggestion for a spelling lesson for the young Prince of Wales:

LESSON I

The Deer is a poor weak Brute, which it is good to Kill. It was once the Plan to Hunt the Deer; but it Runs so fast, that it puts one quite in a Heat to try to Catch it. A PRINCE should not get Hot, or be at much pains to Hunt the Deer, but should have the Deer all Caught, and put in a small Space, which they can in no way get Out of. Then the PRINCE should come with his Gun, and Shoot at the Deer, when he must Kill some. It is fine Sport to see the Deer fall Dead in the Place, where they are all put so Close that a PRINCE, Shoot how he will, must Hit some of them. If you are a good Boy, you shall have a Gun, and some Deer to Shoot at with the Gun; and then they shall be all put Dead in a Row, for you to look at them. Oh! what nice Sport for a PRINCE of the Blood!

Efforts were made to show that the Queen had tears in her eyes during the killing and was with difficulty restrained from leaving her chair. Why then, it was asked, was the British Sovereign exposed to such a sight? Her husband knew exactly what was going to happen, as he had been attending such deer drives since he was a boy. On learning the details from him, she should have declined to take part. The Queen did not therefore emerge unscathed:

Sing a song of Gotha—a pocket full of rye,
Eight-and-forty timid deer driven into die;
When the sport was open'd, all bleeding they were seen—
Wasn't that a dainty dish to set before a Queen?
The Queen sat in her easy chair, and look'd as sweet as honey;
The Prince was shooting at the deer, in weather bright and sunny;
The bands were playing Polkas, dress'd in green and golden clothes;
The Nobles cut the poor deer's throats, and that is all *Punch* knows!

The attacks on the Prince continued in *Punch* for week after week. A full page drawing showed him boasting of his prowess as a marksman to the Queen, while all around his feet deer lay dying and a chasseur cut their throats. It was suggested that the wives of the butchers of London should present him with a blue apron, 'worked with a *couteau de chasse*, and various gouts of blood, in scarlet silk'; and that when the time came for the Christmas presentation of meat to the poor of Windsor, the Prince should slaughter the beasts himself, watched by the Queen. The ingenuity of the versifiers seemed endless:

Some forty Ed of sleak and hantlered dear
In Coburg (where such hanimmles abound)
Were shot, as by the nusepapers I hear,
by HALBERT Usband of the Brittish Crownd.
BRITANNIA'S QUEEN let fall the purly tear;
Seeing them butcherd in their silvn prisns;
Igspecially, when the keepers, standing round,
Came up and cut their pretty hinnocent whizns . . . . .

Fortunately for the holidaymakers in Gotha the London newspapers did not arrive in time to disturb their peace of mind. Now it was time to start the journey home and after a tearful farewell to all the relations, the Queen and Prince drove to Eisenach, at the invitation of the Grand Duke of Weimar. Here they were shown Martin Luther's room, the table at which he translated the Bible and the mark on the wall made by the inkstand which he threw at the devil. At Frankfort they met King Ludwig of Bavaria, who upset the Queen by talking to her with his eyes tight shut.

The royal yacht *Fairy* was waiting for them at Bingen, and slipped silently away downstream. What a contrast was this journey with the slow fight up against the current of only a few weeks before, when the bands had played and the guns thundered from every village. May be the King of Prussia's slight on Prince Albert still rankled, but true it was that the magic of the Rhine had faded clear away. The Queen had left part of her heart at the Rosenau and in the evening of the 5th September she wrote:

Strange to say the Rhine, fine as it is, had lost its charm for us all. First of all, the excitement of the novelty was over—and then, we were

Hochheim on Main

spoiled by the *Thüringer-Wald*. Stolzenfels looked very well, and so did Ehrenbreitstein, and those fine *Sieben Gebirge*; but after passing Bonn, we went down below, and Albert read to me.

★

In the cellars of Windsor Queen Victoria held one of the finest collection of Cabinet Rhine wines in the country. She was very fond of hock. She is credited with saying: 'A little drop of hock keeps away the doc.' When she was at Mayence in 1845 she took the opportunity of learning about the origins of the wine. Guided by members of the Grand-ducal family of Hesse, she drove to the vineyard of Mr George Michael Pabstmann at Hochheim.

The then village of Hochheim lies by the river Main, three miles upstream from the point where it joins the Rhine. From it hock derives its name. Rhenish wines were known as 'hock' as long ago as the sixteenth century. It was probably a case of convenience as the names of the numerous German vineyards were found hard to pronounce. So the label 'hock' was used to designate all Rhine wines, whether red or white. But, in time, home consumption absorbed the output of red and the use of the name hock was restricted to the white.

Queen Victoria and Prince Albert left their carriage at a spot called Dechanten-Ruhe (Dean's Rest) and were shown over the vineyard by Mr Pabstmann. They tasted the grapes and sampled wine. Unfortunately 1845 was not a good year. Winter came in early and the rain was pelting down as the Queen made her way homewards down the Rhine. But 1846 was a very good year indeed.

In 1850 Mr Pabstmann asked the Queen for permission to name his vineyard after her and, in a document dated 5th December 1850, signed at Windsor, she gave the necessary authority. So Königin Victoria Berg was born. Three years later the German authorities agreed to the renaming of

Monument to Queen Victoria at Hochheim

the vineyard and on the Queen's birthday in 1854 a monument was unveiled to celebrate the occasion.

Eight metres high and three wide, the monument looks out over a scene which stretches from busy Mainz to the green-skirted Taunus mountains. It was designed by the Grand Duke of Hesse's architect, Mr Gladbach.

Ornamented with gothic leaves, flowers and ornamental work, the top of the monument ends in four corner towers. In the frieze are the words: 'Queen Victoria Mountain'.

A canopy overhangs the English arms, and the emblems of England,

Scotland and Ireland, and the middle field bears the inscription:

> 'Her Majesty
> VICTORIA
> Queen of Great Britain and Ireland
> etc. has graciously lent her name
> to this vineyard. As an honour to the
> exalted monarch and as a thankful
> remembrance of such graceful distinction,
> this monument was erected by G.
> M. Pabstmann, Hochheim on Main,
> 24th May 1854.'

In 1857 the 'Königin Victoria Weinberg' was entered in the register as a separate winery and through the remaining years of the nineteenth century, and the early years of the next, Queen Victoria's label was to be seen at many a royal occasion.

In 1918 the firm of G. M. Pabstmann & Son changed hands, being purchased by Mr Joseph Neus, a successful winegrower whose son is in charge of the business today.

The two great wars broke many memories and many loyalties. But in 1950, as in 1850, came the royal blessing on the wine from Hochheim. The occasion was the birth of a daughter to the King's elder daughter, Princess Elizabeth. The child was to be called Anne. In time for the christening arrived a case of specially selected 1945 Königin Victoria Berg Auslese, presented by the vintagers and vineyard owner at Hochheim. It was graciously accepted and thus the former contact was re-established.

Journey Nine
1846

Yachting Excursion–Torquay, Dartmouth, Plymouth and Guernsey

On Board the Victoria and Albert, *Dartmouth, Thursday, August 20, 1846.*–We steamed past the various places on the beautiful coast of Devonshire which we had passed three years ago–Seaton, Sidmouth, off which we stopped for ten minutes, Axmouth, Teignmouth, &c.;–till we came to Babbicombe, a small bay, where we remained an hour. It is a beautiful spot, which before we had only passed at a distance. Red cliffs and rocks with wooded hills like Italy, and reminding one of a ballet or play where nymphs are to appear–such rocks and grottos, with the deepest sea, on which there was not a ripple. We intended to disembark and walk up the hill; but it came on to rain very much, and we could not do so. We tried to sketch the part looking towards Torbay. I never saw our good children looking better, or in higher spirits. I contrived to give Vicky a little lesson, by making her read in her English history.

We proceeded on our course again at half past one o'clock, and saw Torquay very plainly, which is very fine. The sea looked so stormy and the weather became so thick that it was thought best to give up Plymouth (for the third time), and to put into that beautiful Dartmouth, and we accordingly did so, in pouring rain, the deck swimming with water, and all of us with umbrellas; the children being most anxious to see everything. Notwithstanding the rain, this place is lovely, with its wooded rocks and church and castle at the entrance. It puts me much in mind of the beautiful Rhine, and its fine ruined castles, and the Lurlei.

I am now below writing, and crowds of boats are surrounding us on all sides.

Plymouth Harbour, Friday, August 21.–We got under weigh by half-past six o'clock, and on looking out we saw the sea so calm and blue and the sun so bright that we determined to get up. It was a very fine day, but there was a great deal of swell. At length at half-past nine we entered the splendid harbour of Plymouth, and anchored again below Mount Edgecumbe; which, with its beautiful trees, including pines, growing down into the sea, looks more lovely than ever.

I changed my dress and read innumerable letters and despatches, and then went on deck and saw the authorities—the Admirals and Generals. I did Vicky's lessons and wrote; and at half-past one we went on board the "Fairy", (leaving the children on board the "Victoria and Albert",) with all our ladies and gentlemen, as well as Sir James Clark,[1] who has joined us here. We steamed up the Tamar, going first a little way up the St. Germans river, which has very prettily wooded banks. Trematon Castle to the right, which belongs to Bertie as Duke of Cornwall, and Jats to the left, are extremely pretty. We stopped here and afterwards turned back and went up the Tamar, which at first seemed flat; but as we proceeded the scenery became quite beautiful—richly wooded hills, the trees growing down into the water, and the river winding so much as to have the effect of a lake. In this it reminded me so much of going up the Rhine,—though I don't think the river resembles the Rhine. Albert thought it like the Danube.

The finest parts begin about Saltash, which is a small but prettily built town. To the right as you go up all is un-English looking; a little farther on is the mouth of the Tavy; here the river becomes very beautiful. We passed numbers of mines at work. Further on, to the left, we came to Pentillie Castle situated on a height most beautifully wooded down to the water's edge, and the river winding rapidly above and below it. Albert said it reminded him of the situation of Greinburg on the Danube. Not much further on we came to the picturesque little village and landing-place of Cothele, at the foot of a thickly wooded bank, with a valley on one side. Here the river is very narrow. We landed, and drove up a steep hill under fine trees to the very curious old House of Cothele, where we got out of the carriage. It is most curious in every way—as it stands in the same state as it was in the time of Henry VII. and is in great preservation—the old rooms hung with arras, &c.

We drove down another way under beautiful trees and above the fine valley; embarked and proceeded down the river. The evening was beautiful, the sun bright, and the sky and sea so blue. We arrived just too late for the launch of the frigate "Thetis". It reminded me so much of when we were here three years ago, as we approached our yacht, surrounded by myriads of boats, and had to row through them in our barge. We returned at half-past five. The evening was delightful—clear, calm, and cloudless, but a good deal of noise in the boats around us. Lord and Lady Mount Edgecumbe[2] and Sir James Clark dined with us.

[1] Royal physician.
[2] 3rd Earl (1797–1861).

The Prince of Wales, 1846, by Winterhalter
(reproduced by gracious permission of H.M. The Queen)

Plymouth, Saturday, August 22.–Albert was up at six o'clock, as he was
to go to Dartmoor Forest. At ten I went in the barge with the two
children, the ladies, Baron Stockmar, and Lord Alfred Paget, and landed
at Mount Edgecumbe, where we were received by Lady Mount Edgecumbe, her two boys, her sister and nieces, and beyond the landing-
place by Lord Mount Edgecumbe. There were crowds where we landed,
and I feel so shy and put out without Albert.

I got into a carriage with the children and Lady Mount Edgecumbe–
Lord Mount Edgecumbe going before us and the other following–and
took a lovely drive along the road which overhangs the bay, commanding such beautiful views on all sides, and going under and by such
fine trees. We had been there three years ago; but it is always a pleasure
to see it again. The day very hot and a little hazy. We came to the house
at eleven. The children went with their governess and the other children
into the shade and had luncheon in the house, and I remained in the
gallery–a very pretty room, with some fine pictures, and with a door
opening on the garden, and commanding a lovely little bit of sea view,
which I tried to sketch. A little after twelve we returned to the yacht,
which had been beset with boats ever since six in the morning. Albert
returned safely to me at one o'clock, much pleased with his trip; and
said that Dartmoor Forest was like Scotland.

At two we went with our ladies and gentlemen, and without the
children, again to the landing-place at Mount Edgecumbe, where we
were received as before, and drove up to the house. There are some of
the finest and tallest chestnut-trees in existence here, and the beech-trees
grow very peculiarly–quite tall and straight–the branches growing upwards. We walked about the gallery and looked into Lady Mount
Edgecumbe's little room at one end of it, which is charming, and full of
pretty little things which she has collected, and there we took luncheon
in a room where there are some fine portraits by Sir Joshua Reynolds[3]
They are all of the Mount Edgecumbe family, one of whom was his
great patron. Sir Joshua was born a few miles from Plymouth. There are
in the same room pictures by him when he first began to paint, which
have kept their colour; then when he made experiments–and these are
quite faded; and again of his works when he discovered his mistakes, and
the colour of his pictures is then beautiful.

We walked about the garden near the house, and then drove to the
"Kiosk", by beautiful stone pines and pinasters, which interested Albert
very much, and put me so much in mind of Mr Lear's drawings. The
view from this "Kiosk", which is very high over the sea and town, is
most beautiful, and the sea was like glass, not a ripple to be seen. We
walked down a very pretty road or path through the woods and trees

[3] 1723–92.

till we met the carriage, and we drove along that beautiful road, which is said to be a little like the Cornice, over-hanging the sea, down to the place of embarkation, where we took leave of them all, and returned to our yacht by half-past four. Poor Lord Mount Edgecumbe is in such a sad, helpless state; but so patient and cheerful. We went on board just to fetch the children, and then on to the "Fairy", and steamed in her round the harbour, or rather bay, in which there are such pretty spots; into the Cat Water, from whence we rowed in one of the barges a little way up the river to look at Saltram, Lord Morley's; after that back to the "Fairy", went in her into Mill Bay, Sutton Pool, and Stonehouse, and returned to the yacht by half-past six.

In Guernsey Bay, off St. Pierre, Guernsey, Sunday, August 23.—On waking, the morning was so lovely that we could not help regretting

The landing at St. Pierre (St. Peter Port), Guernsey

that we could not delay our trip a little, by one day at least, as the Council which was to have been on the 25th is now on the 29th. We thought, however, we could do nothing but sail for Torbay, at half-past nine, and for Osborne on Monday. While dressing, I kept thinking whether we could not manage to see Falmouth, or something or other.

Albert thought we might perhaps manage to see one of the Channel Islands, and accordingly he sent for Lord Adolphus Fitzclarence, and it was settled that we should go to Guernsey, which delighted me, as I had so long wished to see it. The day splendid. The General and Admiral came on board to take leave. Sir J. West is the Admiral, and General Murray, the General; and at about half-past nine we set off, and the sea the whole way was as calm as it was in '43. Plymouth is beautiful, and we shall always be delighted to return there.

For two hours we were in expectation of seeing land; but it was very hazy, and they did not know where we were—till about six, when land was seen by the "Fairy", who came to report it, and then all the other vessels went on before us. As we approached we were struck by the beauty of the Guernsey coast, in which there are several rocky bays, and the town of St. Pierre is very picturesquely built, down to the water's edge. You see Sark (or Sercq) as you enter the harbour to the right, and further on, close opposite St. Pierre, two islands close together—Herm and Jethou. The bay with these fine islands is really most curious.

We anchored at seven, immediately opposite St. Pierre, and with the two islands on the other side of us. We dined at eight, and found on going on deck the whole town illuminated, which had a very pretty effect, and must have been done very quickly, for they had no idea of our coming. It is built like a foreign town. The people speak mostly French amongst themselves.

August 24.—St. Pierre is very picturesque-looking—with very high, bright-coloured houses built down almost into the sea. The College and Church are very conspicuous buildings. This island with its bold point, and the little one of Cornet with a sort of castle on it (close to which we were anchored), and the three islands of Herm, Jethou, and Sark, with innumerable rocks, are really very fine and peculiar,—especially as they then were in bright sunlight. We both sketched, and at a quarter to nine got into our barge with our ladies. The pier and shore were lined with crowds of people, and with ladies dressed in white, singing "God save the Queen", and strewing the ground with flowers. We walked to our carriage, preceded by General Napier,[4] brother to Sir Charles[5] (in Scinde), a very singular-looking old man, tall and thin, with an aquiline nose, piercing eyes, and white moustaches and hair. The people were

[4] General Sir William Napier (1785–1860).
[5] One time Commander-in-Chief in India (1782–1853).

Departure from Guernsey, 24th August, 1846

extremely well-behaved and friendly, and received us very warmly as we drove through the narrow streets, which were decorated with flowers and flags, and lined with the Guernsey militia, 2,000 strong, with their several bands. Some of the militia were mounted.

The vegetation beyond the town is exceedingly fine; and the evergreens and flowers most abundant. The streets and hills steep, and the view from the fort, which is very high, (and where General Napier presented me with the keys,) is extremely beautiful. You look over the bay of Guernsey, and see opposite to you the islands of Herm, Jethou, and Sark; with Alderney, and the coast of France, Cape de la Hague, to the left in the distance, and to the right in the distance, Jersey.

The island appears very flourishing. In the town they speak English, but in the country French, and this is the same in all the islands. They belonged to the Duchy of Normandy, and have been in our possession ever since William the Conqueror's time. King John was the last of their sovereigns who visited them. We drove along the pier, and then embarked amidst great cheering. It was all admirably managed; the people are extremely loyal.

We got under weigh a little before one and in about an hour-and-a-half we came close to Alderney, seeing all the time the French coast, Cape de la Hague, very plainly to our right, and leaving the Casquets Lights to our left. Alderney is quite different from all the other islands, excessively rocky and barren, and the rocks in and under the sea are most frightful.

Journey Ten
1846

Yachting Excursion – Jersey, Falmouth, St. Michael's Mount and Fowey

On Board the Victoria and Albert, *Off St. Heliers, Jersey, Wednesday, September 2, 1846.* – At a quarter-past seven o'clock we set off with Vicky, Bertie, Lady Jocelyn, Miss Kerr, Mdlle. Gruner, Lord Spencer[1] Lord Palmerston[2] and Sir James Clark (Mr Anson[3] and Colonel Grey[4] being on board the "Black Eagle"), and embarked at Osborne Pier. There was a good deal of swell. It was fine, but very cold at first. At twelve we saw Alderney, and between two and three got into the Alderney Race, where there was a great deal of rolling, but not for long. We passed between Alderney and the French coast – Cape de la Hague – and saw the other side of Alderney; and then, later, Sark, Guernsey, and the other islands. After passing the Alderney Race it became quite smooth; and then Bertie put on his sailor's dress, which was beautifully made by the man on board who makes for our sailors, who were all assembled on deck to see him, cheered, and seemed delighted with him.

The coast of Jersey is very beautiful, and we had to go nearly all round, in order to get to St. Heliers. We first passed the point called Rondnez, then Grosnez with a tower, St. Ouen's Bay, La Rocca, a curious old tower on a rock, and then Brelade's Bay. The red cliffs and rocks, with the setting sun gilding and lighting them all up, were beautiful. At last, at a quarter to seven, we arrived in this fine large bay of St. Aubin, in which lies St. Heliers; and after dinner we went on deck to see the illumination and the bonfires.

Off St. Heliers, Thursday, September 3. – A splendid day. I never saw a

[1] Lord Chamberlain.
[2] Foreign Secretary.
[3] Private Secretary to Prince Albert.
[4] Equerry to the Queen.

more beautiful deep blue sea, quite like Naples; and Albert said that this fine bay of St. Aubin, in which we lie, really is like the Bay of Naples. Noirmont Point terminates in a low tower to our left, with St. Aubin and a tower on a rock in front of it; farther in, and to our right, Elizabeth Castle, a picturesque fort on a rock, with the town of St. Heliers behind it.

The colouring and the effect of light were indescribably beautiful. We got into our barge with our ladies and gentlemen, and then went on board the "Fairy", until we were close to the harbour, and then we got into the barge again. We landed at the stairs of the Victoria Harbour, amid the cheers of the numberless crowds, guns firing, and bands playing; were received, as at Guernsey, by all the ladies of the town, very gaily dressed, who, strewing flowers on our way, conducted us to a canopy, where I received the address of the States and of the militia.

We then got into our carriage and drove along the pier; Colonel Le Couteur, my militia aide-de-camp, riding by my side, with other officers, and by Albert's side Colonel Le Breton, commanding the militia, who, 5,000 strong, lined the streets, and were stationed along the pier. The States[5] walking in front. The crowds were immense, but everything in excellent order, and the people most enthusiastic, though not more so than the good Guernsey people; the town is much larger, and they had much longer time for preparations; the decorations and arches of flowers were really beautifully done, and there were numberless kind inscriptions. All the country people here speak French, and so did the police who walked near us. It was a very gratifying reception. There was a seat in one of the streets filled by Frenchwomen from Granville, curiously dressed with white handkerchiefs on their heads. After passing through several streets we drove up to the Government House, but did not get out. General Gibbs, the Governor, is very infirm.

We then proceeded at a quicker pace—the walking procession having ceased—through the interior of the island, which is extremely pretty and very green,—orchards without end, as at Mayence. We passed the curious old tower of La Hougue Bie, of very ancient date, and went to the Castle of Mont Orgueil, in Grouville Bay, very beautifully situated, completely over-hanging the sea, and where Robert, Duke of Normandy, son of William the Conqueror, is said to have lived. We walked part of the way up, and from one of the batteries, where no guns are now mounted, you command the bay, and the French coast is distinctly seen, only 13 miles distant. The people are very proud that Mont Orgueil had never been taken; but I have since learnt it was taken by surprise and held for a few days; Guernsey, however, *never* was taken.

We then returned to our carriage, and proceeded to the pier by a

[5] The Legislative Body.

shorter road, and through a different part of the town. There is a peculiar elm-tree in the island, which is very pretty, and unlike any other,—the leaf and the way it grows almost resembling the acacia. The crowd was very great and the heat very intense in going back.

We re-embarked in the barge, but had only to go a few yards to the "Fairy". The situation of the harbour is very fine,—and crowned with the fort, and covered by numbers of people, was like an amphitheatre. The heat of the sun, and the glare, had made me so ill and giddy that I remained below the great part of the afternoon, and Albert went out for an hour on the "Fairy".

Falmouth Harbour, Friday, Sept. 4.—A beautiful day again, with the same brilliantly blue sea. At a quarter to eight o'clock we got under weigh. There was a great deal of motion at first, and for the greater part of the day the ship pitched, but getting up the sails steadied her. From five o'clock it became quite smooth; at half-past five we saw land, and at seven we entered Falmouth Harbour, where we were immediately surrounded by boats. The evening was beautiful and the sea as smooth as glass, and without even a ripple. The calmest night possible, with a beautiful moon, when we went on deck; every now and then the splashing of oars and the hum of voices were heard; but they were the only sounds, unlike the constant dashing of the sea against the vessel, which we heard all the time we were at Jersey.

Mount's Bay, Cornwall, Saturday, September 5.—At eight o'clock we left Falmouth and proceeded along the coast of Cornwall, which becomes bold and rugged beyond the Lizard Point and as one approaches Land's End. At about twelve was passed Land's End, which is very fine and rocky, the view from thence opening beautifully. We passed quite close by the Longships, some rocks on which stands a lighthouse. The sea was unusually smooth for the Land's End. We went beyond a point with some rocks near it, called the Brisons, and then steamed back; the famous Botallack mine lies here. A little before two we landed in this beautiful Mount's Bay, close below St. Michael's Mount, which is very fine. When the bay first opened to our view the sun was lighting up this beautiful castle, so peculiarly built on a lofty rock, and which forms an island at high water.

In entering the bay we passed the small village of Mousehole and the town of Penzance, which is prettily situated, about one mile and a half from St. Michael's Mount. The day brightened just as we arrived, and the sea again became so blue. Soon after our arrival we anchored; the crowd of boats was beyond everything; numbers of Cornish pilcher fishermen, in their curious large boats, kept going round and round, and then anchored, besides many other boats full of people. They are a very noisy, talkative race, and speak a kind of English hardly to be understood.

The royal yacht off St. Michael's Mount

During our voyage I was able to give Vicky her lessons. At three o'clock we all got into the barge, including the children and Mdlle. Gruner, their governess, and rowed through an avenue of boats of all descriptions to the "Fairy", where we went on board. The getting in and out of the barge was no easy task. There was a good deal of swell, and the "Fairy" herself rolled amazingly. We steamed round the bay to look at St. Michael's Mount from the other side, which is even more beautiful, and then went on to Penzance. Albert landed near Penzance with all the gentlemen, except Lord Spencer (who is most agreeable, efficient, and useful at sea, being a Captain of the Navy) and Colonel Grey, and went to see the smelting of copper and tin, and the works in serpentine at Penzance. We remained here a little while without going on, in order to sketch, and returned to the "Victoria and Albert" by half-past four, the boats crowding round us in all directions; and when Bertie showed himself the people shouted:—"Three cheers for the Duke of Cornwall"! Albert returned a little before seven, much gratified by what he had seen, and bringing home specimens of the serpentine stone.

Mount's Bay, Sunday, September 6.—A hazy, dull-looking morning, but as calm as it possibly could be. At half-past eight o'clock we got into our barge, with Miss Kerr and Lord Spencer, and proceeded without any standard to the little harbour below St. Michael's Mount. Behind St. Michael's Mount is the little town of Marazion, or "Market Jew", which is supposed to have taken its name from the Jews having in former times trafficked there. We disembarked and walked up the Mount by a circuitous rugged path over rocks and turf, and entered the old castle which is beautifully kept, and must be a nice house to live in; as there are so many good rooms in it. The dining-room, made out of the refectory, is very pretty; it is surrounded by a frieze, representing ancient hunting. The chapel is excessively curious. The organ is much famed; Albert played a little on it, and it sounded very fine.

Below the chapel is a dungeon, where some years ago was discovered the skeleton of a large man without a coffin; the entrance is in the floor of one of the pews. Albert went down with Lord Spencer, and afterwards went with him and Sir James Clark (who, with Lord Palmerston and Colonel Grey, had joined us,) *up* to the tower, on the top of which is "St. Michael's chair", which, it is said, betrothed couples run up to, and whoever gets first into the chair will have at home the government of the house; and the old house-keeper—a nice tidy old woman—said many a couple "does go there!" though Albert and Lord Spencer said it was the awkwardest place possible to get at. St. Michael's Mount belongs to Sir J. St. Aubyn. There were several drawings there of Mont St. Michael in Normandy, which is very like this one; and was, I believe, inhabited by the same order of monks as this was, i.e. Benedictines. We walked down again, had to step over another boat in order to get into our barge, as the tide was so very low, and returned on board the yacht before ten.

The view from the top of St. Michael's is very beautiful and very extensive, but unfortunately it was too thick and hazy to see it well. A low ridge of sand separates St. Michael's Mount from Marazion at low water, and the sea at high water. From the sand to the summit of the castle is about 250 feet. The chapel was originally erected, they say, for the use of pilgrims who came here; and it owes its name to a tradition of St. Michael the Archangel having rested on the rock.

At half-past eleven Lord Spencer read on deck the short morning service generally read at sea, which only lasted twenty or twenty-five minutes. The awning was put up, and flags on the sides; and all the officers and sailors were there, as well as ourselves. A flag was hoisted, as is usual when the service is performed on board ship, and Lord Spencer read extremely well.

Albert made a most beautiful little sketch of St. Michael's Mount. Soon after two we left Mount's Bay. About four we came opposite to some very curious serpentine rocks, between Mount's Bay and Lizard Point, and we stopped, that Albert might land. The gentlemen went with him. Lord Spencer soon returned, saying that Albert was very anxious

I should see the beautiful little cave in these serpentine rocks; and accordingly I got into the barge, with the children, and ladies, and Lord Spencer, and we rowed to these rocks, with their caves and little creeks. There were many cormorants and sea-gulls on the rocks. We returned again,

Prince Albert's sketch of St. Michael's Mount

and were soon joined by Albert, who brought many fine specimens which he had picked up. The stone is really beautifully marked with red and green veins.

We proceeded on our course, and reached Falmouth before seven. The fine afternoon was changed to a foggy, dull, cold evening. We have had on board with us, since we left Falmouth, Mr Taylor, mineral agent to the Duchy of Cornwall, a very intelligent young man, married to a niece of Sir Charles Lemon's.

Falmouth, Monday, September 7.—Immediately after breakfast, Albert left me to land and visit some mines. The corporation of Penryn were on board, and very anxious to see "The Duke of Cornwall", so I stepped out of the pavilion on deck with Bertie, and Lord Palmerston told them that that was "The Duke of Cornwall"; and the old mayor of Penryn said that "he hoped he would grow up a blessing to his parents and to his country".

A little before four o'clock, we all got into the barge, with the two children, and rowed to the "Fairy". We rowed through a literal *lane* of boats, full of people, who had surrounded the yacht ever since early in the morning, and proceeded up the river by St. Just's Pool, to the left of which lies Sir C. Lemon's place, and Trefusis belonging to Lord Clinton. We went up the Truro, which is beautiful,—something like the Tamar, but almost finer, though not so bold as Pentillie Castle and Cothele,—winding between banks entirely wooded with stunted oak, and full of numberless creeks. The prettiest are King Harry's Ferry and a spot near Tregothnan (Lord Falmouth's), where there is a beautiful little boat-house, quite in the woods, and on the river, at the point where the Tregony separates from the Truro. Albert said the position of this boat-house put him in mind of Tell's Chapel in Switzerland.

We went a little way up the Tregony, which is most beautiful, with high sloping banks, thickly wooded down to the water's edge. Then we turned back and went up the Truro to Malpas, another bend of the river,

Municipal dignitaries of Penryn introduced to the Prince of Wales, 1846

from whence one can see Truro, the capital of Cornwall. We stopped here awhile, as so many boats came out from a little place called Sunny Corner, just below Truro, in order to see us; indeed the whole population poured out on foot and in carts, &c. along the banks; and cheered, and were enchanted when Bertie was held up for them to see. It was a very pretty, gratifying sight.

We went straight on to Swan Pool outside Pendennis Castle, where we got into the barge, and rowed near to the shore to see a net drawn. Mr Fox, a Quaker, who lives at Falmouth, and has sent us flowers, fruit, and many other things, proposed to put in his net and draw, that we might see all sorts of fish caught, but when it was drawn there was not one fish! So we went back to the "Fairy". The water near the shore in Swan Pool is so wonderfully clear that one could count the pebbles.

Tuesday, September 8.—A wet morning when we rose and breakfasted with the children. At about ten o'clock we entered Fowey, which is situated in a creek much like Dartmouth, only not so beautiful, but still very pretty. We got into the barge (leaving the children on board, and also Lord Spencer, who was not quite well), and landed at Fowey with our ladies and gentlemen, and Mr Taylor, whom we had brought with us from Falmouth. We got into our carriage with the ladies, the gentlemen following in others, and drove through some of the narrowest

The Queen visiting the iron mine near Lostwithiel, 1846

streets I ever saw in England, and up perpendicular hills in the streets—it really quite alarmed one; but we got up and through them quite safely.

We then drove on for a long way, on bad and narrow roads, higher and higher up, commanding a fine and very extensive view of the very hilly country of Cornwall, its hills covered with fields, and intersected by hedges. At last we came to one field where there was no road whatever, but we went down the hill quite safely, and got out of the carriage at the top of another hill, where, surrounded by woods, stands a circular ruin, covered with ivy, of the old castle of Restormel, belonging to the Duchy of Cornwall, and in which the last Earl of Cornwall lived in the thirteenth century. It was very picturesque from this point.

We visited here the Restormel mine, belonging also to the Duchy of Cornwall. It is an iron mine, and you go in on a level. Albert and I got into one of the trucks and were dragged in by miners, Mr Taylor walking behind us. The minders wear a curious woollen dress, with a cap like this:

and the dress thus:

and they generally have a candle stuck in front of the cap. This time candlesticks were stuck along the sides of the mine, and those who did not drag or push the truck carried lights. Albert and the gentlemen wore miners' hats. There was no room for any one to pass between the trucks and the rock, and only just room enough to hold up one's head, and not always that. It had a most curious effect, and there was something unearthly about this lit-up cavern-like place. We got out and scrambled a little way to see the veins of ore, and Albert knocked off some pieces; but in general it is blown by gunpowder, being so hard. The miners seemed so pleased at seeing us, and are intelligent, good people. It was quite dazzling when we came into daylight again.

We then got into our carriage and passed through the small town of Lostwithiel, where an address was presented to us, and then we passed through Mr Agar Robarts' Park, which reminded one of Cothele. We returned by the same road till near Fowey, when we went through some of the narrowest lanes I almost ever drove through, and so fearfully stony. We drove along high above the river to Place, belonging to Mr Treffry, which has been restored according to drawings in his possession, representing the house as it was in former times. A lady of that name defended the house against the French during the absence of her husband, in the fourteenth or fifteenth century. The old gentleman showed us all over the house, and into an unfinished hall, lined with marble and porphyry, all of which came from Cornwall. We then walked down to the place of embarkation and proceeded at once to the yacht. Mr Taylor deserved the greatest credit for all the arrangements. He and his father are what are called "Adventurers" of the mine.

Osborne, Wednesday, September 9. – We got up about seven o'clock and found we had just passed The Needles.

The Fairy at Osborne   *From a Pratt-ware lid*

Journey Eleven
1847

War and Peace at Cambridge

HAVING spent eighteen months at Bonn University, Prince Albert was most anxious to inspect the educational system and way of life at Oxford and Cambridge. He visited the former in 1841, and there heard the under song of Anglo-Catholicism. Such a tune was not for him, and he turned towards Cambridge, where he understood that views were more precise and contemporary. He had the opportunity of finding out in October 1843 when Dr Whewell, Vice-Chancellor and Master of Trinity, knowing of the Prince's interest, invited the Queen to stay at the Lodge of Trinity College, the opportunity being taken to confer the degree of LL.D. upon the Prince.

The Queen and her husband travelled by road, this being one of the last long journeys that they made in this way. Boarding a brand new post-chaise at Paddington, they passed the time between villages by reading to one another from a German novel. Behind them was a most remarkable sight. Two thousand horsemen, farmers, landowners, children on ponies, joined the cavalcade at intervals, so that they might say what they had done that day, royalty being rare travellers indeed on the Cambridge road.

The visit was a great success. The dons had immense fun polishing up royal procedure and practising the air of retrogradation without tripping over the hinder parts of their cassocks. They were delighted with the intelligent questions put to them by Prince Albert. The undergraduates obviously approved of the Queen, those at Trinity laying their gowns upon the ground so that she might walk upon them.

On the way home the Queen and Prince stayed with Lord Hardwicke at Wimpole,[1] a ball being given in their honour.

[1] It was in 1740 that the cultured spendthrift Edward, Lord Harley, 2nd Earl of Oxford, sold Wimpole to Lord Chancellor Hardwicke to rid himself of a debt of £100,000. Harley married Lady Henrietta Cavendish Holles, daughter of John, Duke of Newcastle, and dissipated most of the £500,000 which she inherited. Their only child, Margaret, was the 'noble, lovely little Peggy' of poet Prior, who died at Wimpole in 1721. Margaret married the 2nd Duke of Portland.

Back at Windsor the Queen wrote to King Leopold of the Belgians:

We returned on Saturday, highly pleased and interested with our tour, though a little *done up*. I seldom remember more enthusiasm than was shown at Cambridge, and in particular by the Undergraduates. They received my dear Angel, too, with the greatest enthusiasm. This is useful, as these young people *will all, in time,* have a certain part to play; they are the rising generation, and an event of this kind makes a lasting impression on their minds.

The impression made by the Prince certainly lasted in the minds of the dons of Trinity. After the sudden death of their Chancellor, Hugh, third Duke of Northumberland, on 11th February 1847, fearful that a candidate of Left wing sympathies might be foisted upon them, they decided to thwart such plans by playing checkmate with the Queen's husband.

Prince Albert was both delighted and complimented by the offer. He agreed, provided that there was 'a general manifestation' in his favour, and no competition. When all seemed settled, there came a bolt out of the blue. A rival group of dons had acted independently and persuaded the Earl of Powis, grandson of Clive of India, to stand. An added complication was that the late Chancellor had married Lady Charlotte Florentia Clive, who had been governess to the Queen.

The Prince decided that the best step would be to retire gracefully, and so he informed a deputation that arrived at Buckingham Palace from Cambridge. His supporters at Trinity received the information by telegraph in code, but refused to accept it. They were not going to give up without a fight to St. John's, who had put up Powis. So the battle commenced.

Those who believed that it would be an easy victory for Prince Albert reckoned without the feeling against him in the London newspaper offices. Stories were put out that, if the royal candidate won, there would be no port at the dinner table, and that at his installation those present would either have to kneel or lie prostrate throughout the proceedings.

Punch, not forgetful of the affair of the Coburg battue, gave their cartoonists full pages to lampoon the Prince. It was suggested that, as he had a wife and five children to support, he might also apply for the square-keepership of Golden Square, and that another suitable post might be 'the professorship of Hebrew in the University of Hounsditch'.

Lord Powis decided that it was the support for him in London that could bring him victory, and to encourage this support he ran special trains to Cambridge. The voting continued over three days, and at the end of the first Powis was only sixteen behind.

At this period Evangelicanism was strong at Cambridge, though probably not so marked as the Tractarian movement at Oxford. Here came the undoing of Lord Powis, for the belief was widespread that his religious sympathies lay with Rome. The Prince was the man for the undergraduates and, although they could not vote, they packed the Senate House to give him their support. Their behaviour was described as positively 'hateful'.

The Queen and the Prince Consort

From the galleries came a fusillade of dried peas and such small coins as they could spare. One victim of their attack was Lord Fitzwilliam. When, in his scarlet gown, he entered to vote for Lord Powis, he was met with the cry—'Here she comes—the whore of Babylon.'

On the final count the Prince had a majority of 116—953 votes to 837. The Queen described the affair as an 'unseemly contest' but took satisfaction that 'all the cleverest men were on my beloved Albert's side'. Despite the narrow margin of victory, the Prince was convinced (quite willingly) that this need not deter him from accepting the Chancellorship, the seventy-seven year old Poet Laureate, William Wordsworth, was requested to write an Ode, and the Installation date was fixed. On 5th July the Queen wrote in her diary:

A splendid day, the sky very blue, the sun very, very hot. At Tottenham, we took the Eastern Counties Railway—the great railway king, Mr Hudson himself, going with us—and reached Cambridge station at one.

In the Great Hall of Trinity the Queen received the Chancellor's Address:

I cannot say how it agitated and embarrassed me to have to receive this address, and hear it read by my beloved Albert, who walked in at the head of the University, and who looked dear and beautiful in his robes, which were carried by Colonel Phipps and Colonel Seymour. Albert went through it all admirably—almost absurd, however, as it was for us. He gave me the Address, and I read the answer; a few kissed hands, and then Albert retired with the University . . .

After lunch the Queen went to the Senate House.

It reminded me of Cologne and Bonn having the Prussian Prince

(Waldemar) with us, and driving about from one place to another. Albert received me at the door, and led me up to the seat prepared. He sat covered in his Chancellor's chair. There was a perfect roar of applause, and the heat was over-powering. Some preliminary business was gone through, and then the Public Orator made a long, too long, Latin speech. The three Princes (Prince Waldemar of Prussia, Prince Peter of Oldenburg, and the Hereditary Grand-Duke of Saxe-Weimar), Lords Abercorn, Spencer, and Fortescue, M. Van de Weyer, Prince Löwenstein, the Bishops of Oxford, Tasmania, Cape Town, and Melbourne, were made doctors. So also were Sir G. Grey, Sir Harry Smith (who was much cheered), Sir R. Murchison, Professor Ehrenberg –very odd and very German-looking–and Professor Muhler . . . Got home at twenty minutes to five. Wrote and worked. Such a hot day; but Cambridge looks beautiful in summer, so different from what we saw it at the end of October, and with all its gardens so green, and the flowers in the windows of the colleges, has a very fine effect.

The following morning the ceremony of installation took place in the Senate House. In the afternoon there was a visit to a horticultural show ('the heat was beyond endurance, and the crowd fearful'), and in the evening a great banquet at Trinity. Though the programme of the day was now over, there remained moments that were long to live in the Queen's memory:

The evening being so beautiful, we proposed to walk out, and accordingly at ten set out in curious costumes; Albert in his dress coat, with a macintosh over it; I, in my evening dress and diadem, and with a veil over my head, and the two Princes in their uniform, and the ladies in their dresses, and shawls, and Veils. We walked through the small garden, and could not at first find our way, after which we discovered the right road, and walked along the beautiful avenue of lime-trees in the grounds of St. John's College, along the water and over the bridges. All was so pretty and picturesque–in particular, that one covered bridge of St. John's College, which is like the Bridge of Sighs at Venice. We stopped to listen to the distant hum of the town; and nothing seemed wanting, but some singing, which everywhere but here in this country we should have heard. A lattice opened, and we could fancy a lady appearing, and listening to a serenade.

Journey Twelve
1849

First Visit to Ireland

On Board the Victoria and Albert, *in the Cove of Cork, Thursday, August 2, 1849.* – Arrived here after a quick but not very pleasant passage. The day was fine and bright, and the sea to all appearances very smooth; but there was a dreadful swell, which made one incapable of reading or doing anything. We passed the Land's End at nine o'clock in the morning. When we went on deck after eight in the evening, we were close to the Cove of Cork, and could see many bonfires on the hill, and the rockets and lights that were sent off from the different steamers. The harbour is immense, though the land is not very high, and entering by twilight it had a very fine effect. Lady Jocelyn,[1] Miss Dawson, Lord Fortescue (Lord Steward), Sir George Grey (Secretary of State for the Home Department), Miss Hildyard,[2] Sir James Clark, and Mr Birch[3] are on board with us. The equerries, Colonel Phipps and Colonel Gordon, are on board the "Black Eagle".

Friday, August 3. – The day was grey and excessively "muggy", which is the character of the Irish climate. The ships saluted at eight o'clock, and the "Ganges" (the flag-ship and a three-decker) and the "Hogue" (a three-decker cut down, with very heavy guns, and with a screw put into her), which are both very near us, made a great noise. The harbour is very extensive, and there are several islands in it, one of which is very large. Spike Island is immediately opposite us, and has a convict prison; near it another island with the depôt, &c. In a line with that is the town of Cove, picturesquely built up a hill. The two war-steamers have only just come in. The Admiral (Dixon) and the Captains of the vessels came on board. Later, Lord Bandon (Lord-Lieutenant of the county), Lord Thomond, General Turner, Commander of the Forces at Cork, presented their respects, and Albert went on shore, and I occupied myself in writing and sketching. Albert returned before our

[1] Viscountess Jocelyn, daughter of Lady Palmerston and niece of Lord Melbourne.
[2] Governess.
[3] Tutor.

luncheon, and had been walking about and visiting some of the cabins.

We left the yacht at two with the ladies and gentlemen, and went on board the "Fairy", which was surrounded with rowing and sailing boats. We first went round the harbour, all the ships saluting, as well as numbers of steamers and yachts. We then went into Cove and lay alongside the landing-place, which was very prettily decorated; and covered with people; and yachts, ships and boats crowding all round. The two Members, Messrs. Roche and Power, as well as other gentlemen, including the Roman Catholic and Protestant clergymen, and then the members of the Yacht Club, presented addresses. After which, to give the people the satisfaction of calling the place Queenstown,[4] in honour of its being the first spot on which I set foot upon Irish ground, I stepped on shore amidst the roar of cannon (for the artillery were placed so close as quite to shake the temporary room which we entered); and the enthusiastic shouts of the people. We immediately re-embarked and proceeded up the river Lee towards Cork. It is extremely pretty and richly wooded, and reminded me of the Tamar. The first feature of interest we passed was a little bathing-place, called Monkstown, and later Blackrock Castle, at which point we stopped to receive a salmon, and a very pretty address from the poor fishermen of Blackrock.

As we approached the city we saw people streaming in, on foot, on

[4] Now Cobh.

The Royal yacht in Cork Harbour, 1849

horseback, and many in jaunting-cars. When we reached Cork the "Fairy" again lay alongside, and we received all the addresses: first, from the Mayor and Corporation (I knighted the Mayor immediately afterwards), then from the Protestant Bishop and clergy; from the Roman Catholic Bishop and clergy; from the Lord-Lieutenant of the county, the Sheriffs, and others. The two Judges, who were holding their courts, also came on board in their robes. After all this was over we landed, and walked some few paces on to where Lord Bandon's[5] carriage was ready to receive us. The ladies went with us, and Lord Bandon and the General rode on each side of the carriage. The Mayor preceded us, and many (Lord Listowel[6] among the number), followed on horseback or in carriages. The 12th Lancers escorted us, and the Pensioners and Infantry lined the streets.

I cannot describe our route, but it will suffice to say that it took two hours; that we drove through the principal streets; twice through some of them; that they were densely crowded, decorated with flowers and triumphal arches; that the heat and dust were great; that we passed by the new College which is building–one of the four which are ordered by Act of Parliament; that our reception was most enthusiastic; and that everything went off to perfection, and was very well arranged.

Cork is not at all like an English town, and looks rather foreign. The crowd is a noisy, excitable, but very good-humoured one, running and pushing about, and laughing, talking, and shrieking. The beauty of the women is very remarkable, and struck us much; such beautiful dark eyes and hair, and such fine teeth; almost every third woman was pretty, and some remarkably so. They wear no bonnets, and generally long blue cloaks; the men are very poorly, often raggedly dressed; and many wear blue coats and short breeches with blue stockings.

We re-embarked at the same place and returned just as we came.

Kingstown Harbour, Dublin Bay, Sunday, August 5. – Safely arrived here: I now continue my account. For the first two hours and a half the sea, though rough, was not disagreeable. We entered Waterford Harbour yesterday at twenty minutes to four o'clock. The harbour is rocky on the right as one enters, and very flat to the left; as one proceeds the land rises on either side. We passed a little fort called Duncannon Fort, whence James II embarked after the battle of the Boyne,[7] and from which they had not saluted for fifty years. Further up, between two little villages, one on either side, each with its little chapel, picturesquely situated on top of the rock or hill, we anchored. The little fishing place to our left is called Passage, and is famous for salmon; we had an

[5] James, 2nd Earl. Lord Lieutenant (1785–1856).
[6] William, 2nd Earl (1801–56).
[7] July, 1690.

excellent specimen for our dinner. Albert decided on going to Waterford, ten miles up the river, in the "Fairy", with the boys, but as I felt
giddy and tired, I preferred remaining quietly on board sketching.
Albert returned after seven o'clock; he had not landed.

Viceregal Lodge, Phoenix Park, Monday, August 6.—Here we are in
this very pretty spot, with a lovely view of the Wicklow Hills, from
the window. But now to return to yesterday's proceedings. We got
under weigh at half-past eight o'clock; for three hours it was dreadfully
rough, and I and the poor children were very sea-sick. When we had
passed the Tuscar Rock in Wexford the sea became smoother, and
shortly after, quite smooth, and the evening beautiful. After we passed
Arklow Head, the Wicklow Hills came in sight—they are beautiful.

THE ROYAL TRIP TO SCOTLAND.

THE SUDDEN SEPARATION OF THE ROYAL COUPLE ON THE ANNOUNCEMENT OF DINNER

The Sugarloaf and Carrick Mountain have finely pointed outlines, with low hills in front and much wood.

At half-past six we came in sight of Dublin Bay, and were met by the "Sphynx" and "Stromboli" (which had been sent on to wait and to come in with us), the "Trident", and, quite close to the harbour, by the "Dragon", another war-steamer. With this large squadron we steamed slowly and majestically into the harbour of Kingstown,[8] which was covered with thousands and thousands of spectators, cheering most enthusiastically. It is a splendid harbour, and was full of ships of every kind. The wharf, where the landing-place was prepared, was densely crowded, and altogether it was a noble and stirring scene. It was just seven when we entered, and the setting sun lit up the country, the fine buildings, and the whole scene with a glowing light, which was truly beautiful. We were soon surrounded by boats, and the enthusiasm and excitement of the people were extreme.

While we were at breakfast the yacht was brought close up to the wharf, which was lined with troops. Lord and Lady Clarendon[9] and George[10] came on board; also Lords Lansdowne[11] and Clanricarde,[12] the Primate, the Archbishop of Dublin, and many others. The address was presented by the Sheriff and gentlemen of the county. As the clock struck ten we disembarked, stepping on shore from the yacht, Albert leading me and the children, and all the others following us. An immense multitude had assembled, who cheered most enthusiastically, the ships saluting and the bands playing, and it was really very striking. The space we had to walk along to the railroad was covered in; and lined with ladies and gentlemen strewing flowers. We entered the railway-carriages with the children, the Clarendons, and the three ladies; and in a quarter of an hour reached the Dublin station. Here we found our carriages with the postilions in their Ascot liveries. The two eldest children went with us, and the two younger ones with the three ladies. Sir Edward Blakeney, Commander-in-Chief in Ireland, rode on one side of the carriage and George on the other, followed by a brilliant staff, and escorted by the 17th Lancers and the Carabiniers.

It was a wonderful and striking scene, such masses of human beings, so enthusiastic, so excited, yet such perfect order maintained; then the numbers of troops, the different bands stationed at certain distances, the waving of hats and handkerchiefs, the bursts of welcome which rent the air—all made it a never-to-be-forgotten scene; when one

[8] Dun Laoghaire.
[9] George, 4th Earl. Lord Lieutenant of Ireland (1800–70).
[10] Prince George, afterwards Duke of Cambridge.
[11] Henry, 4th Marquess, 5th Earl of Kerry (1816–66).
[12] Ulick, 1st Marquess (1802–74).

The Queen presenting the royal children, Kingstown Harbour

reflected how lately the country had been in open revolt and under martial law.

Dublin is a very fine city; and Sackville Street and Merrion Square are remarkably large and handsome; and the Bank, Trinity College, &c. are noble buildings. There are no gates to the town, but temporary ones were erected under an arch; and here we stopped, and the Mayor presented me the keys with some appropriate words. At the last triumphal arch a poor little dove was let down into my lap, with an olive branch round its neck, alive and very tame.

The heat and dust were tremendous. We reached Phoenix Park, which is very extensive, at twelve. Lord and Lady Clarendon and all the household received us at the door. It is a nice comfortable house, reminding us of Claremont, with a pretty terrace garden in front (laid out by Lady Normanby), and has a very extensive view of the Park and the fine range of the Wicklow Mountains. We are most comfortably lodged, and have very nice rooms.

Tuesday, August 7. – We drove into Dublin – with our two ladies – in Lord Clarendon's carriage, the gentlemen following; and without any escort. The people were very enthusiastic,[13] and cheered a great deal. We went, first, to the Bank, where the Directors received us, and then to the printing-room, and from thence viewed the old Houses of Lords and Commons, for what is now the Bank was the old Parliament House. From here we drove to the Model-School, where we were received by the Archbishop of Dublin, the Roman Catholic Archbishop Murray (a fine Venerable-looking old man of eighty), and the other gentlemen connected with the school. We saw the Infant, the Girls', and the Boys' Schools; in the latter, one class of boys was examined in mental arithmetic and in many very difficult things, and they all answered wonderfully. Children of all creeds are admitted, and their different doctrines are taught separately, if the parents wish it; but the *only* teaching enforced is that of the Gospel truths, and love and charity. This is truly Christian and ought to be the case of everywhere. About 1,000 children are educated here annually, of which 300 are trained as schoolmasters and mistresses.

From here we visited Trinity College, the Irish University, which is not conducted upon so liberal a system, but into which Roman Catholics are admitted. Dr Todd, the secretary, and a very learned man, well versed in the Irish language, showed us some most interesting ancient manuscripts and relics, including St. Columba's Book (in which we wrote our names), and the original harp of King O'Brian, supposed to be the one from which the Irish arms are taken. The library is a very large handsome room, like that in Trinity College, Cambridge. We then proceeded towards home, the crowd in the streets immense, and so loyal. It rained a little at intervals. Home by a little past one. Albert went into Dublin again after luncheon, and I wrote and read, and heard our children say some lessons.

At five we proceeded to Kilmainham Hospital, very near here; Lord Clarendon going in the carriage with the ladies and myself— Albert and the other gentlemen riding. Sir Edward Blakeney and his staff, and George, received us. We saw the old pensioners, the chapel, and the hall, a fine large room (where all the pensioners dine, as at Chelsea), and then Sir Edward's private apartments. We afterwards took a drive through all the principal parts of Dublin,—College Green, where the celebrated statue of William the III is to be seen; Stephen's Green, by The Four Courts, a very handsome building; and, though

[13] Among the unsuspecting crowds were a large number of London pickpockets, set on easy gain. The police, on satisfying themselves of their place of origin, discouraged charges being made against them. One Dublin lady, who lost her purse, complained bitterly to the magistrate. In defence the constable who had released the thief, explained; 'Please, your worship, we heard that the pickpockets were English, every mother's son, and that this would be in the papers. So we all agreed not to take them up for fear of mortifying the Queen.'

we were not expected, the crowds were in many places very great. We returned a little before seven. A large dinner. After dinner above two or three hundred people arrived, including most of the Irish nobility and many of the gentry; and afterwards there was a ball.

Wednesday, August 8. – At twenty minutes to one o'clock we left for Dublin, I and all the ladies in evening dresses, all the gentlemen in uniform. We drove straight to the Castle. Everything here as at St. James's Levée. The staircase and throne-room quite like a palace. I received (on the throne) the addresses of the Lord Mayor and Corporation, the University, the Archbishop and Bishops, both Roman Catholic and Anglican, the Presbyterians, the non-subscribing Presbyterians, and the Quakers. They also presented Albert with addresses.[14] Then followed a very long Levée, which lasted without intermission till twenty minutes to six o'clock! Two thousand people were presented!

[14] Lord Breadalbane (Lord Chamberlain) was in attendance.

Thursday, August 9.—There was a great and brilliant review in the Phoenix Park—six thousand one hundred and sixty men, including the Constabulary. In the evening we two dined alone, and at half-past eight o'clock drove into Dublin for the Drawing-room. It is always held here of an evening. I should think between two and three thousand people passed before us, and one thousand six hundred ladies were presented. After it was over we walked through St. Patrick's Hall and the other rooms, and the crowd was very great. We came back to the Phoenix Park at half-past twelve—the streets still densely crowded. The city was illuminated.

Friday, August 10.—At a quarter to twelve o'clock we set out, with all our suite, for Carton, the Duke of Leinster's,[15] Lord and Lady Clarendon in the carriage with us. We went through Woodlands, a place belonging to Mr White, in which there are beautiful lime-trees; and we passed by the "Preparatory College" for Maynooth; and not far from Carton we saw a number of the Maynooth students. The park of Carton is very fine. We arrived there at a little past one, and were received by the Duke and Duchess of Leinster, the Kildares, Mr and Lady C. Repton, and their two sons. We walked out into the garden, where all the company were assembled, and the two bands playing; it is very pretty: a sort of formal French garden with rows of Irish yews. We walked round the garden twice, the Duke leading me, and Albert the Duchess. The Duke is one of the kindest, and best of men.

After luncheon we walked out and saw some of the country people dance jigs, which was very amusing. It is quite different from the Scottish reel; not so animated, and the steps different, but very droll. The people were very poorly dressed in thick coats, and the women in shawls. There was one man who was a regular specimen of an Irishman, with his hat on one ear. Others in blue coats, with short breeches and blue stockings. There were three old and tattered pipers playing. The Irish pipe is very different from the Scotch; it is very weak, and they don't blow into it, but merely have small bellows which they move with the arm.

We walked round the pleasure-grounds, and after this got into a carriage with the Duke and Duchess—our ladies and gentlemen following in a large jaunting-car, and the people riding, running, and driving with us, but extremely well-behaved; and the Duke is so kind to them, that a word from him will make them do anything. It was very hot, and yet the people kept running the whole way, and in the thick woollen coats, which it seems they always wear here.

We drove along the park to a spot which commands an extensive view of the Wicklow Hills. We then went down an entirely new road,

[15] Augustus, 3rd Duke. Lord Lieutenant of county Kildare (1791–1874).

Leaving Kingstown Harbour, escorted by the royal squadron

cut out of the solid rock, through a beautiful valley, full of the finest trees, growing among rocks close to a piece of water. We got out and walked across a little wooden bridge to a very pretty little cottage, entirely ornamented with shells, &c. by the Duchess. We drove back in the jaunting-car, which is a double one, with four wheels, and held a number of us—I sitting on one side between Albert and the Duke; the Duchess, Lady Jocelyn, Lord Clarendon, and Lady Waterford, on the opposite side; George at the back, and the equerries on either side of the coachman.

As soon as we returned to the house we took leave of our hosts, and went back to the Phoenix Park a different way from the one we came, along the banks of the Liffey, through Mr Colson's park, in which there were the most splendid beeches I have ever seen—feathering down quite to the ground; and farther along the road and river were some lovely sycamore-trees. We drove through the village of Lucan, where there were fine decorations and arches of bays and laurel. We passed below The Strawberry-beds, which are really curious to see—quite high banks of them—and numbers of people come from Dublin to eat these strawberries; and there are rooms at the bottom of these banks on purpose. We were home a little after five.

On Board the Victoria and Albert, *Sunday, August 12.*—To return to Friday. We left the Phoenix Park, where we spent so pleasant a time, at six o'clock, Lord Clarendon and the two elder children going in the carriage with us, and drove with an escort to the Dublin Railway Station. The town was immensely crowded, and the people most enthusiastic. George met us there, and we took him, the Clarendons, and Lord Lansdowne and our ladies in the carriage with us. We arrived speedily at Kingstown, where there were just as many people and as much enthusiasm as on the occasion of our disembarkation. We stood on the paddle-box as we slowly steamed out of Kingstown, amidst the cheers of thousands and thousands, and salutes from all the ships; and I waved my handkerchief as a parting acknowledgment of their loyalty. We soon passed Howth and Ireland's Eye. The ship was very steady, though the sea was not smooth, and the night thick and rainy, and we feared a storm was coming on.

Saturday, August 11.–We reached Belfast Harbour at four o'clock. The wind had got up amazingly, and the morning was a very bad and stormy one.

We had not had a very quiet night for sleeping, though very smooth. The weather got worse and worse, and blew a real gale; and it was quite doubtful whether we could start as we had intended, on our return from Belfast, for Scotland.

We saw the Mayor and General (Bainbrigg), who had come on board after breakfast.

At a quarter-past one we started with the ladies and gentlemen for the "Fairy". Though we had only two minutes' row in the barge, there was such a swell that the getting in and out, and the rolling and tossing in the boat, were very disagreeable. We had to keep in the little pavilion, as the squalls were so violent as to cover the "Fairy" with spray. We passed between Holywood and Carrickfergus, celebrated for the first landing of William III. We reached Belfast in half an hour, and fortunately the sun came out.

We lay close alongside the wharf, where a very fine landing-place was arranged, and where thousands were assembled. Lord Londonderry[16] came on board, and numerous deputations with addresses, including the Mayor (whom I knighted), the Protestant Bishop of Down and clergy, the Catholic Bishop Denvir (an excellent and modest man), the Sheriff and Members for the county, with Lord Donegal[17] (to whom the greater part of Belfast belongs), Dr Henry, from the new College, and the Presbyterians (of whom there are a great many here). Lady Londonderry and her daughter also came on board. There was some delay in getting the gang-board down, as they had made much too large a one. Some planks on board were arranged, and we landed easily in this way. The landing-place was covered in, and very tastefully decorated. We got into Lord Londonderry's carriage with the two ladies, and Lord Londonderry himself got on the rumble behind with the two sergeant-footmen, Renwick and Birbage, both very tall, large men; and the three must have been far from comfortable.

The town was beautifully decorated with flowers, hangings, and very fine triumphal arches, the galleries full of people; and the reception very hearty. The people are a mixture of nations, and the female beauty had almost disappeared.

[16]Charles, 3rd Marquess (1778–1854).

[17]George, 3rd Marquess (1797–1883).

I have all along forgotten to say that the favourite motto written up on most of the arches, &c., and in every place, was: "Cead mile failte", which means "A hundred thousand welcomes" in Irish, which is very like Gaelic; it is in fact *the* language, and has existed in books from the earliest period, whereas Gaelic has only been *written* since half a century, though it was always *spoken*. They often called out, "Cead mile failte"! and it appears in every sort of shape.

Lord Donegal rode on one side of the carriage and the General on the other. We stopped at the Linen Hall to see the exhibition of the flax and linen manufacture. Lord Downshire[18] and several other gentlemen received us there, and conducted us through the different rooms, where we saw the whole process in its different stages. First the plant, then the flax after being steeped; then the spun flax; lastly, the linen, cambric, and cloth of every sort and kind. It is really very interesting to see, and it is wonderful to what a state of perfection it has been brought.

We got into our carriages again. This time Lord Londonderry did not attempt to resume his uncomfortable position.

We went along through the Botanic Garden, and stopped and got out to look at the new College which is to be opened in October. It is a handsome building. We passed through several of the streets and returned to the place of embarkation. Belfast is a fine town, with some good buildings—for instance, the Bank and Exchange,—and is considered the Liverpool and Manchester of Ireland.

I have forgotten to mention the Constabulary, who are a remarkably fine body of men, 13,000 in number (altogether in Ireland), all Irish, and chiefly Roman Catholics; and not one of whom, during the trying times last year, fraternised with the rebels.

We left amid immense cheering, and reached the "Victoria and Albert" at half-past six. It was blowing as hard as ever, and the getting in and out was as disagreeable as before. We decided on spending the night where we were, unless the wind should drop by three or four o'clock in the morning. Many bonfires were lighted on the surrounding hills and coasts.

[18] Arthur, 4th Marquess (1812–68).

Journey Thirteen
1850

The Ghosts of Holyrood

ON the morning of 27th August the Queen, Prince Albert and their four eldest children left Osborne at the start of the long journey to Balmoral, the old castle in Aberdeenshire which the Prince had leased from the Fife Trustees.

Castle Howard

It was to be a journey of many 'firsts'. It was the first time that they had travelled north by train, and newly completed lines now enabled them to see many fresh places. Among these were Newcastle, where the Queen was to open, officially, the new bridge over the Tyne, and Berwick, where a similar ceremony was to be held on the bridge spanning the Tweed–both notable feats of engineering. At Edinburgh the Royal Family was to stay for the first time in the Palace of Holyrood, and the Prince was to lay the foundation stone of the Scottish National Gallery.

Despite the hindrance of local railway strikes, the royal train reached Yorkshire by evening. There two days were spent at Castle Howard, the home of Lord Carlisle,[1] brother of the Duchess of Sutherland, who was a close friend of the Queen. Then on they went to open the High Level Bridge at Newcastle and the Royal Border Bridge at Berwick, vast crowds greeting them at both places. They continued along the North British Line,

'And reached Edinburgh safe, after no end of speeches,
And was welcomed by folks, some of wich 'ad no breeches . . .'[2]

The Royal Archers, who have the privilege of forming the body-guard while the Sovereign is in Scotland, were waiting at the station, the Duke of Buccleuch at their head. On foot, they accompanied the Queen's carriage to the Palace of Holyrood. The Queen wrote:

The road, the new one under Arthur's Seat, was beautifully kept by cavalry and infantry, and thousands were assembled. The Salisbury Crags were like an anthill, black with people. The sun shone brightly. The sight was a very fine one, and the good Scotch people most enthusiastic. In the court of Holyrood was a guard of honour of the 93rd Highlanders, and Lord Morton, as Captain General of the Royal Archers Guard, received us.

It was near three hundred years since a Queen had trod the halls of Holyrood. On a June evening in 1567 Mary, Queen of Scots, had been escorted from the Palace and taken to the island castle of Lochleven. Now, on a distant summer's evening, a Queen returned. Victoria was so excited that she scarcely stopped to examine the suite of rooms which had been alloted for her use. Taking her daughters by the hand, she ran off to explore, and the staff had not the time to learn whom she was. So she became just one of the ladies who wished to gasp with horror at the stain left by the blood of 'Davie' Rizzio, as it gushed past Darnley's dagger and made a pool upon the floor.

We wandered out with the two girls, and Miss Hildyard, to look at the old ruined Abbey, which adjoins the Palace, and which you see from our windows. It is beautiful inside. One of the aisles is still roofed in, but the other is not. It was originally an Abbey, and the very old tombstones are those of friars. It was afterwards the Chapel Royal, and Queen Mary, my unfortunate ancestress, was married to Lord Darnley at this very altar, of which you see the remains. It was restored in the time of James VII of Scotland and II of England. Later, it was

[1] George, 7th Earl (1802-64).
[2] *Punch*.

Edinburgh from Carlton Hill

used as a parish church. There are many tombs in it—some of the Sutherland and Erroll family, Lord Strathmore, &c. . . . .When we returned, we saw the rooms where Queen Mary lived, her bed, the dressing-room into which the murderers entered who killed Rizzio, and the spot where he fell, where, as the old housekeeper said to me, "if the lady would stand on that side", I would see that the boards were discoloured by the blood. Every step is full of historical recollections, and our living here is quite an epoch in the annals of this old pile, which has seen so many deeds, more bad, I fear, than good. In the long gallery is a collection of most frightful pictures of the Kings of Scotland, beginning with a full-length of a king 330 years before Christ. In Queen Mary's room we saw a piece of her work, the armour and lance of Lord Darnley, and other more doubtful souvenirs. The old housekeeper did not know who I was, and only learned it from Mr Charles Murray[3] afterwards.

[3] Deputy-Keeper of the Palace.

Interior of the Chapel Royal, Holyrood

One of the exhibition halls, from a contemporary album

Milestone 1851 — *The Opening of the Great Exhibition*

April 29, 1851.—We drove to the Exhibition with only the 2 Maids of Honour and 2 Equerries and remained about 2 hours and $\frac{1}{2}$. I came back quite dead beat and my head really bewildered by the myriads of beautiful and wonderful things, which now 'quite dazzle one's eyes. Such efforts have been made and our people have shown such taste in their manufactures, all owing to the impetus given by the Exhibition and by my beloved one's guidance. We went up into the Gallery, and the sight of it from there into all the Courts, full of all sorts of objects of art, manufacture etc. had quite the effect of fairyland . . .

May 1.—This day is one of the greatest and most glorious days of our lives, with which to my pride and joy, the name of my dearly beloved Albert is for ever associated! It is a day which makes my heart swell with thankfulness . . .

The Park presented a wonderful spectacle, crowds streaming through it,—carriages and troops passing, quite like the Coronation, and for *me*, the same anxiety. The day was bright and all bustle and excitement. At $\frac{1}{2}$ p. 11 the whole procession in 9 State carriages was set in motion . . . The Green Park and Hyde Park were one mass of densely crowded human beings, in the highest good humour and most enthusiastic. I never saw Hyde Park look as it did, being filled with crowds as far as the eye could reach. A little rain fell, just as we started, but before we neared the Crystal Palace, the sun shone and gleamed upon the gigantic edifice, upon which the flags of every nation were flying. We drove up Rotten Row and got out of our carriages at the entrance on that side. The glimpse, through the iron gates of the Transept, the waving palms and flowers, the myriads of people filling the galleries and seats around, together with the flourish of trumpets as we entered the building, gave a sensation I shall never forget, and I felt much moved . . . In a few seconds we proceeded, Albert leading me, having Vicky at his hand and Bertie holding mine. The sight as we came to the centre where the steps and chair (on which I did *not* sit) was placed, facing the beautiful crystal fountain was magic and impressive. The tremendous cheering, the joy expressed in every face, the vastness of the building, with all its decorations and exhibits, the sound of the organ (with 200 instruments and 600 voices, which seemed nothing) and my beloved husband, the creator of this peace festival 'uniting the industry and art of all nations of the earth', all this was indeed moving, and a day to live for ever. God bless my dearest Albert, and my dear Country, which has shown itself so great today.

Journey Fourteen
1851

Liverpool and Manchester

ON 22nd August a colossal statue of Queen Victoria was placed on
its plinth before the Palace of Holyrood. It was Edinburgh's way of
commemorating the visit of the previous year. The following
description appeared in a contemporary report:

> The folds of the drapery are disposed so as to show the entire figure; and the
> back view, difficult in such heavy draping, is well managed. Her Majesty's
> left hand is pressed to her breast, and in her right hand she bears a palm branch,
> emblematic of her peaceful rule. Her countenance is marked with simplicity
> and dignity . . .

Five days later the Court left Osborne for Balmoral, the Queen having
decided on a night stop at Edinburgh en route so that she might inspect
the likeness of herself in double size.

Again it was to be a journey of historic interest. As far as York the
track of the new Great Northern Railway was to be used, and a new level
of luxury to be sampled. After lunch at Buckingham Palace, the royal
party left in a procession of carriages for the terminus at King's Cross.
There awaited the special train which had been provided by the Company.
It was made up of eight carriages, three of which had been especially
built for the occasion. They were for the Queen and her husband; the
Prince of Wales and his brother and sisters; and the suite. Of the same
basic design, the Queen's saloon was the more luxurious. The mouldings
were of gilt, the doors bore the royal arms, and over each was a gilt
crown. At one end was a couch, and at the other a withdrawing-room,
with full length mirror and washstand etc. While the carriage of the Queen
was lined with 'the richest white brocaded Indian silk', the other two had
to be content with 'plain drab brocaded silk'. All windows were counter-
balanced with weights, allowing finger-tip control.

The engine was driven by Mr Sturrick, superintendent of the locomotive department, and the first stop was at Peterborough. Here the

The Queen arriving at the Angel Hotel, Doncaster

Queen was greeted by old Dr Fisher, the Bishop, who twenty years before had helped with her lessons in the schoolroom at Kensington Palace. Congratulatory addresses on the success of the Great Exhibition were handed in at Boston and Lincoln, and Doncaster was reached at half past six. Here the Royal Family were to spend the night, at the Angel hotel, and they were greeted with a display of Yorkshire military might, a phalanx of schoolchildren, decorations, triumphal arches and illuminations, and a banquet at the Mansion House.

Leaving Doncaster at nine next morning, the journey was uneventful until Nottingley was reached. Here lay a hazard, in the form of an osier-bed. The line crossed this bed at a considerable height, and a reporter commented that the traversing of it called for considerable caution on the part of the driver and that the carriage 'went very slowly past this ugly spot'. At York there was a change of company's track, and Edinburgh was reached in time for tea. As the Deeside line was not yet in operation, the rail journey the following day was only as far as Stonehaven. There carriages were waiting to take the holidaymakers on the last stage to Balmoral.

The return journey south was through Lancashire, and great receptions were prepared by both Liverpool and Manchester. At Lancaster, on 8th

October, the Queen was presented with the keys of the Castle at John of Gaunt's gateway. Leaving the train at Prescot, the royal party drove through Knowsley park to spend the night with the Earl of Sefton[1] at Croxteth.

That evening it appeared as if the Queen had brought 'Queen's weather' with her, and that the sun would be shining for her tour of Liverpool on the morrow. But during the night there was a sudden change and the rain poured down relentlessly.

Thursday, October 9.–To our despair, a wet morning, and hopelessly so! At ten o'clock we started in closed carriages, Vicky and Bertie with us, the two others in the next carriages. It poured; the roads were a sea of mud, and yet the whole way along was lined with people, and all so wet! The atmosphere was so thick, that we could see a very little way before us. Still, the reception was most enthusiastic. The preparations were beautiful. Liverpool is three miles from Croxteth, but there are houses almost the whole way . . . I cannot attempt to describe the route or detail the fine buildings. The streets were densely crowded, in spite of the horrible weather, everything extremely well arranged and beautifully decorated, but the poor people so wet and dirty! We were obliged to spread Albert's large cloak over us to protect us from the rain and the splashing of the mud.

We drove along part of the Docks, and got out at the place of embarkation, which was covered over; there we went on board the *Fairy*, with our whole party, the Mayor, and gentlemen connected with the Docks and Harbour, and went along all the Docks, which are magnificent. The mass of shipping is quite enormous. We went round the mouth of the Mersey, but could hardly make out anything that was at any distance, and we had all to remain in the Pavilion. We disembarked at the same place, and proceeded to the Town Hall. I must mention here the Seamen's Refuge–a magnificent stone building, of which Albert laid the first stone five years ago. The Town Hall is a very handsome building, beautifully decorated inside, and with fine large rooms. We proceeded to the Council Room, where we stood on a throne and received the addresses of the Mayor and Corporation, to which I read an answer, and then knighted the Mayor, Mr Bent, a very good man . . .

We remained nearly half-an-hour afterwards in the Town Hall, as there was too much time,–a rare occurrence. At a little before four we re-entered our carriages, and drove to St. George's Hall, one of the finest of modern buildings. It is worthy of ancient Athens; the elevation is so simple and magnificent. It is well raised, and approached by a

[1] Charles, 3rd Earl. Lord-Lieutenant of Lancashire (1796–1855).

Reception at the Town Hall, Liverpool

splendid flight of steps. We got out here and examined the interior, which is quite unfinished, but will be very fine,–the taste so good and pure . . . The Law Courts are to be held here, and in the centre is the magnificent Hall, intended for concerts . . . Albert, who is always so ready to admire whatever is simple and grand, was delighted. He never really admires what is small in purpose and design, what is frittered away in detail, and not chaste and simple . . . We stepped out in order to gratify the great multitude below. We also appeared on the balcony at the Town Hall.

The night was to be spent at Worsley Park and the journey as far as Patricroft was made by rail. Amongst those waiting to receive the Queen at the station was the Duke of Wellington, now eighty-two years old, and the Queen invited him to join her procession for the morrow. In

this he proved somewhat of a liability, as he was continually dozing off
and a lady-in-waiting was permanently employed in nudging him to
ensure that the cheers of the crowd were acknowledged.

We walked through a covered and very prettily ornamented corridor
to the boat, which was waiting on the (Bridgewater) Canal. It was a
very elegant barge, to which a rope was fastened, drawn by four horses.

The state barges on the Bridgewater Canal

Ourselves, the ladies, Lady Ellesmere, Lady Brackley and her little boy,
the old Duke, and Captain Egerton (the second son), came into it with
us. Half was entirely covered in, the other half had an awning over it.
The boat glided along in a most noiseless and dream-like manner,
amidst the cheers of the people who lined the sides of the Canal, and
passed under the beautifully decorated bridges belonging to the villages
connected with the vast coal-pits belonging to Lord Ellesmere[2] In

[2] Francis, 1st Earl (1800–57).

half-an-hour we were at the landing-place in Worsley Park, and in five minutes at the hall-door, where Lord Ellesmere, who is lame with the gout, and walked with a stick, and Lord Brackley,[3] who is terribly delicate, received us. The evening was so wet and thick, that one could see nothing beyond the windows. It is an Elizabethan house, finished only five years ago, very handsome and comfortable[4] . . .

Friday, October 10.—From one o'clock in the morning Albert was very unwell,—very sick and wretched, and I was terrified for our Manchester visit. Thank God! by eight o'clock he felt much better, and was able to get up . . . At ten we started for Manchester. The day was fine and mild, and everything to a wish. Manchester is called seven miles from Worsley, but I cannot think it is so much. We first came to Pendleton, where, as everywhere else, there are factories, and great preparations were made. School-children were there in profusion. We next came to Salford, where the crowd became very dense. It joins Manchester, and is to it, in fact, as Westminster to London. The yeomanry which escorted us, and which is a very fine regiment, was relieved by a regiment of Lancers,—Lord Cathcart and his staff riding near the carriage.

The mechanics and work-people, dressed in their best, were ranged along the streets, with white rosettes in their button-holes; both in Salford and Manchester, a very intelligent, but painfully unhealthy-looking population they all were, men as well as women. We went into Peel Park, before leaving Salford—the Mayor having got out and received us at the entrance—where was indeed a most extraordinary and I suppose totally unprecedented sight—82,000 school-children, Episcopalians, Presbyterians, Catholics (these children having a small crucifix suspended round their necks), Baptists, and Jews, whose faces told their descent; with their teachers. In the middle of the park was erected a pavilion, under which we drove (but did not get out), and where the Address was read. All the children sang "God Save the Queen" extremely well together, the director being placed on a very high stand, from which he could command the whole Park.

We passed out at the same gate we went in by, and through the principal street of Salford, on to Manchester, at the entrance of which was a magnificent arch. The Mayor, Mr Potter, who went through the proceedings with great composure and self-possession, beautifully dressed (the Mayor and Corporation had till now been too Radical to

[3] Lord Ellesmere's son, who had been injured in a hunting accident.
[4] During the evening the Queen was introduced to Mr Nasmyth, the inventor of the Steam Hammer, who had works at Patricroft. He exhibited and explained the maps in which he had embodied the results of his investigations of the conformation and atmosphere of the moon.

have robes) received us there, and presented me with a beautiful bouquet. We drove through the principal streets, in which there are no very fine buildings—the principal large houses being warehouses—and stopped at the Exchange, where we got out and received the Address again on the throne, to which I read an answer. The streets were immensely full, and the cheering and enthusiasm most gratifying. The order and good behaviour of the people, who were not placed behind any barriers, were the most complete we have seen in our many progresses through capitals and cities—London, Glasgow, Dublin, Edinburgh, &c., for there never was a running crowd. Nobody moved, and therefore everybody saw well, and there was no squeezing . . . We returned as we came, the sun shining brightly, and were at Worsley by two . . .

Saturday, October 11.—We started at eleven, every one going with us,—entered the barge, and were towed up the canal to Patricroft as the other evening, only this time in beautiful, but too mild weather. The Mayor[5] told me last night, that he thinks we saw a million of people between Manchester and Salford. There are 400,000 inhabitants in Manchester, and every one says, that in no other town could one depend so entirely upon the quiet and orderly behaviour of the people as in Manchester. You had only to tell them what ought to be done, and it was sure to be carried out. We took leave of the Ellesmeres and party at the station, and steamed off.

It was a very pleasant and interesting visit. We went through Manchester, and had an opportunity of seeing the extraordinary number of warehouses and manufactories it contains, and how large it is. We came next to Stockport, then Crewe, Stafford (where Lord Anglesey was), Rugby, Weedon, Wolverton, and lastly Watford, which we reached at five. Lord Grey took leave of us here, and we got into our carriages, and posted to Windsor.

The evening was soft and beautiful, without any autumnal feel;—the day had been very hot, particularly in the railway. Everywhere our reception had been most kind. We changed horses at Uxbridge, and soon after shut the carriage; a fine moonlight night. We arrived at Windsor at half-past seven, and found the three little children[6] at the door, well and pleased.

[5] Sir John Potter. He had been knighted after presenting the Manchester Address.
[6] Princess Helena, born 1846; Princess Louise, born 1848; Prince Arthur, born 1850.

Journey Fifteen
1852

A Dutch Sunday Afternoon

IN August the Queen and her husband decided that they would pay a short visit to King Leopold of the Belgians. Their uncle had once again been widowed, his wife, Louise, having died two years before, and he was in need of cheering up. To the royal horror, gales swept the Channel, and it was not until the 10th that the captain of the yacht was able to take advantage of a lull and make direct for the haven of the Scheldt. But once Flushing was passed the storms returned, and it was in a hurricane of wind and rain that the King received his guests at Antwerp.

The Queen had given strict instruction that there was to be nothing in the shape of state receptions during the short stay, and that no dignitaries were to appear. Thus four peaceful days were spent at the King's country seat of Laeken and on the 14th he drove back with his guests to the royal yacht which awaited them at Antwerp. But still the gale blew, and the night was spent at anchor eight miles from Flushing. So foul was the weather the following morning that the Captain refused to go out into the open sea. He attempted to land his passengers at Flushing, so that they might while away the hours by exploring Middelburg, but the swell was such that landing was impossible. Accordingly the yacht returned and anchored close off Terneusen. Here the pilot managed to conjure up a carriage, 'a wonderfully primitive affair without springs'. At five o'clock, the Queen and Prince set out on a drive of exploration. Suddenly it seemed as if they were in a world of two centuries gone by:

> *Sunday, August 15.*–The little town is very narrow, but most beautifully clean, the houses looking as though newly washed. The women's dress is very neat, peculiar, and ancient-looking. The colours of their handkerchiefs and jackets are very bright, their petticoats very full, of a thick woollen texture, coming directly out, as it were, almost from under their arms. Their little white caps and golden pins are very pretty and peculiar, as well as the way of arranging the hair in a curl on the forehead. The dresses altogether are like those of the time of James or

Charles I. Young and old, and quite little children wear them. The dress of the men, though you see some ugly attempts at our modern dress, is likewise very characteristic. The low and very small brimmed hat, the full leathern trousers with the belt, and large silver buttons and clasps, remind one of the German peasants, as indeed do the women also.

We drove to one of the farms, a rich one, in the neighbourhood. The pilot went in to ask the owners, if we might look at their farm, and immediately they came out, and welcomed us most kindly. They were fine and striking specimens of the Dutch peasantry. The man, Peter Feiter, was a tall, very dark and handsome slim young man, dressed in the strict costume of the country, and the woman, his mother, was a very fine, tall, hearty old woman, the picture of cleanliness. Albert said, she reminded him of the Tyrolese women. They took us into their house, which was beautifully clean, and charmingly arranged, – all the walls covered with Dutch painted tiles. In the parlour everything was decked out. There were the dishes, the china, a handsome mahogany press, a large book with massive clasps, containing (as Lady Gainsborough thought, who looked into it) the pedigree of the family. They insisted on our sitting down and taking some fresh milk. The old lady brought out a number of smart glasses for the purpose, and, like the Scotch, seemed not satisfied that we did not take it all. They then showed us their cowsheds, which in the summer they fill with their corn, and afterwards a pretty garden.

There were great dignity and independence in the deportment of the young man. A sister-in-law, with two little children, all in complete costume, joined us in the garden, and several other men, dressed in precisely the same way, came to the farm. There is a solidity and respectability about the people which was very striking; and, as well as their cleanliness, showed them at once to be Protestants. When travelling in Germany, I have observed the same difference between Protestant and Catholic villages, and in the people's appearance. This is certainly the case with the Dutch; and though the Belgians are by no means dirty or slovenly in their appearance, – quite the contrary – still there is a great difference.

It was a very interesting and pleasant little expedition, which seemed to take one back two centuries; but the return to the yacht in the barge was very disagreeable. It was very rough and wet, but our men pulled splendidly. Though blowing very hard and raining, they assured us it would be fine to-morrow, as the wind had gone to the north.

Journey Sixteen
1853

The Great Exhibition of Dublin

THE Dublin Great Exhibition was opened in May. The Queen and Prince Albert were most eager to see it, not only so that they might compare it with the Exhibition in Hyde Park of 1851, but also that the utmost assistance might be given to Irish industry. Accordingly, at the end of August, they travelled by train to Holyhead, taking their two eldest boys, the Prince of Wales and Prince Alfred with them, and boarded the royal yacht on the 29th.

Staying at Viceregal Lodge, they visited the Exhibition on each of the mornings of their four day visit. The Queen was intrigued with the poplins, lace and pottery, but for the Prince the choice was different. His wife wrote in her diary; 'By the novel process of hatching salmon, exhibited here for the first time, Albert was especially interested, as he is by every new and useful discovery.'

One afternoon they drove to Mount Annville, overlooking Dublin Bay, the home of Mr and Mrs Dargan. William Dargan was the moving spirit behind the Exhibition–he had guaranteed £100,000 to cover the cost of the erection of the building. As in the case of Brassey, he had made his fortune out of railway contracts, and had employed Irish labour to an extent never rivalled in the country's history. The Queen offered Mr Dargan a baronetcy, but he and his wife were Quakers, and declined, being satisfied with the success of their efforts. When Mrs Dargan was asked by a friend why her husband had turned down the honour, she replied that 'the fount of all true honour is within oneself'.

One incident led to a sharp rise in the Queen's popularity with the Dublin people. She was driving to the Exhibition with her two sons, and the crowds were dense. She was smiling and bowing. The Prince of Wales held his white-banded flat cap gracefully in his hand and behaved impeccably, as he always did when on display. But young Alfred was in one of his most awkward moods. A rebellious child, he was permanently in mischief and had no respect for his own safety. At a very early age he had narrowly escaped serious injury by sliding down a stair rail at Balmoral,

The exhibition buildings, Dublin, 1853

and had been known to stick coloured flags on pins in the padded calves of gentlemen attending Court. He was a worry to his mother and she kept a wary eye on him. But on this morning she gave no outward sign that she was watching him. Obviously Alfred did not relish another visit to the Exhibition. His expression was surly and he kept his hat upon his head. Suddenly those near the carriage saw the Queen move. With one hand she whipped the cap off his head, and with the other she caught him a resounding smack across the cheek. The crowd loved it.

At the Exhibition the Princes strayed away from her, probably looking at engines or such things as appeal to boys. The Queen stopped before a picture of young King Louis XVII dying in prison. She sent for her sons and there and then gave them a history lesson. It later came to light that she was impressing upon them the hard truth that 'heedless sovereigns, thinking only of their own pleasure, must look out for disasters'.

On the 3rd September the Royal Family left Ireland for Scotland:

A beautiful morning, and this the very day we are going away, which we felt quite sorry to do, having spent such a pleasant, gay, and interesting time in Ireland . . . At half-past five we started for Kingstown. We drove gently, though not at a foot's pace, through Dublin, which was unusually crowded (no soldiers lining the streets,) to the station, where again there were great crowds. In eight minutes we were at Kingstown, where again the crowds were immense, and most enthusiastic. The evening was beautiful, and the sight a very fine one—all the ships and yachts decked out and firing salutes, and thousands on the quay cheering . . . It was a gay, fine evening, and the hum and singing and noise made by the people made one fancy oneself in a foreign port in the South.

Journey Seventeen
1857

Sight-seeing at Cherbourg

WHEN Prince Louis Napoleon seized absolute power in France in 1851, and the following year was proclaimed Emperor of the French, the Queen and Prince Albert viewed his action with aversion and his motives with distrust. They were already convinced that Beelzebub strolled the boulevards of Paris, and now it seemed that he had a companion, for the love life of Napoleon was both varied and dynamic.

The new Emperor, on the other hand, was determined that there should be a cordial relationship between the British Royal Family and himself. He knew London well, and had many friends there, and he so chose his advances that total resistance to them might end in peril.

He opened up his friendly overtures with the suggestion that he should marry the Queen's niece, Adelaide. This thunderbolt caused Victoria to take firm and immediate measures to save the girl from such a fate and such a religion. Undismayed, Napoleon returned with a counter proposition—that his cousin, Prince Jerome, should marry the Queen's cousin, Princess Mary of Cambridge. It was left to the Princess to decide. Already developing the features which were later to lead to her being dubbed 'Fat Mary', she stamped upon the idea with heavy foot.

The matrimonial impasse was solved when Napoleon married Eugénie de Montijo, a twenty-six year old Spanish countess, of great beauty and Scottish descent. As he obviously wished to start a new dynasty, a mantle of respectability now clothed the Tuileries.

Continuing his line of personal introduction, the Emperor invited Prince Albert's brother, Ernest, to visit him in Paris. The Duke of Coburg was fêted and injected with strong doses of flattery about the wonderful example of life at Windsor. Ernest passed on what he had heard, although his impressions were more than a trifle suspect since he was even more of a rake than his host. It was the feminine angle that won the day. The Empress Eugénie, he said, was most anxious to meet Queen Victoria's children.

Not yet daring to risk his wife to contagion, Prince Albert decided

The Emperor Napoleon III

that he would travel alone to France to make his appraisal of the little Frenchman. He accepted an invitation to inspect troops being trained for the Crimean war at a camp at St. Omer. During long talks together Prince Albert formed the opinion that the Emperor 'spoke very sensibly', and the only point of criticism sent back to Windsor was that he smoked cigarettes. Again the admiration for Victoria was stressed and this, coupled with the attention lavished on the Prince, tipped the scales. State visits should be exchanged.

On 16th April 1855 the Emperor and Empress of the French arrived at Windsor. The success of the visit surpassed all expectations. The experienced Napoleon knew exactly how to handle the Queen. Adroitly he flattered her, and attained familiarity without losing respect. Delighted, she bestowed upon him the Order of the Garter. Eugénie charmed Prince Albert as no other woman, bar his wife, was ever to do. The Queen saw this and wrote in her journal: 'Albert who is seldom much pleased with ladies or princesses, is very fond of her and her great ally.' Playing safe, the Prince assured Baron Stockmar: 'Our relation rests upon an honourable, moral basis.' This was fortunate indeed, for if it had been otherwise there would have been no Albert Hall. Yet the Prince was in no danger, for Eugénie would not have had it so, even if he had wished it so.

Victoria and Eugénie were immediately attracted to one another and formed a friendship that was to endure until the Queen's death. It was an attraction of opposites. Victoria admired the willowy beauty and the sense of dress that was unrivalled in Europe. Eugénie was impressed with the solidarity and the regality, seeing in the Queen the only woman in the world who could, without an instant of reflection, adopt the sitting position with the assured knowledge that a chair would be waiting under her posterior. In later years malicious tongues were to attribute the friendship to sapphism, which, if only on the score of the Queen's ignorance on such matters,[1] was absurd. It was more the relationship of the elder, more responsible sister, to the younger and more volatile one. Over tea cups, and in confidence, Eugénie would relate, with delicious giggles, little anecdotes about her friend, particularly in the sphere of John Brown, on whom French and Windsor views were widely divided.

On an intimate point which was troubling both Napoleon and Eugénie, the Queen was able to be of practical assistance. Advice was needed on how to have a baby, and what better mentor could there be than Victoria, who already had eight—her latest, Leopold, having been born in 1853. Whilst no full and technical record of the advice given, survives, the tip was imparted that the immersion of the body in hot water should be avoided.

[1] When Labouchere placed before her a paper dealing with the homosexual act between consenting males and females, the Queen struck out 'females'. Her curt reason for doing so was the one word—'Impossible'.

Queen Victoria at the Tomb of Napoleon by E. M. Ward, R.A.
(reproduced by gracious permission of H.M. The Queen)

In August of the same year the visit was returned, the Prince of Wales and the Princess Royal accompanying their parents. Queen Victoria was abominably dressed when she entered Paris. She wore a plain straw bonnet and carried a parasol of glaring green. A white poodle was embroidered on her massive handbag. Notwithstanding, she received a greater ovation than was awarded to Napoleon I on his return from Austerlitz.

The Prince of Wales contributed greatly to the success of the visit. In Highland dress, he knelt before the tomb of the great Napoleon. At this moment a clap of thunder rolled over Paris, followed, fittingly, by a rain of tears from the eyes of the elderly generals who surveyed the scene.

The young Prince fell in love with both Paris and the Empress. He asked her if he could stay with her and, on being told that his parents might object, replied that there were so many brothers and sisters at home that he would not be missed.

This interlude in Paris remained ever fresh in the Queen's memory. She confided all the details to her Journal, and in 1881 circulated a printed copy privately among her relatives. Much of it has since been re-published. Despite the political differences that came between the Emperor and herself, her letters to him were always in the cordial strain that had existed in 1855.

These political differences were soon to arise. They centred round Napoleon's policy of rearmament, his strengthening of coastal defences, and his attitude to Balkan affairs, which conflicted with that of the British

Government. Determined that he would remain on friendly relations with the British Queen, Napoleon suggested that he should visit her and discuss matters. Accordingly he and the Empress were invited to Osborne early in August 1857. As a side issue, there were baby matters to compare. Eugénie had given birth to a son the previous year, and Victoria's last born, Beatrice, was but four months old.

The Emperor lavished his customary charm upon the Queen, seemingly met her on obstinate points, and put her mind at rest. He did not succeed so well with the Prince Consort,[2] who saw only a practical use for the fortifications now being erected at Cherbourg. Blandly, the Emperor suggested that they should take a trip over in the royal yacht, and see for themselves. He could not be there himself, but they were free to wander as they wished. This bland invitation was acted upon. As the sun was setting on the 19th August the *Victoria and Albert* glided, unannounced, into Cherbourg harbour. The Queen recorded:

> The evening was splendid, the sea like oil, and the sun throwing over everything a beautiful golden light. The breakwater is of great extent, and extensive works are going on all round; the only shipping, two or three small trading vessels. The small town is picturesquely situated, with an old church,—a fort with a high cliff commanding it on one side, and hills rising behind the town . . .

The Prince Consort went ashore and returned with the *Préfet Maritime*, who was asked to stay for dinner. Afterwards arrived a posse of officials and officers, and the English Consul, Mr Hammond. After small talk and speeches of welcome, the party retreated, upon which, the Queen commented, she and her husband went below and played. Six of their children were on board with them.

> *August 20.*—At twenty minutes past nine the Consul arrived, and Albert, to my great delight, consented to remain here to-night, so that we might visit an old château. Presently the Admiral arrived and preceded us in a fine large boat,—we following with the three eldest children and the ladies and gentlemen (the three youngest remaining to go on shore with the governesses). Rowed up under salutes and the well-known *fanfare*, or *Battre aux armes* of the different guards of honour. The reception was half private—no troops being drawn up—but all the generals and officers of different kinds were there; General Borel, in high boots, and on horseback, riding near our carriage. We and the two girls were in the Admiral's little open carriage—the ladies and gentlemen and officers, in others, following. The docks and "bassins"—

[2] The title conferred upon Prince Albert on 25th June 1857.

of which there are three enormous ones in course of construction—are
magnificent, formed of the finest granite of the country, and all executed
in the best manner.

It makes me very unhappy to see what is done here, and how well
protected the works are, for the forts and the breakwater (which is
treble the size of the Plymouth one) are extremely well defended. We
got out twice to examine the construction, and look at the enormous
depth of the docks. There are at least 8,000 workmen employed, and
already millions have been spent. The works were commenced in the
time of Louis XIV. We then proceeded through the town—leaving the
arsenal and fortifications, and passing by the *Corderie* (rope manu-
factory)—and ascended a hill outside the town. The town itself is very
picturesque, but small, humble, and thoroughly foreign-looking;
streets narrow, "*pavé*" bad; all the windows, without exception,
casements, opening quite back, leaving the whole space open, as if
there were no windows, and with outside shutters. All the women in
caps, many in the regular costume caps—many in smaller ones, and
wearing full woollen petticoats and aprons, generally dark blue or
violet—also coloured handkerchiefs. With hardly an exception, the
caps were of dazzling white. Some (in mourning evidently) in black,
with black ribbons round their caps. Very friendly, and making a great
noise; many nice fat children and babies . . . We wound up a hill,
looking over a beautiful country, to an old deserted fort called "*Fort
d'Octeville*", where we all got out and scrambled up, and looked over
the town and port, with the beautiful blue sea—a very fine sight—and
the view very extensive. An extremely hot sun and no air . . .

We lunched at two. The three younger children—delighted with
their expedition—had seen town, shopped, seen soldiers, forts, &c.
Arthur much excited . . . At three we left with precisely the same party
as in the morning; landed at same place, and got into an open *char-à-
bancs*, with three seats and drawn by four horses. Albert and Mr Hammond in front, I and Vicky next, Alice and Affie behind. The regular
French *poste*, driven by one *postillon* on the wheel horse, harnessed
with ropes, no springs to carriage, so that we bumped along on the
pavement pretty roughly. The others were in two carriages following,
closed, odd sort of carriages, each with a pair of horses. Drove through
town, streets much fuller, some flags out, people very friendly, calling
Vive la Reine d'Angleterre, and the post-boys making a terrible noise,
cracking and flourishing their whips.

We drove to Bricquebec, twenty-two kilomètres from Cherbourg;
and by Octeville, a very small village, along a beautiful hilly, rich
wooded country, with cornfields, but very small ones, and literally
not one village, only detached cottages and farms, some close to the

road. Everything most picturesque and primitive—all the women in white caps, often with children in their arms, but many weighed down with the weight of corn which they carried on their backs; many sitting and resting on the door-sill, knitting; children running about, lattices open, showing in some cottages nice pewter-pots and platters, loaves, and here and there a ruddy, healthy *paysanne*, with her snow-white cap, looking at the strangely filled carriages passing before her. The horses and carts most picturesque, with sheepskins over them. The road, quite straight, turning to neither right nor left after leaving Octeville, up and down the long steep hills, so that a sort of drag had to be constantly let down on both sides to keep back the wheel. Intensely hot and dusty, but too delightfully interesting for one to feel tired. We could hardly believe we were really driving in this quiet way in France.

Half of the way the country was very like Devonshire. Beautiful beech and elm trees, and everything very green, and thoroughly rustic and unsophisticated . . . It grew later and later, and it seemed as though we should never reach our destination. At length, at the bottom of a hill, surmounted by the high old tower of the château, appeared the little town of Bricquebec. Most picturesque, the outskirts with good houses, well-dressed peasant women and fat babies at doors and windows. Then came a narrow street with shops, two old figures of saints in a conspicuous place, and people working and knitting at doors; picturesque groups without end. We stopped at an old narrow gateway

Cherbourg, c. 1860

and walked into the yard of the old château, part of which is now a very humble country inn called Le Vieux Château; and close to the gateway rises the very high old château. Got out, had very tired horses to feed, walked about, and finally climbed portion of the castle, and went into the only portion of the interior which remains entire. The château is of the date of the eleventh century, and very curious. The somewhat tipsy mayor of the town conducted us over it; and then, as our horses had to rest, we walked a little about the outskirts, and began to be surrounded by the *gamins, moutards,* and little beggar-boys of the village.

By the time we returned to the inn, the inhabitants of the village came up and surrounded us, chatting away and staring at and rather mobbing us. The horses, to our despair, not yet being rested, we decided to wait in a room upstairs—a small one with two beds—where we sat with the children and ladies, Vicky and I sketching the picturesque women and children standing below, in agony how and when we were to get back. It was near seven before we got into our carriage. We had only three horses, and fearing the others could not keep up with us, and wishing to be back as soon as possible, having people to dinner, we took Colonel Biddulph and Lady Jocelyn into our carriage, instead of Affie and Mr Hammond.

The drive back was charming, sun setting, air deliciously fresh, and horses getting along very well. Many people coming home or at their supper. At last we stopped to light our lanterns at Montinvart, a third part of the way. Most amusing to see people running out with candles, which they held up trying to get a sight of us. Great crowd at Octeville, when we stopped to adjust harness, and many gathering round and trying to see "qui est donc la Reine?" ('which is the Queen'?) Cherbourg very full, but very dark, streets only lit by a lantern here and there slung across. Drove on to Port, and then pushed with great difficulty into barge, through a loudly talking crowd, and left General Bouverie with a lantern in his hand on the steps. People cheering.

Long past nine when we got back, only to dinner at a quarter to ten! Général d'Herbillon (who sat next to me), Général Borel, and the Admiral, dined with us. Général d'Herbillon is an agreeable man, very dark and weather-beaten; he talked much of the Crimean War, and of their having lost 90,000 men! He was fifteen years in Algeria without coming home.

It was nearly eleven when dinner was over, and we retired shortly afterwards. Beautiful night. This expedition, the object of many wishes of mine, had been delightful. Some singers came out in a steamer and sang very prettily. Strange to say, hardly a single boat came out while we were in the harbour. In an English port we should have been beset with them.

Milestone
1858

The Wedding of the Princess Royal and Prince Frederick William of Prussia at the Chapel Royal, St. James's Palace

Monday, January 25. – The second most eventful day in my life as regards feelings. I felt as if I were being married over again myself, only much more nervous, for I had not that blessed feeling which I had then, which raises and supports one, of giving myself up for life to him whom I loved and worshipped – then and ever! . . . Got up, and, while dressing, dearest Vicky came to see me, looking well and composed, and in a fine quiet frame of mind. She had slept more soundly and better than before. This relieved me greatly . . . Gave her a pretty book called *The Bridal Offering* . . . The Chapel, though too small, looked extremely imposing and well, – full as it was of so many elegantly-dressed ladies, uniforms, &c . . .

The drums and trumpets played marches, and the organ played others as the procession approached and entered. There was a pause between each, but not a very long one, and the effect was thrilling and striking as you heard the music gradually coming nearer and nearer. Fritz looked pale and much agitated, but behaved with the greatest self-possession, bowing to us, and then kneeling down in a most devotional manner. Then came the bride's procession, and our darling Flower looked very touching and lovely, with such an innocent, confident, and serious expression, her veil hanging back over her shoulders, walking between her beloved father and dearest Uncle Leopold, who had been at her christening and confirmation, and was himself the widower of Princess Charlotte, heiress to the throne of this country, Albert's and my uncle, Mama's brother, and one of the wisest kings in Europe!

My last fear of being overcome vanished on seeing Vicky's quiet, calm, and composed manner. It was beautiful to see her kneeling with Fritz, their hands joined, and the train borne by the eight young ladies, who looked like a cloud of maidens hovering round her, as they knelt near her. Dearest Albert took her by the hand to give her away,—*my* beloved Albert (who, I saw, felt so strongly), which reminded me vividly of having in the same way, proudly, tenderly, confidently, most lovingly knelt by him, on this very same spot, and having our hands joined there . . .

The Princess Royal and Prince Frederick William of Prussia, from a contemporary commemoration plate

Journey Eighteen
1858

Birmingham in the Sun

THE summer of 1858 was exceedingly hot. *Punch* said of it:

The sunshine is baking—thermometer making
Attempts up to tropical figures to climb . . .

In addition there was a drought, and the river Thames stank:

Bake, bake, bake,
O Thames, on thy way to the sea!
And I would that thy stink could poison
A Bishop, Peer, or M.P.

Queen Victoria did not like the heat. She said that it made her feel as if she was going to swoon—but she never did. Out of doors she defended herself under powder and parasol, and indoors she attempted to counteract it by having buckets of ice placed under the chairs, a practice which was the cause of a venerable and unsuspecting cleric developing inflammation of the hip, from which she never recovered.

It was therefore with some trepidation that she boarded the train for Coventry on the stifling afternoon of 14th June. She was bound for Stoneleigh Abbey, Kenilworth, the home of Lord and Lady Leigh,[1] and thereafter for the crowded streets of Birmingham.

It was overpoweringly hot in the compartment, and there was little relief at Coventry station where vast crowds had gathered. But at least there was light relief. The *Morning Post* described how, after the address of the Mayor and Corporation had been presented, 'Lord Leigh now threw himself into the saddle, and galloped off in advance of Her Majesty's carriage'.

Contrast came as the horses turned into the park of Stoneleigh. In the

[1] 2nd Baron, Lord-Lieutenant of Warwickshire. He married 1848, Caroline, daughter of 2nd Marquess of Westminster.

shade of the centuries' old oaks, the air was delicious and cool and the grass bright green. The Queen looked with delight at the terrace garden, the river Avon flowing before it, and, behind, the high curtain of trees. The cool of the river could be felt at her bedroom window.

Among the guests at dinner were two of particular interest to her. They were Mr and Mrs Bracebridge, friends of Florence Nightingale, 'who were always with her in the Crimea, and at Constantinople, elderly, plain, most excellent worthy people'.

June 15.–After half-an-hour's broiling in the railway, we were soon after noon at Birmingham, which shone clear and bright, without a particle of smoke. It was as hot as Paris; but Paris had not the dense and closely packed multitudes, and it had less heavy air. The arrangements were magnificent–the best I ever saw–the thousands all stationary, behind barriers, and the decorations most beautiful and full of taste. There were endless inscriptions of the most loyal kind, banners, flags, "*guidons*", wreaths of flowers across the streets in every direction, and so abundant as to have at every turning the most beautiful effect. There were Prussian flags, Vicky's and Fritz's initials, and a flag with Fritz and Vicky on it, and underneath, "Long live the Prince and Princess of Prussia". Then, along the front of a house was a scroll with "Victoria the People's Friend" in flowers wrought on cloth, and then "The Prince Consort, Long may he Live"–"The Queen, our Nation's Pride"–"God Bless our Queen! a Pattern to the World!"–"Victoria, the Queen of Peace"; others for my beloved Albert, and one as follows: "God Bless Prince Frederick of Prussia's bright Star! Health to the Blooming Rosebud afar!" Then there were inscriptions on flags, and on almost every house either our cypher or inscriptions. All was admirably done–handsomer even than Manchester. The cheering was tremendous.

We went to the Town Hall, where the heat was fearful. Here we received on a throne two Addresses, one to Albert and one to myself, and I knighted the Mayor,–"God save the Queen" having been first sung to the fine organ. Then the procession continued through countless thousands to old Aston Hall and Park, now to be converted into a people's museum and park, and to obtain which the working people have worked very hard, and subscribed very largely. Here we were received by the managers, and taken upstairs to rooms prepared for us. Many fine old pictures had been lent, and Vicky's picture (a copy of Winterhalter's) had been placed in the recess of our retiring-room. The room where we lunched with our party–Sir C. Scott (a young Baronet who has had the management of the whole proceedings, and has excellent taste), Sir H. Smith, and Mr Bracebridge–was full of fine

The inauguration of Aston Park

pictures, and beautiful things by Elkington ornamented the table. Luncheon over, we went into the Gallery, where we received Addresses (of course we read answers to them), and the managers were presented, including the working men themselves, to six of whom I said a few words. We next stepped out on the balcony, from which the park was proclaimed open. Then we went downstairs, and through the Exhibition rooms, and walked once down and back along the terrace, the people cheering us very warmly. Dear Albert is so beloved here—as, indeed, everywhere—having been here, I think, on three previous occasions for different purposes, and his love for the Arts and Sciences, and the moral improvement of the working and middle classes, and the general enlightenment of all, being so well known. A person called out in the crowd, "Quite a pattern lady"! Another, "What a darling"!

I felt much oppressed with the heat by the time we left the hall. I had been here as a child in 1830, when it belonged to a Mr Watts,— also at Birmingham, and at Guy's Cliff. The day became fearfully oppressive. Leaving the railway we drove to Kenilworth Castle. Albert got out to see the beautiful ruins. I had seen them as a child, and, being very tired, returned to Stoneleigh at half-past five . . . At a little after eleven we retired, and found but little air in our rooms. We watched some people on the water, and the young ladies sang; and we listened to the band, and the distant hum of voices, and the people (the crowd) sang "God save the Queen" as they had done yesterday. It reminded us of a similarly hot night in July, at Cambridge, on the occasion of Albert's Installation in 1847, when we took a walk with poor Waldemar of Prussia, Charles of Weimar, and the Duchess of Sutherland, after a fearfully hot dinner, and when it was so fine, and the garden of the College, with the bridge over the river, looked so picturesque.

The following day the Queen and Prince, with an escort of the Warwickshire Yeomanry, drove through Leamington to Warwick Castle, where they lunched with Lord and Lady Warwick. Their train for home was to leave from the Great Western station at Warwick. As they reached the platform, as if in salute, came a mighty clap of thunder.

Warwick Castle

We had barely got into the railway carriage, before the rain came down with fearful violence. We soon got out of it, and the journey, though not cool, was not so bad as Monday's. We got to Buckingham Palace a little before eight. So hot, it had been 90° in the shade, and people half smothered.

Journey Nineteen
1858

The Palaces of Potsdam and Berlin

IN this year of many comings and goings, Queen Victoria's thoughts were, in the main, concentrated around the fate of her married daughter in Germany—in the event a child in exile, for the seventeen year old Princess Royal was not yet ready to digest the solid *schloss* pudding of Potsdam.

During the schoolroom period there had been no close bond between mother and daughter. The former's sudden switch from the dull routine of Kensington Palace to the glories of Buckingham Palace and Windsor, coupled with the emotional tide of her love for Albert, had been largely responsible for that. Then, too, there was a touch of bitterness when the Queen compared the hard days of her own childhood with the gilt which had surrounded her daughter from birth—at the age of three 'Vicky' had proclaimed: *'Voilà le tableau qui se déroule à mes pieds.'* There was also a tinge of jealousy over the brilliant mind of 'Vicky', and that when mother, father and daughter were alone together, it was the mother who was out of company.

The Queen had begun matrimonial plans with a Prussian groom when her daughter was only two, and allowed her to become engaged at fourteen. Having brought her plan to fruition, she found that she had lost not only control, but also happy years of companionship that would have come, of natural course, from the maturing girl. The Queen, therefore, tried to retain her control by means of a series of instructional letters to Germany, and to find an emotional safety valve and a feeling of companionship by means of the written, in place of the spoken, word.

These letters, which left for Germany at the rate of two or three a week, were crammed with advice about cough medicines and draughts, drains and lavatories, and the plagues and miseries that are the lot of a newly married woman—all of course to be as nothing when dissolved in the radiance of a husband's love. There were reproaches about orders not complied with, questions not answered, and the paucity of correspondence with her brothers and sisters and former governesses. There were lectures on how young married women should conduct their conversation and how to deal with lecherous Princes who told bawdy stories at the dinner table. Intermixed was political propaganda on the Coburg line, leaving the impression that Victoria and Albert considered that they had taken over Prussia's future by bestowing their daughter in marriage.

As was only to be expected, a fraction of that which Princess Frederick William read in these letters found its way into her attitude, and conversation, at Potsdam. One habit which was found particularly irritating, was that of referring to England as 'home'. The Prussians, now in the embryonic dream that was to materialise in the desire for world mastership, set about the task of cutting down 'Miss' Princess Royal to the size in which they wanted her. Jealous of the large allowance which she had brought with her, they were determined that she should adopt the traditional role of Prussian women. The result was argument and some miserable moments, and a general upsetting of the nervous system, which was most undesirable during the period of procreation of a child.

The information that the Princess was pregnant reached Osborne at the end of May. 'Horrid news', the Queen described it, adding, in her reply, that she was almost certain that nothing would come of it. Why she should have thought so, is difficult to understand, as she herself had been married on 10th February and given birth to the Princess Royal on 21st November, thereafter complaining bitterly that she had been 'caught' so early.

The Prince Consort was about to leave for a short visit to Coburg, and had arranged to meet his daughter there. But now, although the baby was not due until January, it was decided by the Prussian hierarchy that the Princess could not travel, a bad foot being given as the excuse. The Prince Consort, determined that nothing should stop him seeing his beloved daughter, cut short his time in Coburg and made the return journey via Potsdam. He found the newly married couple much in love and in perfect harmony together. But beyond the grounds of the palace a different feeling prevailed. Two high officials saw the Prince Consort driving by, and one asked the other whom he was. On learning of the identity, the first commented: 'Why did you not tell me? I would have thrown him in the river.'

Of the forthcoming event, Princess Frederick William took the ecstatic view of a novice in such matters, and was full of pride that she was the vehicle that was to give 'life to an immortal soul', a view with which the end-product would doubtless have fully agreed, if he had been in a position to have an opinion since, in later years, he was to make it abundantly clear that he looked upon himself in this light.

Queen Victoria took a very different stand. To her the relevant period levelled one to the status of a cow in a similar predicament, just animal and no ecstasy. But as, in April, she had been convinced that she was set on the path to increase her own brood to the target figure of ten—hopes that came to nothing—her attitude may have been biased.

Determined to see her daughter before the summer was out, the Queen laid her plans to travel to Germany in August. But she ran into opposition over points in the plan. Her suggestion for a rendez-vous on the Rhine was amended to read Potsdam. Her wish to take with her Princesses Alice and Helena, was vetoed by Miss Hildyard, their governess, and by the Prince Consort, on educational grounds. The Queen gave way, but, as whenever she was thwarted, someone was pricked with the sharp end of her fork. This time the victim was the unfortunate Princess Frederick William. She was informed that, as a child, she had been insubordinate and bad tempered, and that she and her brother, 'Bertie', had been a constant worry to their parents. The Queen went on to wonder whether six months of marriage had wrought any changes for the better—whether she still stood on one leg, crammed food into her mouth, and waddled when she walked?

Before the German excursion, the Queen and Prince Consort had another overseas engagement to fulfil. Early in August they sailed to Cherbourg once again, this time to meet the Emperor and Empress. Napoleon, who appeared to be out of sorts, did his Gallic best to explain away the multitude of ships and the menacing and mammoth fortifications. Eugénie was apologetic. The Prince Consort commented that what he had seen made his blood boil. The Queen wrote to her Prime Minister demanding urgent action on the home side of the Channel.

Although there were clouds on the political horizon, the summer sky was untrammelled as the royal couple entrained for Berlin at Antwerp on 11th August. 'Blazingly hot, with a stifling haze', wrote the Queen. The temperature rose high into the eighties, and the carriages were like ovens.

At intervals along the line the Queen was subjected to 'stoppages', as she called them. At these halts relations were waiting to greet her with embraces, and notabilities with addresses. After spending the night at Dusseldorf, Hanover was reached the following noon. The Queen had a raging headache by the time she alighted at the capital over which she would have reigned if she had been born a boy. She was met by her blind cousin, King George, and his wife, and driven to their country palace of Herrenhausen, where family associations were thick about her. Here Electress Sophia had dwelt and died, and here George I was living when he succeeded to the British Throne.

Endless people to meet . . . more stoppages . . . At eight o'clock Prince Frederick William (dear Fritz) joined the train at Magdeburg, with the news that 'Vicky' was awaiting them at the Wildpark station:

It became gradually dark, and the time seemed very long as we approached nearer what we had come for. One more stoppage at Brandenburg, and we arrived at the Wildpark station. There on the platform stood our darling child, with a nosegay in her hand. She stepped in, and long and warm was the embrace, as she clasped me in her arms. So much to say, and to tell, and to ask, yet so unaltered, looking well–quite the old Vicky still! It was a happy moment, for which I thank God!

Another five or six minutes brought us to the Potsdam station, where were a band and a guard of honour of gigantic guardsmen with pointed caps, and all the princes and princesses . . . Then at the door of the station were the dear Princess of Prussia and the Princess Charles (her eldest sister) . . . After waiting a few minutes we got into open carriages; I with the dear Princess and Vicky, and drove up to Babels-berg. The Castle was beautifully lit up. The Princess and Vicky took us to our rooms, which are very comfortable. It was eleven! Many well-known faces appeared among the servants, and I felt half at home . . . We supped with our children and the Prince and Princess,[1] and then went up to bed, wishing our dear child, as of old, good-night. Very pleasant.

Babelsberg, which had been lent to Prince and Princess Frederick William, had been built by the Prince of Prussia as a summer residence, and was a welcome change from the cold and depressing Berlin *schloss* in which they had spent the first months of their marriage. Situated on a wooded hill some three miles from Potsdam, water lay before it and, beyond, the view was of pleasant countryside. The Queen wrote of it:

Everything there is very small, a Gothic *bijou*, full of furniture, and flowers (creepers), which they arrange very prettily round screens, and lamps, and pictures. There are many irregular turrets and towers and steps . . . My sitting-room commands splendid views of the lake (the Havel), the Bridge, Glienicke (Prince Charles's Château), the Marmor-Palaise, Pfingst-Berg, and looks on one of the lovely terraces . . . There are charming walks under trees, and fountains on all the terraces . . . Vicky came and sat with me. I felt as if she were my own again . . .

Yet, away from Babelsberg, the holiday was not to provide the Queen with the relaxation and fun which had hitherto been woven into the excursions that she had made with her husband. Part reason was the gloom caused by the illness of King Frederick William IV. A paralytic stroke had robbed him of his reason, and he lived in seclusion in the Palace

[1] William and Augusta of Prussia, parents of Prince Frederick William. Afterwards King and Queen of Prussia, and Emperor and Empress of Germany.

Babelsberg

of Bellevue. In the event only a few weeks were to pass before the Prince of Prussia took over as Regent.

The Prussian idea of daily entertainment consisted of large and heavy dinners, military reviews and conducted tours round tombs and empty castles. Not everyone whom the Queen met at the dinners was friendly—General Manteuffel she described as being 'most unpleasant, cross and disagreeable'. But, dutifully, as she tramped round the sights in the heat, she made her notes.

The King's Palace, Berlin

We went across an open gallery (very cold and inconvenient in winter) to the King's apartments—strange, dark, vaulted, dull rooms, left just as he used them, full of pictures of the interiors of churches, busts, &c.; then to the Queen's rooms, fine and spacious, but very cold, full of family pictures and busts, and everywhere Russian memorials, showing quite a *culte* (worship) for the Emperor Nicholas. From the Queen's window the first shot on the 18th March, 1848 was seen . . . [The series of State apartments were then visited.] The last of all these is the Weisser Saal, nearly though not quite so large as our Ball-room (at Buckingham Palace), with a gallery at the top and fine frescoes all round. Here the state dinner on Vicky's arrival was given and the Polonaise took place. From this you descend by a staircase, over which there is a fountain, into the magnificent new chapel which the King has built, all of the finest marble, with a dome and endless paintings of saints and great men on a gold ground. Very fine, but very peculiar . . . This concluded the sight-seeing.

Potsdam Palace and Frederick the Great's Tomb

First we went to Frederick the Great's rooms, left just as he used them, blue and silver, rich Louis XV style, silverframes, everything silver, and well preserved. Several relics of his were shown, all carefully kept his hat, and flute, a book of his, an old piano, &c. . . . Then we went to the late Queen's (Louise's) rooms, which have been left entirely untouched, everything in its place, even to her parasol, *all* sad and cheerless, for the colour is gone out of everything, and the whole is so old-fashioned. Thence we went to the late King's rooms, and to the present King's and Queen's—not very comfortable, the present King's in particular . . .

We got into our carriages and drove to the Garnisonkirche, where we went to the tomb of Frederick the Great, the anniversary of whose death (seventy-two years ago) it was. His father is also buried here in a marble sarcophagus. Thence we went upstairs to see the uniforms of the late King of Prussia, the Emperor Alexander (of Russia), and Emperor Francis (of Austria), the three allies, kept in glass cases. The old custos was present at Frederick the Great's funeral.

The visit to Frederick the Great's tomb recalled to my recollection a circumstance which had been mentioned to me many years before by my dear mother. As she was born the very day Frederick died, her

The New Palace, Potsdam

grandmother, the old Duchess of Coburg (a Princess of the House of Brunswick), whose sister had been Frederick the Great's wife, would never allow the Duchess of Kent's birthday to be celebrated, which, as the Duchess said, gave her an early dislike for the Prussians. This old Duchess of Coburg was also sister to Queen Ulrica Juliana of Denmark, who behaved so unkindly to poor Queen Caroline Matilda.

Neue Palais, Potsdam

A splendid building that reminded me much of Hampton Court, the same colour, same style, same kind of garden, with splendid orange trees, which in the cool calm evening sent out a delicious smell . . . We got out for a few minutes and saw one side and a suite of rooms of this enormous Palace. The Garten-Saal, one enormous hall, all in marble, with incrustations of stones, opening into a splendid room or gallery, reminded me of the Salle des Glaces at Versailles. We went into Frederick the Great's room, and wrote our names down, as we had done at Potsdam.

The Palace of Sans Souci, Potsdam

It is quite in the rococo style—built by Frederick the Great, who died there. It is all on the ground-floor, merely one story, low and dark, damp and cheerless . . . Here also are rooms all in silver, which was Frederick the Great's taste . . . The terraces, with the splendid orange-trees, which everywhere here are magnificent, and with festoons of creepers drawn from one to the other, are lovely. There are 400 orange-trees here, two hundred years old . . . The view from the Belvedere, which we next visited, is very fine, and the new Orangerie is magnificent, really one of the finest pieces of architecture that can be imagined—but what an expense!

The Palace of Charlottenberg, Berlin

This is another Palace, and, though the situation is not pretty, it is, to my taste, far the most cheerful of the Palaces. It was built by Frederick William I (the first King), who married George I's sister, Sophie Charlotte, after whom it is called. You enter a hall below, where there is a fine marble statue of the Empress-mother of Russia. The *culte* for her is wonderful, as indeed it is for the whole Russian family, and quite artificial, as the country hate all that is Russian.

We saw first the rooms of Queen Sophie Charlotte, and the curious old chapel in which all the Princes and Princesses have been confirmed, and some christened and married. Thence we went through the garden along a fine avenue of silver firs, to the Mausoleum, where the late King and Queen are buried. In the beautiful chapel, which is all of marble, with admirably selected inscriptions in large golden letters upon the walls, are the noble recumbent figures, by Rauch, of the King and Queen, sleeping peacefully. Blue glass from above sheds a beautiful soft light upon these monuments. I admire the King's most . . . The Prince (of Prussia) took us down into the vault, where stand the two stone coffins of the King and Queen, covered with wreaths of immortelles placed there by the family. Vicky and Fritz placed the last . . . We returned to the Schloss, and there went upstairs and saw the King's and Queen's rooms and their reception-rooms—all beautiful and cheerful. The poor King's everywhere contain such a curious mixture of things: Russian and scientific portraits and souvenirs, views of churches, &c. In the bedroom I was touched to see the prints of our children, as also Bertie's picture. Melancholy to see in all these Palaces the poor King's and Queen's deserted rooms, with all their little things left just as if they were there.

We then visited the late King's and Queen's rooms, also left quite untouched, time alone showing its melancholy traces. Here was the Queen's unfinished work—she died in 1811—the King's coat, &c. There are curious life-size pictures of Frederick the Great's Guardsmen, the very tallest he had, in some rooms below-stairs. Upstairs there is a most beautiful *salle* in a suite of fine reception-rooms, called "Der Trompeter-Saal", on account of a curious sort of organ with trumpets which stands in it, and which was wound up, and set off playing and making an overpowering noise. Returning to the hall below, we went through a long gallery with wood carving and pictures, reminding me forcibly of Hampton Court, and through some smaller apartments, in one of which is the celebrated picture of Frederick the Great and his sister as children, he playing a drum and still in petticoats.

The Friedenskirche, Potsdam

We went next to the Friedenskirche, close to Sans Souci—a beautiful Italian church with a campanile and open cloisters. In the first court is a colossal bronze statue of Our Saviour by Thorwaldsen. In a small niche or side building, open in front, there is a beautiful marble Pietà by Rietschel, with a very fine painted dome over it. The church is entirely marble, of different colours, in the Byzantine style; so also are two lovely little side chapels, in one of which is a font. There are some beautiful things, too, in the colonnade.

The visit ended on 28th August. For the Queen the parting from her daughter was poignant, for the two would not meet again until after the birth of the grandchild? In truth, State duties precluded the absence of

[2] Prince William, the future German Kaiser, was born on 27th January 1859.

the Sovereign at the expected time, but it had also been made clear in
Berlin that the event was looked upon as a purely Prussian affair. So the
Queen wrote in her diary:

> Our tears flowed fast, and so did Vicky's, but our last words were,
> "*Auf baldiges Wiedersehn!* (To a speedy meeting again!)" All would be
> comparatively easy, were it not for the one thought, that I cannot be
> with her at that very critical moment, when every other mother goes
> to her child!

Frederick the Great's chinoiserie *tea-house, Potsdam. Built 1754*

Journey Twenty
1858

Overture at Leeds

STRANGE to relate, no Sovereign had visited Leeds prior to Queen
Victoria's arrival at the station on the evening of 6th September 1858.
The occasion which called her thither, was the opening of the new
Town Hall. She was accompanied by her husband, her daughters, Alice
and Helena, and Miss Hildyard, governess to the Princesses. It was estimated that the crowd which had gathered to meet them, was the largest
ever to pack the streets of the town.

The success of the visit was assured in the first few moments on the
platform, as the Mayor, Mr Peter Fairbairn, stepped forward to greet the
Queen. He reminded her of a painting by Titian. She wrote:

> . . . a perfect figure of a fine old man, with dark eyes, snowy hair, and
> flowing beard. He was dressed in crimson velvet robes, with a gold
> chain; his bearing and manner were excellent, and he looked the
> personification of a Venetian Doge.

Miss Hildyard immediately fell in love with him.

Her two charges were very much on their best behaviour. Having been
refused permission to take part in the Berlin excursion on the grounds of
youth and lessons, they were now having their baptism of public adulation.
The occasion was of particular importance to fifteen year old Alice, who
was now the eldest Princess at home and was being prepared to play
support role to her mother. A fun loving and flirtatious girl, little did
those thousands who watched her dream that but three short years ahead,
she would be the only link between the Sovereign and Her Ministers, an
experience which was to drain all the high spirits from her being.

The Mayor had lent his home, Woodley House, for the occasion, and
here the staff learned that being royal did not entail lying late in bed in
the morning. By eight o'clock next day the Prince Consort was exploring
the local Exhibition of Social Industry. On display was Mr Donisthorpe's
wool-combing machine. In one room the many parts which made it up

Driving past Sunday School children, Woodhouse Moor

were laid out on a table, whilst, in another, the assembled machine could be seen working.

The Prince remembered the machine from the time of the Great Exhibition of 1851. Now he inspected the laid out parts, and then, with the inventor to guide him, moved off to see the finished article. The Prince watched it for a time and then pointed out to Mr Donisthorpe that a wheel was missing—a fact which the inventor had to admit was correct, and one that he was never to forget.

By half past ten half a million people, controlled by 29,000 volunteers, were waiting for the Queen:

The day, though not very bright, was very warm. We made the entire tour of the town, which took us more than an hour. Nothing could be more enthusiastic than our reception, or better behaved than the people. The streets were beautifully decorated with countless wreaths and festoons of flowers in paper, hung from side to side, and along the houses were flags innumerable (the Prussian included), and inscriptions, with here and there triumphal arches. Nowhere have I seen the children's names so often inscribed. On one large arch were even in large letters "Beatrice and Leopold", which gave me much pleasure – then Vicky's and Fritz's.

'Both inside and out it is a splendid building', was the Prince Consort's opinion of the new Town Hall. On entering, the Queen and he ascended a dais, and the proceedings began with a prayer from the Bishop of Ripon – 'a very lengthy and tedious one' was the royal opinion. An exchange of Addresses followed. The Mayor then knelt before the Queen and became Sir Peter Fairbairn.[1] The Prime Minister, Lord Derby, stepped forward, and, at the Queen's command, declared the Hall opened. There followed a tour of the main apartments and lunch with Sir Peter and Lady Fairbairn. In the afternoon the journey towards Balmoral was resumed.

That evening the first Leeds Musical Festival was held in the Town Hall.

[1] His son, Sir Andrew Fairbairn, was Mayor of Leeds, 1866–8.

Journey Twenty-one
1860

Escape in Coburg

THE Prince Consort longed to see Coburg once again. He wished to
talk with his old mentor, Baron Stockmar, realising that this might
be the last opportunity to do so. He yearned to walk through the
woods and over the hills that he had known as a child, and to savour the
true peace that he found only there. He also wanted to see his grandson.

In this last wish he had the urgent backing of his wife. William was now
over eighteen months old and had already been joined in the nursery by a
sister, Charlotte—a name of whom Queen Victoria did not approve, rating
Victoria the obvious selection. Princess Frederick William had of purpose
kept the child away from his grandparents, hoping against hope that the
withered arm with which he had been born would grow stronger and less
obvious with the passing months. But now no further excuses could be
made, and a rendez-vous at Coburg was fixed for the end of September.

Although only just past his forty-first birthday, Albert was in poor
state physically. He was subject to violent attacks of cramp in the stomach,
and the condition of his nerves was clear from the bouts of sickness that
preceded the major speeches that he was called upon to make. He was
overworking, and not even allowed to do so in comfort. In his fireless
study he would wear a wig to keep the cold from his head.

His wife was not being helpful—nursing was not her strong line. Emotional troubles that had existed between the two prior to the birth of
Princess Beatrice in 1857, had lapsed in the fun of having about them this
imp of a child, who had no respect for Queen or Consort. But by now
the tantrums and complexes of the Queen were once again coming to the
surface. She attributed the depressions and lack of energy of her husband,
to a diminution of his passion for her and a general lack of trust. She
would trot around the corridors after him, pleading her non-existent case.
She would bombard him with notes, and bang upon his door when he
locked himself in in self-defence. She seemed incapable of realising that
her own fount of physical strength and courage was not issued as a standard ration to all human beings.

Albert saw a visit to Coburg as a remedial measure both for his wife and himself. Yet, from the outset, it would appear as if a curse had been put upon the journey.

The departure date was fixed for 22nd September. Ten days prior to this an incident, minor in itself, occurred in Germany. It blew up to such an extent that for a time it was feared that relations between Britain and Prussia might be severed.

On the 12th September Captain Macdonald, on holiday in Germany, entered a railway carriage at Bonn and occupied a seat which had already been reserved. On refusing to quit his place, he was ejected by superior native forces. The ejection necessitated a certain amount of violence. The Captain was committed to prison and while there—he was later to complain—he was treated harshly. On the 18th he was tried, and fined twenty thalers and costs. But it was the words of the Public Prosecutor that precipitated the international crisis: '*The English residing and travelling are notorious for the rudeness, impudence and boorish arrogance of their conduct.*' This was altogether too much for Lord Palmerston, who demanded reparations for the Captain, and punishment for the Public Prosecutor.

Yet the Prussian allegation was not without some foundation. One has only to regard the guide books of the period to appreciate the basic attitude of the English abroad: 'This is my seat—relinquish it at once'; 'I have been overcharged—fetch the manager'; 'Extinguish that pipe/cigar—I abhor the smell of tobacco'. And the Queen herself admitted that, while foreign Governments could be both arbitrary and violent, 'our people are apt to give offence, and to pay no regard to the laws of the country'. Princess Alice, travelling incognito to Italy a few years later, was appalled by the conversation and behaviour of English holidaymakers with whom she shared a carriage.

While the Prince Consort did his utmost to pour oil on the troubled waters, *The Times* did the very reverse. Under the editorship of Mr Delane, its circulation had risen to over fifty thousand, and no opportunity of sticking pins into Prussia was missed. The Macdonald affair provided the ammunition for a fusillade of pins. Behind the policy of *The Times* was a deep dislike and mistrust of matrimonial alliances between the royal houses of Great Britain and Germany, as had been made abundantly clear at the time of the marriage of the Princess Royal. As the Prince Consort's concept of a peaceful Europe rested on cordial relations between Germany and Britain, he viewed the newspaper attacks with alarm and deep concern. He told his eldest daughter: 'What abominable articles *The Times* has against Prussia! . . . a total estrangement between the two countries may ensue, if a newspaper war be kept up for some time between the two nations.' He struggled to keep an argument over a reserved seat apart from *la haute politique*, but the spark of Captain Macdonald's ire was but one of many that led towards the final holocaust. Albert had no more chance of extinguishing it than had Canute of stopping the waves.

Yet the Queen was in high spirits, in anticipation of the holiday, as she left Buckingham Palace for Gravesend with the Prince Consort and Princess Alice, on the sunny afternoon of 22nd September. They were accompanied by Lady Churchill, Miss Bulteel, General Grey, Sir Charles Phipps and Colonel Ponsonby, with Lord John Russell and Dr Baly to advise politically and medically.

> At half-past five we embarked on board the *Victoria and Albert*. Many people there. A number of volunteer cadets, pretty little boys, nicely set up, lined the way to the vessel. We started almost immediately, and dropped anchor at the Nore about a quarter to seven.

In the early hours the royal yacht crossed to the Scheldt through smooth waters. The Queen came on deck to comment that the scenery was 'really too hideous' compared with the glorious Highlands which she had so lately left behind.

> But I am so thankful for the admirable passage, the best, I think, we have ever had to Antwerp, that I can complain of nothing, and feel full of gratitude to be so far on our journey! May the rest be equally prosperous!

But, as they passed through Belgium, a message was handed to the Prince Consort telling him that his step-mother, the Dowager Duchess of Coburg, was dead. The news hit Albert hard. The divorce of his lovely mother, Louise, when he was seven, had upset the whole balance of his childhood. When his father married Marie of Wurttemberg in 1831, he found in her a friend and adviser who did much to mitigate the effects of the years without a mother.

Yet there was distraction in the beauty of the day's journey. From Bonn the train ran over the newly constructed line along the left bank of the Rhine:

> You see from the railway admirably all the beautiful parts upon the river, and pass sometimes through, sometimes close behind the picturesque little towns and villages on the Rhine. We saw and admired the Drachenfels, Königswinter (where Bertie spent six months in 1857) decked out with flags . . . the numerous beautiful castles and vine-clad hills . . . The mountains are very pretty, and were beautifully lit up, but they are not our dear hills, and the vineyards are stiff . . . At about seven we reached Frankfort, where, to our regret, we were received by a guard of honour and a band.

Lichtenfels

After spending the night at the Hotel d'Angleterre, the royal party left at nine, the route lying through the valley of the Main to Aschaffenburg and Lichtenfels, where a switch was made to the Thuringian line for the last stage to Coburg:

> The country is charming: fields and valleys, vineyards with crucifixes and little picturesque chapels in the vineyards and along the roads; and women working in the fields, with handkerchiefs over their heads, reminding me so much of the Highland women. They carry baskets on their backs, with immense loads of fruit, &c. reaching over their heads. The carts drawn by oxen, none by horses . . .
>
> I felt so agitated as we approached nearer and nearer, and Albert recognised each spot. At last we caught the first glimpse of the Festung, then of the town, with the cheerful and lovely country round, the fine evening lighting it all up so beautifully. At five we were at the station. Of course all was private and quiet; Ernest (Duke of Coburg) and Fritz (Prince Frederick William) standing there in very deep mourning. Many people out, but they showed such proper feeling – all quiet, no demonstrations of joy, though many kind faces. Felt so moved as we drove up to the door of the Palace under the archway. Here stood, in painful contrast to fifteen years ago, when so many dear ones, in the

brightest gala attire, received us at the door, Alexandrine (Duchess of Coburg) and Vicky, in the deepest German mourning, long black veils with a point, surrounded by the ladies and gentlemen! A tender embrace, and then we walked up the staircase . . . Could hardly speak, I felt so moved, and quite trembled. We went at once through the large rooms to ours, where my dear Mama used to live . . . The view from them is on the Festung and the Platz, which is now so pretty, with Papa's (the late Duke of Coburg's) statue, surrounded by a garden. One of the sitting-room windows also looks up one of the very picturesque narrow streets of the town, with high gabled red-roofed houses, and commands a glimpse into the market-place.

We remained together for some little time, and then our darling grandchild was brought. Such a little love! He came walking in at Mrs Hobbs's (his nurse's) hand, in a little white dress with black bows, and was so good. He is a fine, fat child, with a beautiful white soft skin, very fine shoulders and limbs, and a very dear face, like Vicky and Fritz, and also Louise of Baden. He has Fritz's eyes and Vicky's mouth, and very fair curly hair. We felt so happy to see him at last.

September 27.—Was wakened at six by the "Currenden Schüler" (boys belonging to a school) singing as they passed under the window *"Ein feste Burg ist unser Gott"*. It was beautiful and touching, as it came nearer and then died away. Dear little William came to me as he does every morning. He is such a darling, so intelligent . . . We went at ten to the *Schloss-Kirche* (in the Palace), a fine large and richly-decorated chapel like some of those old chapels in England. We went in veils with the points on the forehead. Every one in the church in mourning. They were singing when we went in, and so beautifully, it quite upset us all. The service was very like the Scotch, only more form; but we did not stand up for the prayers, which I believe we ought to have done. They sang two hymns, consecutively, at two different times. One, to the tune "O Jerusalem!" was exquisite. The Superintendent Meyer prayed and preached upon the death of my poor Mama-in-law; but what he said did not move me greatly. It was too general, too much a mere eulogy . . .

Saturday, September 29.—Again such a beautiful day. I feel so happy to be here, to visit all these loved places again, and to see my dearest Albert so happy! Market-day again—a gay scene, of which we got a glimpse from our windows—so many of the peasants in their best dresses coming into the town . . . Very bad weather we hear at Osborne— very beautiful at dear Balmoral. A fortnight to-day we left it. It seems so far off!

At a quarter to one we drove in four carriages with our dear relations and children, and also Lady Churchill, the Countess Brühl (Vicky's

lady), and Lord John Russell, to the Rosenau. Our English people are
enchanted with everything, with the beauty of the country, and of the
palaces, the quiet and simplicity of the people, &c., and certainly nowhere could you see a more charming, cheerful country, with such
pretty valleys, and so much fine distant scenery, as here. We got out
at the bottom of the hill, and walked about the charming grounds,
which I knew so well, and then went into the dear old house, and over
all our dear rooms, and the salons, all which are quite unaltered. There
was the room painted by dear Mama, &c . . . After luncheon Vicky and
I sat in front of the *Marmorsaal* (Marble Hall), drawing the beautiful
view of the Festung and Oeslau, the air like a warm summer's day, and
listening to the tinkling of the cow-bells.

The Queen began her diary entry for 1st October with the words:

Before proceeding I must thank God for having preserved my adored
one! I tremble now on thinking of it . . . The escape is very wonderful,
most merciful! God is indeed most gracious.

That afternoon the Prince Consort had some business matters to attend
to in Coburg, so his wife and daughters decided that they would take their
sketch books out into the country. The Prince was driving in an open
carriage drawn by four horses. A leader took fright, and bolted. As the
carriage raced towards the railway crossing, he saw that the bar was down
and that a waggon was waiting to cross. He flung himself out on to the
road. As he struggled to his feet, wiping the blood and dirt from his face,
he saw the wreck of the carriage, one horse lying dead beside it and the
others galloping away in their traces, and the coachman writhing in
agony on the road. The Queen takes up the story:

Our drawings (the distant view of Coburg, which is beautiful) being
finished, we ladies walked down (the gentlemen were gone elsewhere)
through the *Hahn* to the Parkthor, going along merrily, and much
amused by a pretty peasant woman, who told Vicky how dirty her dress
was getting by trailing on the ground, and advising her to take it up,
and expecting our carriages to overtake us, when we met a two-seated
carriage, with Colonel Ponsonby in it, who said Albert had sent him
to say there had been an accident to the carriage, but that Albert was
not hurt, having only scratched his nose; that Dr Baly happened to
meet him, and said it was of no consequence. This prevented my being
startled or *much* frightened. That came later, when Colonel Ponsonby
explained that the horses had run away, and that Albert had jumped
out!

Ketchen Tor, Coburg

Drove back in this carriage with Alice, Colonel Ponsonby sitting on the box beside the coachman. We were told by an excited *Postbeamter* (Post-official) not to go where the carriage still was, one of the horses being seriously hurt as well as the coachman, and then drove by the "Pappel-Allee" and the Barracks home. I went at once to my dearest Albert's rooms, and found him lying quietly on Löhlein's (his valet's) bed, with lint compress on his nose, mouth, and chin, and poor good old Stockmar (who, I feared, would be terribly alarmed) standing by him, and also Dr Baly. He was quite cheerful, and talking, and giving an account of this fearful accident, and, as it proved, merciful and providential escape. Dr Baly said Albert had not been the least stunned, that there was no injury, and the features would not suffer. Oh God! What did I not feel! I could only, and do only, allow the feelings of gratitude, not those of horror at what might have happened, to fill my mind . . . Every one in such distress and excitement, and such anxiety in Coburg. I sent off many telegrams to England, &c., fearing wrong messages.

In front of the Queen the Prince made little of the matter. She noted: 'Albert in high spirits, talking away . . . Dearest Albert at dinner, of course, as usual.' But in the ensuing days the shock of what might have happened chilled her . . . the thought that her husband might have been crippled for life, or even that the saga of their days together might have ended. But what she did not realise was how much the incident, which had caused but surface damage physically, had affected his mental condition. Old Baron Stockmar saw the truth. 'God have mercy on us!' was his comment. 'If anything serious should ever happen to him, he will die.' Duke Ernest also learned of it. He saw his brother dabbing his face with a handkerchief. He thought at first that Albert was attending to his scratches, but then saw that he was crying. Albert then broke down, sobbing that he was certain that he would never see Coburg again.

Five days later the prayers of thanksgiving for a merciful escape were over, the Prince's cuts healed and his spirits apparently back to normal, strengthened by the anticipation of the thrill of the chase. The Queen, disregarding criticism at home of her participation in blood–letting, drove out with the guns:

Saturday, October 6.—A dull and threatening morning, which soon turned to rain. The dear little boy is so intelligent and pretty, so good and affectionate. So much to do every day . . . The day cleared, and we made a charming expedition. We all started at twenty minutes past twelve, I and Alexandrine, with our daughters, Ernest in front, Albert, Fritz, and the suites following. Sir Charles Phipps and General Grey had gone to Gotha and Reinhardtsbrunn.

We drove by the *Schweizerei*, through Oeslau, to Mönchröthen, a village with an old monastery, most picturesquely situated. We got out at the entrance of the Park, where two of Ernest's Jägers met us. We went on to the Häslich, which quite caused me an emotion, reminding me, as it did, of our beloved Highlands, for there were Scotch firs, and we gathered blaeberries and cranberries, and their little flowers, and the heather.

We walked quietly and noiselessly on, up a small path, into a lovely valley, where a stand was arranged, into which we and the ladies got, and also Albert and Ernest, Fritz, and Lord John Russell, with guns and rifles. The drive of wild boars then took place, and was most successful, no less than seven being killed, very fine large ones too. It was very exciting. They are fine wild-looking beasts. Albert shot three (I think more), and each time gave them the mortal wound; Fritz one; and Lord John Russell and Colonel Ponsonby (who was below), one. The gentlemen ran to see their sport, and little *Dachshunde* were sent into the woods to bring out any wounded boars. The gentlemen carried spears to kill those which had not fallen at once. Albert was much

Schloss Ehrenburg, Coburg

pleased, no one having killed more than one before. We wished Grant (head-keeper at Balmoral) had been there . . . According to German custom, we each received a *Bruch*, viz., a small branch of oak and of spruce, to put in our hats. Oak is the *spécialité* of wild boars.

Sunday, October 7. – We went past the *Schweizerei* to get a good view of the dear Rosenau, a short way from Oeslau. We found a good place, and I made a successful sketch, to my great satisfaction. A nice old woman in her Sunday dress coming past, we stopped her, and she stood with her basket on her back while I made a sketch of her. When finished, I showed it to her, and she was delighted; she called her grandson to look at it, and then shook hands with me. They are so good, so simple, and unaffected, these people. Elizabeth Korn was her name. A funny, rather tipsy old man in Sunday dress, with silver buttons to his plush waistcoat, came up to the carriage, and was not pleased at being sent off. '*Sie thun mir Nichts, ich thue Ihnen Nichts*' – ('You don't meddle with

me, I don't meddle with you'), was his observation, when the footman
sent him away.

Then, with the end of the holiday, the rain came down and the first cold
of winter caught the Queen unawares. She developed a sore throat and
felt wretched, but the integral courage and determination of the woman
showed in her insistence on following the programme that had been set
for her. On the return journey a halt was made at Coblenz, where the
royal party was entertained by the Prince and Princess of Prussia. Even at
the end of a tiring day, when obviously she would have been better off
in bed, she was present at dinner and the musical entertainment afterwards.

> *October 12.* – A rather better morning . . . At eleven we walked out
> with the Princess, Vicky, Alice, and Fritz of Baden, first in the garden,
> and then along the Rhine, where the Princess has made a really lovely
> promenade with statues, figures, and flowers, and afterwards in the
> town, to look at the bridge (near the confluence of the Moselle and
> Rhine). Could hardly stand, – felt so weak and full of aches when we
> came back, and had to lie down and rest; but before doing so, we went
> to see the fine chapel, and also the small English one, which the Princess
> has arranged for the English residents – both in the Schloss . . . Soon
> after luncheon we dressed to go out. It rained and hailed heavily just
> before we drove out, and this drive it was which increased my cold so
> much . . . We drove up to the Stolzenfels, got out at the Castle, and
> went over all this really beautiful place . . . I remembered it all so well,
> and was much pleased to see it again. Our rooms and everything re-
> minded me of the poor King. The chapel is now finished, and the
> painting by Däger very beautiful. But oh! it was dreadfully, bitterly
> cold and damp. However the beams of light on the Rhine, and the
> view on Ehrenbreitstein lit up by the setting sun, were splendid . . .
> Only home by ten minutes past six. Felt thoroughly chilled, for it was
> very damp and cold. Vicky came over to us, and remained with us, it
> being, alas! our last day together, and the darling little boy was with us
> for nearly an hour, running about so dearly and merrily.

By the time that Belgium was reached next day the Queen was really ill:

> I had to lie down, and only got up about a quarter of an hour before
> we reached Brussels. At the station dear Uncle received us. I could
> hardly walk when we got out, and with difficulty got up stairs . . .
> Dr Baly found my throat very bad, that I had much fever; so I was
> ordered to remain lying down in my room and to see no one . . . Not
> since Ramsgate in 1835 did I feel so ill as I did this day . . . It was

provoking, as Uncle gave a very large dinner in honour of myself. By opening the door I could hear the fine band of the Guides. Later, Jane (Lady) Churchill came and read to me out of *The Mill on the Floss*.

It was not until the 16th that the Queen was fit enough to board the royal yacht. After a night spent at anchor riding out a storm, at eight o'clock next evening the carriages rattled up the hill to Windsor:

> Found all the dear children well, and delighted to see us, including our precious Beatrice. Already a week since we left Coburg, and the dear happy days there belong to the treasured recollections of the past!

But not all the recollections were allowed to remain in the roseate sunset of the past. *Punch* had been keeping a sharp eye open to see if blood was spilled in the Coburg arena. The letting of the Prince Consort's was commemorated with the following levity:

> It is an extraordinary thing that any sort of vehicular indiscretion should have been manifested in the case of a Prince who has always been so remarkably Prudent in his Carriage.

But the target that *Punch* was really waiting for was the letting of the blood of animals, and the hunting of the boars exactly fitted the bill. On 27th October a letter was published from one Giles Joulter, a Hampshire farmer. It was headed 'A PIG AND A POKE':

> Mr Punch, Sir, The other morning, as I were a going to kill our pig, in steps our parson. My wife she were a standing by me, quite pleased to see the pig weighed so handsome—and our two little lads was a laughing like mad, for really the pig did squeak quite unnecessary loud. So says the parson, says he, quite sharp like to my wife, 'I do wonder, Mary, that you should be here at all, and still more that you should allow your boys to make diversion of a poor dumb animal's sufferings. (Dumb he warn't, no how, by the bye, but that's nought). Why can't you let Giles kill the pig by himself, and why don't you give those two brats a couple of boxes on the ear for taking a pleasure in seeing such sights?'
>
> Those were our parson's very words, Sir, and I do believe he were right; so I told my wife to go indoors and mind her own business, and then I took the stick to Jem and Billy, and sent 'em scampering like afore I finished the pig, which died beautiful.
>
> A few days after, my wife she was a reading out to us after supper an old penny paper as the cheese had come home in, she reads capital well, for she was in service at the parson's before she married me, and I'll be hanged if she didn't read out *this*:-

"From the *Court Circular*"

"Yesterday Her Majesty The Queen, with their Royal Highnesses the Prince Consort, the Duke and Duchess of Saxe-Coburg Gotha, the Prince and Princess Frederick William, of Prussia, and Princess Alice, accompanied also by Lord John Russell, and attended by the Ladies and Gentlemen of the Household, drove to the Wald Parc at Mönckröden, where, the gentlemen being posted, the forest was driven for wild boar. The sport was very successful, seven boars being killed. Luncheon was afterwards served to the Royal party in one of the forester's houses."

Only fancy, Sir, our Gracious Queen, and the little Princess Alice, and all the rest of the Royal folk, amusing of themselves killing pigs, and being very successful; and getting an appetite for their dinners that way . . .

Baron Stockmar

The Lakes of Killarney

THE motive for the visit of the Queen and Prince Consort to Ireland in the summer of this year was to inspect the progress and behaviour of 'Bertie', Prince of Wales, who was in camp with the Guards at the Curragh. A second reason, and a more relaxing one, was to see the lakes of Killarney. Their beauty was to exceed all expectation and Albert tramped beside the waters, repeating to himself and anyone who cared to listen – 'This is sublime! This is perfectly sublime!'

This was his swan-song, for it was his goodbye to Ireland. Nearly forty years were to pass before the Queen visited her western subjects again. Whilst her advisers advanced the safety of her person as an excuse, she herself remained petulant and irritated by the paucity of Albert memorials on the other side of St. George's Channel. Thus much of the good that had been achieved in a decade of visits was washed away. In the event the Irish would have been more sympathetic with the tragedy of her widowhood than were the English.

Yet Victoria was a great feuder, and for the past three years she had been at loggerheads with her eldest son. 'Sinful, idle, lazy and imprudent', were words she used to describe him in letters to her daughter in Germany. Sometimes she could not even bring herself to use his name, referring to him as 'You know Who'. His clever remarks and jokes irritated her beyond measure. She disliked the way that he pasted down his hair, thus exaggerating his small head and 'enormous features'. His large mouth and nose were ever a subject of maternal regret – it was said that she saw in him a cartoon of herself. He wore his clothes 'frightfully'. Yet the chief argument against him, made by both parents, was his obvious objection to work. While the rest of the children made birthday presents for their mother and father with their own hands, 'Bertie' would slip out to a shop and return with a gift. As his brothers and sisters wrestled with their spades and hoes in the vegetable patch at the Swiss Cottage at Osborne, 'Bertie' would stand on the path, hectoring and giving advice, but contributing no active part to the operation. Matters reached a point at which the Princess Frederick William decided that she would have to warn her mother of the grave dangers of a rift between the Sovereign and her heir. And this she very bravely did, but, it may be said, not without adverse reaction.

While admittedly 'Bertie' was an awkward person to have about the house—he threw a bottle of ink over a new valet assigned to him—much of the trouble was because he was being crammed with more learning than he could assimilate and that he was being denied the lighter side of life. As his sister saw, a little sympathy and understanding would have cured most of his faults.

Yet 'Bertie' belonged to that segment of the Royal Family, appearing before his time and after, who shed their tantrums and their weaknesses once they set foot upon the stage of their public duties. For most of 1860 he had been in America and Canada. He was a riotous success, and praise flowed back across the Atlantic. The Press hoped, and forecast, that he would bring back a wife from the United States—rumours were born and lived a long time—but his governor, General Bruce, stayed too close to his 'coat tails' for that. When he returned he was sarcastically referred to by his father as 'Our hero', and told that his success was entirely due to his being the son of his parents. History was to repeat itself. When the Duke of York, his lovely Duchess beside him, ended his triumphal world tour of 1927, George V met him at Victoria station and said: 'When you kiss Mama, take your hat off.'

So that no inflated ideas of his own importance might pollute the poor Prince of Wales, he was despatched to terms of virtual imprisonment and hard labour at Oxford and Cambridge. Then, most unexpectedly, in the spring of 1861, his dragon of a governor suddenly decided that he should join the Guards at camp at the Curragh in August. By so doing, the General handed 'Bertie' the latch-key to life.

He must have regarded with some trepidation the intrusion of his parents into the programme of field-days, for the year had gone badly for them. The previous December the Prince Consort had been laid low with an attack of what he described as 'English cholera'. In January mad King Frederick William had died, spreading an unnecessary pall of Prussian gloom over royal circles. A few weeks later Dr Baly, who alone knew the truth about Albert's medical state, was killed in a railway accident between Wimbledon and Malden, being mangled by the carriage wheels. In March the old Duchess of Kent, long a sufferer from cancer, succumbed at Frogmore. As a result the Queen had a nervous breakdown, firmly believing that, like her grandfather, she was going mad. As she had once confided in Lord Melbourne that she did not believe that her mother had ever really loved her, and as the two had not been in a carriage together from the date of her marriage until 1860, the exaggerated grief appeared out of focus. May be part of it was recrimination and part tantrum with God for taking matters into His own hands. In any case, it was most wearying for her husband who now had the additional work of sorting out the Duchess's papers, wherein rested secrets which posterity certainly must not know. Even by August Victoria was still liable to explode into tears if a chance remark reminded her of 'the dear dead past'.

On the 21st the Queen and Prince Consort, with Prince Alfred, Princess Alice (who had recently become engaged to Prince Louis of Hesse and the Rhine) and Princess Helena crossed from Osborne to Southampton and travelled by train to Holyhead. There the royal yacht was waiting for them. At Kingstown they were received by the Lord-Lieutenant, Lord Carlisle, who escorted them to the Viceregal Lodge in Phoenix Park.

Friday, August 23.—A fine morning. Breakfasted downstairs. Everything is good, and in good taste here. The pretty cups and china make me feel that Lord Carlisle is the brother of the dear Duchess of Sutherland.[1] Albert left for the Curragh at ten, to see Bertie at work. Walked with Jane (Lady) Churchill in the pretty gardens and pleasure-grounds. Received the Lord Mayor, who presented the Corporation Address, when I said a few civil words in return, Jane Churchill, Lord Carlisle, Lord Granville, and others being present . . . Very busy writing all day, but miss so dreadfully the writing to dearest Mama . . .

Albert back at four. It was beautiful and bright all day. At five, we and the girls planted trees (Affie was out shopping), and then we drove into Dublin—Alice and Lord Carlise in the carriage with us—through the principal streets, and back by the Circular Road and the Park. The streets and buildings are really very fine. There were many people out, and they cheered loudly. Lord Carlisle is, as he well deserves to be, exceedingly popular. We then walked for some time, and looked at a pretty little monument raised by Lord Carlisle on the site of a tree which poor Lady St. Germans planted, and which died about the time she did, with a pretty little verse inscribed on it, written by Lord Carlisle himself. I think of her here very often; she was so kind, so good, and amiable.[2]

Saturday, August 24.—A gray morning; but still we hoped for the best. At half-past nine we started for the railway, Alice and Affie in the carriage. The railway-carriage was a fine one, and very easy. At the Curragh station we found our carriages. Albert, Affie, and the other gentlemen, all in uniform, rode. Our own carriages and horses had all

[1] The Duchess was a connoisseur of china, and provided the services used in the inns on the Sutherland estates.

[2] Lord St. Germans was Lord-Lieutenant when the Queen and Prince visited Ireland in 1853.

been sent here. Such a crowd, such a scamper and scramble! Alice, Lenchen, and Jane Churchill were in the carriage with me. The position of the camp is splendid,—with the Wicklow Hills in the distance, and an immense amount of turf, which nothing can spoil.

We drove up to where the troops were assembled, and received the royal salute, after which Sir George Brown rode up and delivered to me the State. Then we drove down the line. As we approached the cavalry, they began to play one of dearest Mama's marches, which they did again in marching past. This entirely upset me, and the tears would have flowed freely, had I not checked them by a violent effort. But I felt sad the whole day, except when we came to Bertie, who looked very well. I recognised many Aldershot acquaintances. During the march-past à violent shower came down, which obliged us to close the carriages. We did not get wet; neither did Albert; but the troops were soaked.

A field day followed, which we watched, as we usually do, from a distance, moving about from place to place, and occasionally near some portions of the troops. Albert, Affie, and the gentlemen rode about, and kept close to the principal manoeuvres. There were crowds of people in every direction, ladies, common people, &c., on foot and on horseback,—and jaunting-cars driving in every direction. We had one more heavy shower, but otherwise it was very fine.

At a little before three we went to Bertie's hut, which is in fact Sir George Brown's. It is very comfortable—nice little bedroom, sitting-room, drawing-room, and good-sized dining-room,—where we lunched with our whole party, and Sir George Brown, General Ridley (in command at the camp), Colonels Wetherell, Browning, and Percy. The latter commands the Guards, and Bertie is placed specially under him. I spoke to him, and thanked him for treating Bertie as he did, just like any other officer, for I know that he keeps him up to his work in a way, as General Bruce told me, no one else has done; and yet Bertie likes him very much.

The next day, being Sunday, was devoted to occupations beneficial to the souls of the young. The Prince took his two sons on an exhaustive tour of the prisons, while the Queen and her daughters visited the Kilmainham hospital. Monday was Albert's birthday. After the customary elaborate ceremony of present giving, the royal party drove to the station of the Great Southern and Western railway and set off for Killarney:

It was very hot. The country for some distance was very unattractive, except for the outline of distant hills which were visible from time to time. It is astonishing how wanting in population this part of the country is—large plains, a good deal cultivated, here and there a small house,

LAKES ✚ OF ✚ KILLARNEY.

By her Most Gracious Majesty's Special Permission.

The Royal Victoria Hotel,

OPEN THROUGHOUT THE YEAR.

Patronised by H.R.H. the PRINCE OF WALES ; by H.R.H. the DUKE OF CONNAUGHT ;
by the ROYAL FAMILIES OF FRANCE, BELGIUM, &c.; and LEADING AMERICAN FAMILIES.

THIS HOTEL is delightfully situated on the shore of the Lower Lake, close to the water's edge, within ten minutes' drive of the Railway Station, and a short distance from the far-famed Gap of Dunloe. It is lighted with Gas made on the premises, and is the Largest Hotel in the district. A magnificent Coffee Room, a public Drawing Room for Ladies and Families, Billiard and Smoking Rooms, and several suites of Private Apartments, face the Lake.

TABLE D'HOTE DURING THE SEASON.

CARS, CARRIAGES, BOATS, PONIES, & GUIDES, AT FIXED MODERATE CHARGES.

Drivers, Boatmen, and Guides are paid by the Proprietor, and are not allowed to solicit gratuities.

THE HOTEL OMNIBUS AND PORTERS ATTEND THE TRAINS.

POSTAL TELEGRAPH OFFICE IN THE HOUSE.

BOARDING TERMS FROM OCTOBER TO JUNE INCLUSIVE.

It is necessary to inform Tourists that the Railway Company, Proprietors of the Railway Hotel in the town, send upon the platform, as *Touters for their Hotel*, the Porters, Car-drivers, Boatmen, and Guides in their employment, and exclude the servants of the Hotels on the Lake, who will, however, be found in waiting at the Station door.

JOHN O'LEARY, PROPRIETOR.

B 2

with a few cabins, but no villages, and hardly any towns, except the few close upon the railway.

The Lord Lieutenant of the county received us at Portarlington, where General Bruce joined us. We passed Maryborough. We stopped at Thurles, close to the town. The crowd was tremendous – very noisy – the people very wild and dark-looking, – all giving that peculiar shriek which is general here instead of cheers, – the girls were handsome, with long dishevelled hair. Here we saw fine hills to the left. Our next stoppage was at the Limerick Junction, where we found Lord Lismore, Lieutenant of this county. The large plains and distant hills were not unlike the country about Tarland. The last station we stopped at was Mallow, a small town on the Blackwater, in a beautiful valley. Soon after this, the line enters a mountain region, and winds along below woods. At half-past six we reached the Killarney Station, where we were received by Lord Castlerosse,[3] Mr Herbert of Muckross, the General commanding the district and the Mayor, who presented an Address.

There was a great crowd, and troops lined the place. There was likewise an escort. We entered our carriage, with Alice and Bertie, and drove along a rather circuitous road to Lord Castlerosse's Park. Great numbers of people were out, cheering very enthusiastically. We drove through the pretty and much-wooded grounds up a fine avenue of trees to the house, which stands on a terrace, with steps leading down from it, at the foot of which stood Lady Castlerosse and her aunt, Lady Downe. The house looks like a French château, the roof being high. We were taken at once to our rooms, which were very pretty, and most charmingly and elegantly, though simply, furnished. The view from the bedroom towards the lake, with its islands, across a lawn, with two long borders of flowers, and walks stretching from the house to the water, was lovely. I sketched it.

Tuesday, August 27. – At eleven o'clock we all started in our own sociable, and another of our carriages, and on ponies, for Ross Castle, the old ruin which was a celebrated stronghold, and from which the Kenmare family take their name. Here there was an immense crowd and a great many boats. We got into a very handsome barge of eight oars – beautifully rowed. Lord Castlerosse steering. The four children, and Lady Churchill, Lady Castlerosse, and Lord Granville were with us.

We rowed first round Innisfallen Island and some way up the Lower Lake. The view was magnificent. We had a slight shower, which alarmed us all, from the mist which overhung the mountains; but it suddenly cleared away and became very fine and very hot. At a quarter to one

[3] 3rd Earl (1789–1871). Created a peer of the United Kingdom, 1856, with the title of Baron Kenmare.

The Lower Lake, Killarney, by Jonathan Fisher

we landed at the foot of the beautiful hill of Glena, where on a small sloping lawn there is a very pretty little cottage. We walked about, though it was overpoweringly hot, to see some of the splendid views. The trees are beautiful,—oak, birch, arbutus, holly, yew,—all growing down to the water's edge, intermixed with heather. The hills, rising abruptly from the lake, are completely wooded, which gives them a different character from those in Scotland, though they often reminded me of the dear Highlands. We returned to the little cottage, where the quantity of midges and the smell of peat made us think of Alt-na-Giuthasach.[4] Upstairs, from Lady Castlerosse's little room, the view was towards a part of the Lower Lake, the outline of which is rather low. We lunched, and afterwards re-embarked, and then took that most beautiful row up the rapid, under the Old Weir Bridge, through the channel which connects the two lakes, and which is very intricate

[4] Shiel on the Balmoral Estate.

and narrow. Close to our right as we were going, we stopped under the splendid hill of the Eagle's Nest to hear the echo of a bugle; the sound of which, though blown near by, was not heard. We had to get out near the Weir Bridge to let the empty boats be pulled up by the men. The sun had come out and lit up the really magnificent scenery splendidly; but it was most oppressively hot. We wound along till we entered the Upper Lake, which opened upon us with all its high hills— the highest, The Reeks, 3,400 feet high—and its islands and points covered with splendid trees; such arbutus (quite large trees) with yews, making a beautiful foreground. We turned into a small bay or creek, where we got out and walked a short way in the shade, and up to where a tent was placed, just opposite a waterfall called Derricaunihy, a lovely spot, but terribly infested by midges. In this tent was tea, fruit, ice, cakes and everything was most tastefully arranged. We first took some tea, which was very refreshing in the great heat of this relaxing climate. The vegetation is quite that of a jungle—ferns of all kinds and shrubs and trees,—all springing up luxuriantly. We entered our boats and went back the same way we came, admiring greatly the beauty of the scenery; and this time went down the rapids in the boat. No boats, except our own, had followed us beyond the rapids. But below them there were a great many, and the scene was very animated and the people very noisy and enthusiastic. The Irish always give that peculiar shrill shriek—unlike anything one ever hears anywhere else.

Wednesday, August 28.—At a quarter-past eleven we started on a most beautiful drive . . . We drove with Mrs Herbert and Bertie in our sociable, driven from the box by Wagland; and, though the highest mountains were unfortunately occasionally enveloped in mist, and we had slight showers, we were enchanted with the extreme beauty of the scenery. The peeps of the lake; the splendid woods full of the most magnificent arbutus, which in one place form, for a few yards, an avenue under which you drive, with the rocks,—which are very peculiar—all made it one of the finest drives we had ever taken. Turning up by the village and going round, the Torc mountain reminded us of Scotland— of the woods above Abergeldie, of Craig Daign and Craig Clunie. It was *so* fine. We got out at the top of the Torc Waterfall and walked down to the foot of it. We came home at half-past one. At four we started for the boats, quite close by. The Muckross Lake is extremely beautiful; at the beginning of our expedition it looked dark and severe in the mist and showers which kept coming on, just as it does in the Highlands. Mr Herbert steered. Our girls, Mrs Herbert, Lady Churchill, and Lord Granville were in the boat with us. The two boys went in a boat rowed by gentlemen, and the rest in two other boats. At Mr and Mrs Herbert's request I christened one of the points which runs into the lake with a bottle of wine, Albert holding my arm when we came close by, so that it was most successfully smashed.

When we emerged from under Brickeen Bridge, we had a fine view of the Lower Lake and of the scenery of yesterday, which rather puzzled me, seeing it from another *point de vue*. At Benson's Point we stopped for some time, merely rowing about backwards and forwards, or remaining stationary, watching for the deer (all this is a deer forest as well as at Glena), which we expected the dogs would find and bring down into the water. But in vain: we waited till past six and no deer came. The evening had completely cleared and became quite beautiful; and the effect of the numbers of boats full of people, many with little flags, rowing about in every direction and cheering and shouting, lit up by the evening light, was charming. At Darby's Garden, the shore was densely crowded, and many of the women in their blue cloaks waded into the water, holding their clothes up to their knees.

We were home by seven o'clock, having again a slight sprinkling of rain.

The Prince Consort had long wished to see more of Wales, and he took the opportunity to do so on the journey from Ireland to Balmoral. When the royal yacht reached Holyhead, he left his wife and daughters on board and set off with Prince Alfred for a long day's excursion. They

Ladies' View, Killarney

travelled by rail to Caernarvon, where they visited the castle. Then they drove through the Vale of Llanberis and over the pass to Beddgelert. It was a perfect day and Snowdon was clear against the sky. Thus it was that, on his last holiday, the Prince was able to enjoy some of the finest scenery of Ireland, Wales and Scotland.

Meanwhile 'Bertie' soldiered on at the Curragh, but under a tighter rein, as his father, in conversation with Lord Carlisle, had expressed doubts as to whether his son was sufficiently serious about his military duties. The camp was to break up on 12th September. On the evening of the 11th the Prince attended a ball in his honour at the Mansion House in Dublin. On his return to his hut he found a girl in his bed. Her name was Nellie Clifden and she was an actress.

This unfortunate incident may simply have been a prank born out of the high spirits and revelry indelibly associated with the last night in camp; but there may have been more to it than that. The Prince Consort, a Field-Marshal, had made other remarks at the Curragh, remarks not limited to the ears of Lord Carlisle. He had condemned 'the idle tendencies of English youth'. He had deplored that military matters were not discussed in the Mess, on the grounds that they were 'shop'. In past years he had often criticised the Army, and had been accused of interfering with War Office matters. In addition the members of the British aristocracy did not like him, nor he them, sharing the Teutonic opinion that they were profligate and unprincipled. May be Nellie Clifden was a way of settling old scores.

Looking back at his inheritance, to the sons of George III on the one hand, and Ernest of Coburg on the other, it is difficult to imagine 'Bertie' adopting a course divergent from that which he followed. Yet, for a particular reason, he would have been well advised to push that pretty miss out into the Irish night.

From the Curragh the Prince of Wales proceeded direct to Germany, there to further his military training by attending the autumn manoeuvres of the German army around Coblentz, under the guidance of his brother-in-law, a professional soldier, or so it was made to appear. In the event a more important and personal motive summoned him to the Rhine. He was to meet the girl whom it had been decreed should become his wife.

The quartet of selectors, the Queen, the Prince Consort, the King of the Belgians and Baron Stockmar, had been busy with their task for the past three years, Stockmar being of the opinion that, if 'Bertie' was not married early, 'all would be lost'. The names put forward had been narrowed down to a short list of seven. After careful consideration the quartet unanimously agreed Alexandra of Denmark to be the winner, despite objection from members of the family not included in the final consultation.

Just seventeen, Alexandra was the daughter of Prince Christian of Schleswig-Holstein-Sonderburg-Glucksburg, next heir to the throne of Denmark. His income was £800 a year and his daughters served at table and made their own clothes.

The couple were brought together, as if by chance, in the cathedral at Speyer. The rest of the party drifted away, one eye on the objects of architectural and religious interest, the other on the boy and girl. 'Bertie' and Alexandra chatted shyly and spasmodically, and exchanged photographs. He thought that her nose was too long and her forehead too low. Owing to her penurious background, it was not incumbent upon Alexandra to think at all. The general impression of the meeting appeared to be favourable.

'Bertie' entrained once more, reporting to Balmoral on 30th September. Any hopes that the Queen might have fostered of observing a spring from which would flow a river of eternal love, were quickly smashed. Her son was evasive and non-committal. Under pressure, he blurted out that the mere thought of becoming a father filled him with horror—a feeling which his mother considered to be most unnatural. On the 13th October the Prince returned to his studies at Cambridge.

Once again the Scottish holiday ended, with the customary sighs and regrets, and the Queen returned to 'gloomy' Windsor. On 12th November Albert received a letter from Stockmar in Coburg. Usually such letters were most welcome, but this one drained the blood from his face. The Baron reported that the Continent was buzzing with the story of Nellie Clifden. Albert went into seclusion while he checked the facts. He developed a cold, accompanied by sleepless nights, shivering fits and rheumatic pains. He travelled to Cambridge and back in the day to have the matter out with his son. On his return the fever came upon him.

Milestone
1861

The Death of the Prince Consort

December 14. – The day was very fine and bright. I asked whether I might go out for a breath of air. The doctors answered "Yes, just close by, for a quarter of an hour". At about twelve I went out upon the Terrace with Alice. The military band was playing at a distance, and I burst into tears and came home again. I hurried over at once. Dr Watson was in the room. I asked him whether Albert was not better, as he seemed stronger, though he took very little notice, and he answered, "We are very much frightened, but don't, and won't give up hope". They would not let Albert sit up to take his nourishment, as he wasted his strength by doing so. "The pulse keeps up," they said. "It is not worse." Every hour, every minute was a gain; and Sir James Clark was very hopeful – he had seen much worse cases. But the breathing was the alarming thing, it was so rapid. There was what they call a dusky hue about his face and hands, which I knew was not good. I made some observation about it to Dr Jenner, and was alarmed by seeing he seemed to notice it. Albert folded his arms, and began arranging his hair, just as he used to do when well and he was dressing. These were said to be bad signs. Strange! as though he were preparing for another and greater journey.

Statue of Queen Victoria and the Prince Consort by W. Theed in the Royal Mausoleum, Frogmore (reproduced by gracious permission of H.M. The Queen)

"ALLURED TO BRIGHTER WORLDS, AND LED THE WAY."

Journey Twenty-three
1862

Love and Tears in Belgium

FOR Victoria, the spring of 1862 was the spring that never was. Always she had welcomed the coming of the flowers and the sun with pure delight and into her diary she had poured the story of their beauty. Now those few people who reached her looked into still, unseeing eyes, blinded by sadness. In February she wrote to Lord Derby: '*She* sees the trees budding, the days lengthen, the primroses coming out, but *she thinks* herself *still* in the month of December.' Many years were to pass before, on her travels, she could look from her carriage or train window and bring into clear focus the distant church tower, the sun on the forest, the reapers in the harvest and the dogs and children playing by the stream— to see with the same clarity that had been her gift when Albert was by her side.

In May she went to Balmoral, but to her, the leaves on the birch were those that she had left behind in the autumn, and the burns, singing and dancing on their way to the Dee, were running with tears from the weeping patches of mountain snow.

Now her sole determination was to transfer into reality the desires and wishes that had been confided to her by her husband. One such wish was that Alice should marry Prince Louis of Hesse. Another was that the Prince of Wales should make a tour of Egypt and the Holy Land and thereafter marry Alexandra of Denmark. Thus it should be.

Sometimes it happened that the wishes of the Prince Consort coincided closely with the convenience of the Queen. So it was in the case of 'Bertie's' tour. She remembered vividly her husband's journey to Cambridge in order that he might remonstrate with his son over the Nellie Clifden affair, and it was to this exertion that she contributed the beginning of his illness. Although 'Bertie' had extracted a promise from his father that the 'sordid details' would be kept from his mother, the Queen had managed to extract them, as she always succeeded in getting her way when she set her mind to it. Now, she said, she could not look at him without a shudder. That was one reason why she wanted him out of the way.

Another was that the Press were urging—even taking for granted—that the Prince of Wales would now play a more important part in public life and would lift some of the burden from the shoulders of his widowed mother. This the Queen was determined should not happen. Not only did she remember her husband's fear about the catastrophe that would ensue if 'Bertie' was in a position of power, but she was adamant that no part of the mantle of Albert should pass to his son. She wanted time to take certain steps. She took those steps, and most effective they proved.

Princess Alice was married to Prince Louis of Hesse at Osborne in July and the foundation stone of the House of Mountbatten was laid in funereal gloom. The Queen switched immediately to the next bridal arrangements. Speed was necessary, as she had heard that the Russians had their eyes on the Danish Princesses. Having written to Alexandra's parents, she called Uncle Leopold into her scheme.

The Queen had arranged to visit Coburg in September. Now, and for many years after, she had the deep conviction that, when she returned to some spot which she and Albert had loved, she would find him waiting for her there.

On the way to Germany she was to pass through Brussels. She therefore asked her uncle to arrange that she meet Princess Alexandra and her parents at his palace of Laeken. Efficient as ever, King Leopold laid on a seaside holiday for Prince and Princess Christian and their daughter at Ostend. They could thus be summoned quickly to headquarters on the arrival of the Queen. The call came.

LAEKEN, *September 3.*—At half past 1 went down to luncheon with the girls, going first to the Drawing-room where Marie B[1] and Mrs Paget[2] introduced Princess Christian, who presented her two daughters Alexandra and Dagmar,[3] and Prince Christian.[4] I had seen him last twenty-four years ago. The Brabants and Philip[5] were also there. Alexandra is lovely, such a beautiful refined profile, and quiet lady-like manner, which made a most favourable impression. Dagmar is quite different, with fine brown eyes. Princess Christian must have been quite good-looking. She is unfortunately very deaf. Uncle soon came in, and after a rather stiff visit they all (excepting myself) went to luncheon. I spoke to Mrs Paget in the next room and told her I was favourably impressed. Baby lunched with me.

[1] Duchess of Brabant. Married to King Leopold's elder son, afterwards King Leopold II.
[2] Mrs 'Wally' Paget, wife of Mr (later Sir) Augustus Paget, Minister at Copenhagen. Before her marriage she was Countess Walburga Hohenthal, lady-in-waiting to the Princess Royal.
[3] Afterwards Empress Marie of Russia.
[4] He succeeded to the Throne of Denmark in autumn, 1863.
[5] Count of Flanders, younger son of King Leopold.

Afterwards Marie B. brought Prince and Princess Christian upstairs, leaving them with me. Now came the terribly trying moment for me. I had *alone* to say and do what, under other, former happy circumstances, had devolved on us both together. It was not without much emotion that I was able to express what I did to the Princess: my belief that they knew what we wished and hoped, which was terrible for me to say *alone*. I said that I trusted their dear daughter would feel, should she accept our son, that she was doing so with her whole heart and will. They assured me that Bertie *might hope* she would do so, and that they trusted *he* also felt a real inclination, adding that they hoped God would give their dear child strength to do what she ought, and that she might be able to pour some comfort into my poor heart, that they were sure she would become quickly attached to me, and be a good wife to Bertie. I replied I would do all I could to be a *real* mother to her, but I feared she was entering a very sad house. Thus ended this most trying meeting. Feodore afterwards came to my room and I told her all. She spoke with great admiration of the young Princess.

Dined as yesterday, and afterwards Prince and Princess Christian and Princess Alexandra came upstairs. She looked lovely, in a black dress, nothing in her hair, and curls on either side, which hung over her shoulders, her hair turned back off her beautiful forehead. Her whole appearance was one of the greatest charm, combined with simplicity and perfect dignity. I gave her a little piece of white heather, which Bertie gave me at Balmoral, and I told her I hoped it would bring her

Laeken Palace, Brussels

luck. Dear Uncle Leopold, who sat near me, was charmed with her. Very tired, and felt low and agitated.[6]

The mission accomplished, the Queen proceeded on her slow way to Coburg. There she stayed at Reinhardtsbrunn, the hunting lodge in the forest which had entranced her in 1845. Although she had no marital company, at least there were children partly to fill the gap. 'Baby' Beatrice, her youngest daughter, was on her first trip abroad, and prattled incessantly. Three year old William of Prussia was waiting for her at Coburg. He was led into her presence riding on an ass and bearing an unfurled parasol.

On 7th September the Prince of Wales, home from his tour, arrived at Ostend and strolled on the sands with the Christians. Two days later King Leopold summoned 'Bertie' and Alexandra to Laeken, and stage-managed the formal betrothal. 'Bertie' spoke with 'Wally' Paget, who was much of his age and whom he had come to know well through visits to his sister. He said: 'I shall now take a walk in the garden with Princess Alexandra for three-quarters of an hour; then I shall take her into the grotto and propose to her, and I hope everything will turn out to everybody's satisfaction.' 'Wally' was somewhat taken aback at the exactness of the time-table.

The news was certainly to the satisfaction of his mother, but it was anything but welcome to her German hosts. Duke Ernest of Coburg described it as 'a thunder clap for Germany'. Bismarck, whose star was rising in Berlin, viewed it with displeasure, for reasons that were to become abundantly clear two years later, when Prussian forces occupied Denmark.

On her return journey home the Queen was delayed in Belgium by violent storms in the Channel. It had happened so often before, when she had been with Albert, but then it had been rather exciting and fun. He had looked after all the emergency arrangements and organised excursions to while away the time. A feeling of utter loneliness swept over her. She wrote to her eldest daughter in Germany.

LAEKEN, *October 22.*—Here we are quite weather-bound and blowing so fearfully that it is utterly impossible to get across! We might just have got over if we had gone straight on board on Saturday 18th and sailed Sunday morning—but at dear Uncle's age and especially after his illness I could hardly—particularly as we had announced ourselves—go by, without seeing him, and so we settled to go either Sunday evening or Monday morning. Well that very Sunday (Saturday it poured the whole afternoon) it began blowing most fearfully, and so

[6]This and succeeding extracts from the Journal of Queen Victoria are from *The Letters of Queen Victoria, Series II and III,* are are reproduced by gracious permission of H. M. The Queen.

it has done ever since—and we had after constant telegrams and con-
sultations with General Grey etc. to give up first Monday morning and
afternoon; the same yesterday and after a very quiet night the same
today as it is worse even today and with such deluges of rain! No
packets have gone across either way from Ostend the last two days,
and poor Arthur is at Ostend on board the *Black Eagle* since Monday
morning !!!

Oh! and here I am with all the children all alone without beloved
Papa's counsel and advice and love and feel lonely and so wretched,
in this terribly dull place—where really I feel as if one would lose one's
intellects. The quiet and the repose I seek are not being shut up in a place
like this, cut off from every thing, surrounded by canals, nothing but
pavé to drive on, no streets to go into, which are so dreadfully jarring
and clashing to my poor sad, wretched nerves. Nothing quieting or
"Gemütlich" and so terribly Catholic!

This afternoon (a dreadful evening) I walked about here with Augusta
and visited the stables and greenhouses in dreadful weather and it made
me feel quite sick, for how often I went with adored Papa about in
this way, and whenever we were in a strange place—how we used to
walk about and look at every thing, which was his greatest delight,
and so often out in the rain![7]

[7] *Dearest Mama.* P. 114.

Leopold I, King of the Belgians

Milestone
1863

The Wedding of the Prince of Wales and Princess Alexandra of Denmark at St. George's Chapel, Windsor

There was a pause, and then the trumpets sounded again, and our boy, supported by Ernest C[oburg] and Fritz, all in Garter robes, entered; Bertie looking pale and nervous. He bowed to me, and during the long wait for his Bride kept constantly looking up at me, with an anxious, clinging look, which touched me much. At length she appeared, the band playing Handel's Processional March, with her eight Bridesmaids, looking very lovely. She was trembling and very pale. Dearest Albert's Chorale was sung, which affected me much, and then the service proceeded. When it was over, the young couple looked up at me, and I gave them an affectionate nod and kissed my hand to sweet Alix.

Journey Twenty-four
1866

A First at Wolverhampton

T HE statue of the Prince Consort in the market place at Wolverhampton was the first to be raised by an English municipality.

WINDSOR CASTLE, *November 30.* – A bright morning, though
very cold. Shortly before 10 started by train for Wolverhampton, with
Lenchen, Louise, Christian, etc. . . .

With a sinking heart and trembling knees got out of the train, amidst
great cheering, bands playing, troops presenting arms, etc. Was received
by Lord Lichfield, Lord Lieutenant of the County (who presented the
Mayor), and Lady Lichfield, looking so young and handsome, who
was standing with Lady Waterpark. When we were told all was ready
entered our carriages, I driving with my daughters and Christian,[1] with
an escort of the 8th Hussars. The postilions wore the Ascot livery.
Lord A. Paget and General Grey rode just behind the carriage. All
along the three or four miles we drove, the town was beautifully
decorated, with flags, wreaths of flowers, and endless kind inscriptions.
There were also many arches. It seemed so strange being amongst so
many, yet feeling so *alone*, without my beloved husband! Everything
so like former great functions, and yet so unlike! I felt much moved,
and nearly broke down when I saw the dear name and the following
inscriptions – "Honour to the memory of Albert the Good", "the good
Prince", "His works follow him", and so many quotations from
Tennyson. There were barriers all along, so that there was no over-
crowding, and many Volunteers with bands were stationed at different
points.

The arrangements on the spot where the statue stood were extremely
good and the decorations very pretty. There were high galleries all
round, and a covered daïs for me, but the cold wind made it fearfully
draughty. The Prayers and Address were both long, and trying to many.

[1] Princess Helena had married Prince Christian of Schleswig-Holstein in July.

Princess Christian of Schleswig-Holstein in her wedding dress

I made several very deep curtsies when I got out of the carriage and stepped forward. The enthusiasm was very great.

The Mayor was completely taken by surprise when I knighted him, and seemed quite bewildered, and hardly to understand it when Lord Derby told him. There was some slight delay in the uncovering of the statue, but it[2] fell well and slowly, amidst shouts and the playing of the dear old Coburg March by the band. How I could bear up, I hardly know, but I remained firm throughout. At the conclusion of the ceremony I walked round the statue followed by the children. I had seen it before at Thornycroft's studio, and it is upon the whole good. I spoke to the Bishop of Lichfield, Lord and Lady Lichfield, Lady Waterpark, the Mayoress, who gave me a bouquet, the General, Mr C. Villiers, the member, etc.

We drove back through quite another, and the poorest, part of the town, which took half an hour. There was not a house that had not got its little decoration; and though we passed through some of the most wretched-looking slums, where the people were all in tatters, and many very Irish-looking, they were most loyal and demonstrative. There was not one unkind look or dissatisfied expression; everyone, without exception, being kind and friendly. Great as the enthusiasm used always to be wherever dearest Albert and I appeared, there was something peculiar and touching in the joy and even emotion with which the people greeted their poor widowed Queen!

[2] i.e. the covering sheet.

Journey Twenty-five
1868

Switzerland via Paris

IN August of this year, members of the Royal Family were on Swiss
territory in force. Prince Arthur, with suitable escort, was on a walking
and climbing tour. Queen Victoria, the Princesses Louise and Beatrice,
and Prince Leopold, were at Lucerne.

This was the Queen's first visit to Switzerland, and it was very different
from the previous trips that she had made to the Continent. In France she
had been the guest of King Louis Philippe or Emperor Napoleon. In
Belgium and Germany she had stayed with rulers or relations, with only
an occasional night in an hotel for variation. But now she had hired a
villa, and was travelling incognito as the Countess of Kent. She was a
mother on holiday with her children.

During the preceding five years many changes had come to the Europe
which she had known with her husband. Two wars—the Schleswig-
Holstein dispute and the Seven Weeks war, both victories for Bismarck—
had upset the balance and brought in their train the heartache of divided
loyalties to her married son and daughters. Both King Leopold of the
Belgians and Baron Stockmar were dead, and so the sentimental ties with
Brussels and Coburg were severed.

A change had also come into her domestic life, a change which part
filled the void that had existed since December 1861. Once again there
was an interest and a sense of security. In the dark years which followed
their father's death the elder Princesses had been distressed by their mother's
grief and loneliness, the manner in which she preserved her bedroom as a
shrine for her husband, falling asleep with his red dressing-gown clutched
close to her, and her obvious longing for male companionship that shone
clear in her written outpourings. Particularly did this upset Princess Alice,
whom the Queen was for ever begging to make her home in England,
so that she might have a son-in-law about the house. As such a step was
impossible, the Princess decided on an alternative plan. With the conni-
vance of others, she arranged that the duties of John Brown, her mother's
regular attendant in Scotland, should be extended beyond the spring and

autumn visits to Balmoral. Accordingly, in December 1864 the gillie arrived at Osborne, and the tonic effect was immediately apparent. The following year he was promoted to become an upper servant and the Queen's permanent personal attendant. The demands for visits from her married daughters ceased.

Excellent and faithful servant as Brown proved to be, the disadvantages of taking him abroad soon became apparent. Firstly, having spent all his life on Deeside, he did not take kindly to changes in language, climate, or ways of life. Secondly, his peculiar position was liable to misunderstanding. While travelling to Coburg for the unveiling of the statue of Prince Consort in 1865, the Queen had been displeased with the treatment of Brown in Brussels. At Coburg Duke Ernest had banished him to a servants' wing. This, added to her brother-in-law's contrary attitude at the time of the engagement of the Prince of Wales and his constant *affaires*, caused the Queen to boycott her husband's birthplace for many a year.

An amendment that the Queen now made to her Continental excursions was to change the line of approach. She decided to make the crossing to Cherbourg in the royal yacht, and thereafter take the train to Paris. To this route she remained faithful for the rest of her life.

Although she was travelling incognito, the Swiss holiday attracted great attention in Britain. The interest was fanned by the presence of John Brown and the fear that the Fenians might make an attempt on her life.

Two years earlier a Swiss newspaper had carried the rumour that the Queen and Brown had been secretly married. Long after the holiday was over an irresponsible section of the British Press printed the story that the Queen had gone to Lucerne so that she could have a baby. She was forty-nine years old at the time. When the rumour was repeated to her, she just laughed.

The Queen planned her holiday with infinite care and had arranged for Sir Howard Elphinstone to make a reconnaissance the previous summer. The situation, she stipulated, must be in true mountain scenery, and the air must be fresh and cold. Two houses would suit, one for herself and her children, the maids and two menservants, and the other for the ladies and gentlemen. She would take two cooks. Ponies–including her favourite, 'Sultan'–together with their attendants and her sociable, would be provided by Balmoral. If suitable, local carriages would be used, but there must be room on the box for Brown beside the driver. She would take her own bed.

The Villa Wallace at Lucerne was at last agreed upon, Napoleon's offer of his Imperial train was accepted, and, in early August, the caravan collected. The public was able to follow its every movement.

Her Majesty the Queen—travelling incognita, as the Countess of Kent—embarked on Wednesday, August 3 from Osborne Pier, shortly afternoon, in the Royal yacht Victoria and Albert, Captain his Serene Highness the Prince of Leiningen, which immediately afterwards sailed for Cherbourg.

The Royal yacht was attended across the Channel by the Enchantress, Government steam-yacht, Staff Commander John E. Pettey, R.N., and by the Black Eagle steam-yacht, Staff Commander Thomas J. Whillier, R.N. The Royal flotilla arrived off Cherbourg at six p.m.

Her Majesty and the Royal Family dined on board the yacht and disembarked at eleven p.m. on the Government jetty, where a flying bridge, leading direct from the arsenal to the departure-platform of the station of the Chemin de Fer de l'Ouest, had been especially constructed, to obviate the necessity of using carriages for the conveyance of the Royal party from the dockyard to the railway station. The Emperor placed at the disposal of the Queen an Imperial train, consisting of ten vehicles, several of which are fitted up with luxurious magnificence.

The Queen and the Royal party left Cherbourg at eleven p.m. The distance from Cherbourg to Paris is 230 miles, the route traversing Normandy, and passing in succession the important towns of Bayeux, Caen (where refreshments were provided), Lisieux, Evreux, and Nantes. Her Majesty arrived in Paris at seven o'clock on Thursday morning.

At the station of the Chemin de Fer de l'Ouest, in Paris, her Majesty was received by his Excellency Lord Lyons, British Ambassador at the Court of Paris, with his staff; and by several French officers of distinction.

The Queen and the Royal party proceeded in the Ambassador's carriages from the railway station to the hotel of the Embassy, where her Majesty remained during Thursday. The Empress Eugenie visited the Queen at a quarter past three in the afternoon, and remained with her Majesty until four o'clock. The Duke of Edinburgh arrived in the morning by way of Calais, and immediately on his arrival paid a visit to the Queen.

Her Majesty continued her journey on Thursday evening, leaving Paris at nine p.m. by the Chemin de Fer de l'Est, using the same Imperial train which conveyed the Royal party from Cherbourg to Paris. The distance from Paris to Bâle, on the Swiss frontier, is 323 English miles—the route, except on the hilly wine districts, having little of a picturesque character to recommend it. At Bâle her Majesty and the Royal party partook of breakfast, and here the officials of the Chemin de Fer de l'Est resigned charge of the train to the officers of the Central Swiss Railway, over which her Majesty travelled henceforward to Lucerne . . . This railway, the works of which were executed by Mr Brassey, traverses the district of the Jura, through very beautiful scenery, to Olten, at which point branches diverge to Lucerne and other Swiss centres. The Queen, after breakfasting, proceeded on her journey through exquisite scenery, and arrived at Lucerne yesterday (Friday) morning.

The Queen and the Royal family will occupy, during their stay at Lucerne, a beautifully-situated residence, called the Villa (Pension) Wallace. It stands on a hill overlooking the town, with the Rhigi on the left, and Mont Pilatus, distinguished by its serrated ridge, upon the right, and the lake and snowy

Royal residence at Lucerne

St. Gothard range of Alps immediately in front.

The Queen and the Royal family, with the ladies in waiting, will occupy the villa, and the other members of the Royal suite will be accommodated in a pretty châlet, situated in the grounds, and closely adjoining the lake. Altogether, the spot chosen for her Majesty's residence has charms of scenery of the most sublime character, probably not to be equalled in Europe.[1]

The only incident on the journey concerned the Queen's bed. On arrival in Switzerland Brown decided to check on its whereabouts. Not being able to locate it, he became loquacious in his native tongue, which was entirely incomprehensible to the Swiss officials. At first it was assumed that the strangely attired gentleman required a bed in a local hotel, and, when this proved not to be the case, the sad conclusion was reached that the beds of Switzerland were not comfortable enough for Her Majesty the Queen. In due season the missing bed was unloaded from the train.

By the time that the royal party was ensconced every corner of the

[1] Illustrated London News.

Villa Wallace and its chalet was occupied. Thus the announcement that Prince Arthur and his party were on their way there was greeted with alarm. The Queen sent a message that ,'we have no room to spare for a mouse', and that no meals could be provided but breakfast. But, undaunted, the Queen's favourite son arrived, quarters being found in the town.

The Swiss authorities made every effort to ensure that their visitor's holiday was a success. The steamer *Winkelried* was waiting for her when

The steamer Winkelreid

she wished to make a trip along the lake and the Town Council put the Belvedere, on the Guetsch, at her disposal. Sightseers did not disturb her peace, and if she wished to stop at a wayside café for a cup of tea, or something stronger, she was treated as an ordinary tourist. She spent three days at a quiet inn at Flüelen, and found it almost as peaceful as a shiel at Balmoral. She made a number of climbs, amongst them being that of Mont Pilatus. This feat earned the following despatch from Lucerne:

Queen Victoria has made a pleasant ascent of Mount Pilate. Of the two rival mountains that guard the entrance of the St. Gothard gorge, near this town, the most frequented by travellers is the Righi; but the grandest by far is Mount Pilate. Its wild precipitous aspect, however, is sufficient to deter mere excursionists from approaching it, and it is even said that there was formerly a cantonal law forbidding the attempt in consequence of its dangers. A still more deterrent cause is, probably, the frequency of fogs and clouds on the summit, which destroy all chances of a view. A weird legend that Pilate, seized with remorse while traversing the spot, drowned himself in a little lake cradled in one of the ravines, has given its name to the mountain; and, according to the popular belief, his spirit still haunts the neighbourhood. But modern philosophers have dared to doubt the truth of the legend of Pontius Pilate, and ascribe the true derivation of the name to Pileatus, or capped (with clouds). The best road from the plain to the summit leads from Hergiswyl, and the traveller obtains magnificent views as he zigzags upwards. After passing the Klimsenhorn he will have to climb a ladder through a tunnel cut in the rock, called the Krisiloch, and on emerging will be repaid for his toil by a prospect of extraordinary grandeur. The other road to the summit leads from Alpnach; and it was by this that the Queen ascended. Princess Louisa was with her Majesty as well as Prince Arthur, who has already earned for himself a reputation as an Alpine climber. The Queen rode her English pony, and was escorted by her Highland attendants, who, if report speaks truth, have outdone the Swiss hillmen in mountain-walking. Hoffman, the well-known guide, led the way to the top, and accomplished the distance in four hours. The highest peak here is the Esel, reached by a precipitous path, and so narrow on the summit that there is scarcely room for a dozen people to stand together; but the view is inexpressibly grand, the whole range of the Alps from the Glarnitsch to the Blumlis Alp stands out clearly on the horizon to the south, while the low ground and lakes are stretched out like a map at the foot of the precipices. If the view at mid-day is glorious, it is doubly so when the sun sets or rises, and colours the whole of the snowy peaks with molten gold; but the Royal party did not remain till the evening. The following names were inscribed in the travellers' book at the Bellevue Hotel:- The Countess of Kent, Lady Louise Kent; Lieutenant the Hon. Arthur Kent, R.E.; The Marchioness of Ely; Colonel Henry Ponsonby, G.G. The route taken for the descent was the same as that for the ascent, and its gentle declivities enabled the horses to proceed without difficulty.[2]

[2] From *Galignani*.

Mount Pilatus, Lucerne

A sensational newspaper story about the Queen's holiday described
how a Fenian had attempted to enter her private quarters. In 1868 all
outrages were attributed to this source. The Fenian Brotherhood was an
Irish-American revolutionary society, the avowed intent of which was to
overthrow the English rule in Ireland. The previous year in Manchester a
police sergeant had been shot when Fenians attempted to free two of their
companions from arrest. Three of the rescuers were hanged, and became
known as 'the Manchester martyrs'. About the same time an attack was
made on Clerkenwell prison, the object being to free a Fenian awaiting
trial. The wall was blown down by gunpowder, and the explosion killed
twelve people and wounded some 120. There was good reason to fear
the activities of these men, and no one was more aware of the danger
than John Brown, ever at the Queen's side.

It was the *Gazette de France* which first reported that a Fenian had
arrived at Lucerne, with the intention of making an attempt on the
Queen's life. 'But', the report continued, 'he was arrested on Wednesday
in front of the Swiss Hotel by two English Police Agents. The incident
caused great excitement among the English residents here and it is believed
the man did not come alone. It is said that Her Majesty was informed of
the plan to assassinate her before her departure from England.'

The British Press took up the story and two days later a London paper
came out with 'the truth of what had happened'. A man named William
Wood had tried to gain access to the apartments occupied by the Queen.
He was arrested, found to be mentally unstable, and taken to Berne to be
handed over by the police to the British Legation. On 29th August the
following official announcement appeared in the Court columns:

> We are requested to contradict on authority a report which has appeared
> in the public press of a man having been arrested at Lucerne on suspicion of
> being a Fenian with designs against the life of the Queen. Her Majesty has
> been subjected to no annoyance of any kind during her stay in Switzerland,
> and nothing has occurred to interfere with the excellent arrangements made for
> her comfort by the Federal and local authorities.

Perhaps the real truth behind the contradictory reports can be traced
to events which occurred in Switzerland eighty years before. Then twenty
year old Prince Edward, afterwards Duke of Kent and father of Queen
Victoria, was studying at Geneva. He fell in love with a married woman,
Madame Julie de St. Laurent, Baronne de Fortisson. She followed him
when his military service took him to Gibraltar and North America. In
Quebec a son was born. George III had already attempted to keep the
couple apart. Prince Edward was fearful of the effect upon his father of the
news that he had had a child by a woman who was not only already
married, but also a Catholic. He therefore arranged that a friend, a naval

Statue of William Tell at Altdorf, near Lucerne

officer named Wood, should adopt the child, who would have the name of Wood. What more natural, therefore, that the son of this Wood, on hearing that his father's half-sister was in Switzerland, should call at the Villa Wallace to pay his respects. In any case, there was no mistake of identity during the next two reigns, both Edward VII and George V addressing Colonel William Wood, of Quebec, as 'Dear Willie', in their letters to him.

The incident had no effect on the holiday spirit of the Queen. Never since the Highland expeditions of 1861, had she been so talkative and cheerful. The change came as an emotional safety valve to those around her, who had passed through countless silent dinners in the unrelenting gloom. Gleefully she recounted the feats of the day. She teased and she argued. She believed strongly in the reality of the legendary figures of history and, after a visit to Tell's Chapel, defended the story of William Tell and the apple against the sceptics. And she laughed again, without restraint and until the tears ran down her face, as if she was trying to catch up with all the years that she had lost. Out of character as it may appear, the subject that made her laugh the loudest during her widowhood was centred around the matrimonial bed.

Included in the royal party was Fraulein Bauer, the German governess of Princess Beatrice. Miss Bauer was plain of face and unexciting in figure. One day Sir William Jenner, the physician in attendance, and the governess found themselves excluded from the Queen's excursion. The doctor therefore suggested that the two of them should ride up the Rigi. And off they went.

At dinner that evening the Queen carried out her usual cross-examination of how the members of her party had passed the day. Sir Henry Ponsonby asked Jenner what the tourist and guides had considered the relationship between the two to be. On learning that everyone considered that they were man and wife, the diners began to giggle. The doctor went on to say that, so convinced were the guides of this, that they

The Queen's room at Lucerne

had insisted that the two made the descent *tête-à-tête* in a chair. Now for unmarried couples to be completely alone together was not countenanced by the Queen, and she had an eagle eye. But now here was admission that doctor and governess had been very much alone together. Convulsions shook the soup. Lady Churchill tried to redeem the position by asking: 'Was it comfortable?' That was the undoing of Queen Victoria.

On 9th September the Queen began her journey home, travelling to Paris through the night in the Imperial train. She rested at the British Embassy and, in the afternoon, drove out to the Palace of St. Cloud. She walked in the park and the gardens but did not enter the Palace. The ghost of Albert was there and memories of an evening thirteen years before came back as fresh as if there had been no days between.

It was on 18th August 1855, that the Queen had first seen Paris. She had immediately dubbed it 'the most beautiful and gayest of cities'. She had driven with Napoleon and Albert through decorated streets, echoing endlessly with the cry: '*Vive la Reine d'Angleterre*'. Porte St. Dennis – la Madeleine – the Place de la Concorde – the Arc de Triomphe – de l'Etoile – the Bridge of Boulogne – St. Cloud – and the Empress Eugénie waiting to greet them, in a blaze of light from lamps and torches, while the canons fired and bands played. Only thirteen years later she walked alone on the drying grass.

It was this lone walk that involved the Queen in trouble with the French Press. As the Empress had taken considerable trouble to meet her on the way to Switzerland, it was considered discourteous on Victoria's part that she did not ask Eugénie to walk with her now at St. Cloud, or at least to ask her to tea at the Embassy. Particularly was this so, as a boulevard had been named after the English Queen, and she had been to see it. As Disraeli was to point out, the etiquette of travelling incognito did not demand such a call being made, but at the same time – 'Perhaps Your Majesty was not well advised in receiving the visit of the Empress as such a reception was equally inconsistent with incognito.' Although the Empress was at first inclined to ignore the discourtesy, the Ministers and Court so insisted upon it that at last she came to think that she had been slighted.

The Queen was delighted with the manner in which she was received at the Paris Embassy and thereafter made many calls up to the time of the death of John Brown. Lord Lyons, who had succeeded Lord Cowley in 1867, was a most tactful diplomat, and held the appointment until 1887, the year of his death. He was brother of the Duchess of Norfolk, governess to the royal children, and therefore knew well how the Queen liked John Brown to be housed. While the other servants were lodged at Unthank's Hotel across the road, Brown was given a small room at the head of some private stairs, only a few doors away from the Queen. This suited the

La Madeleine, Paris

Ambassador's book, as there were a number of Fenians in Paris and the presence of the stalwart Scotsman was an added security measure. In the event the only sign of anti-British feeling came when a leading Fenian named O'Brien shook his stick at Princess Louise and called out, '*À bas les anglais*'.

As the Imperial train bore Queen Victoria safely towards Cherbourg, she took her last look at the France of the Second Empire. In reality she had deeply appreciated the kindness of Napoleon and Eugénie and that kindness was shortly to be repaid.

Journey Twenty-six
1871

Crisis in Norfolk

IT was not until ten years after the death of the Prince Consort that
Queen Victoria visited Sandringham. Then, in December 1871, she
became almost a commuter between Windsor and Wolferton, making
the journey three times in a month. The reason behind the exertion was
the illness of the Prince of Wales.

It is difficult to understand why the Queen was so tardy in calling upon
her son and daughter-in-law, posing the question of how much longer the
delay would have been but for the illness. On the official side, a visit to
East Anglia was overdue, would have helped to cement the position of
the Prince, and given her the chance of showing her appreciation of the
generosity of the people of Norfolk in presenting the main gates of
Sandringham as a wedding present to the newly married couple.

On the private side, even more reasons were apparent. There was the
curiosity of a mother-in-law to see how the rooms were decorated and
arranged, and the way of life ordered; the desire to see how faithfully
the detailed plans left behind by the Prince Consort had been carried out;
and the interest to see her grandchildren of Wales in their nursery, an
interest which had been overwhelming in the case of the Prussian brood.
Why, then, were these curiosities subdued?

It was certainly not the journey that deterred the Queen, as she was
never more content than when watching the fields go by from the carriage
window. Perhaps an early reason was the aversion that she had towards
her son as a result of the Nellie Clifden affair, coupled with the objection
to seeing a family home run on rules not laid down by the Prince Consort.
There may also have been a jealousy, and an increased sense of loss, at the
thought of seeing a married couple engrossed in one another while she
had to endure the grief of a widow.

A later reason may possibly be found in the permanent attendance of
John Brown. 'Bertie' heartily disliked the gillie, who had treated him with
scant respect as a boy. He also took exception to the position of the Personal
Servant, who apparently was more in the confidence of the Sovereign

The entrance to Sandringham, December, 1871

than was the Heir. Quite naturally he was disturbed at the scandal which surrounded Brown's name. The Queen would not travel without Brown, and Brown would obviously be unwelcome at Sandringham. Those who did not treat Brown as the Queen considered he should be treated, were cut from her visiting list. But in December 1871 the case was different, as the Prince was confined to his sickroom.

Although the Queen had never been to Sandringham, she knew much about the estate. The property deal had been arranged by the Prince Consort. When 'Bertie' was eighteen, his parents, urged on by Stockmar, had decided that, if he was to be 'saved', he must marry early and have an establishment of his own in the country to hold his interest. The Prince Consort, in his reasoned way, therefore made two lists, one of brides and one of houses. One by one, and each for a good reason, names were crossed out on both sheets. While Alexandra easily came out the winner of the short list of brides, the choice of a house was less simply decided. At last three names remained – Sandringham, Houghton in Norfolk, and Bramshill in Hampshire. Sandringham proved a somewhat curious choice, as it was but a shooting lodge in mock Elizabethan style and in a poor state of repair. May be the Prince Consort was looking forward into the years when he could descend on Norfolk and, after lecturing his son, enjoy some of the best shooting in the country. £220,000 was paid for the 7,000 acre estate, the price on the previous change of owners being £75,000. Some people considered that the Prince Consort was losing the astuteness that he had showed over the purchase of Osborne and Balmoral, but time was to prove him very right.

The Prince of Wales had no more to do with the purchase of Sandringham than he had in the selection of a wife. He did not see it until 4th February 1862, when he travelled there and back in a day from London under the watchful eye of his Governor. He was allowed one look, as later he was allowed one look at Alexandra at Speyer. The letters of both the Queen and Prince Consort during the years 1859–61 make it abundantly clear that they did not consider 'Bertie' capable of making the most minor decisions on his own account. His every move was watched and guided and, as he was not considered capable of travelling from Oxford to London unattended, he would certainly not have been allowed to handle a quarter of a million pound property deal. The Queen explained the parental control with the excuse that 'Bertie was different'.

Having despatched her son to the Near East a few weeks after his father's death, it fell upon the Queen to implement the detailed plans which the Prince Consort had made for Sandringham. Some of the plans were welcome in the Norfolk outpost—some were very definitely not.

The old steward from Osborne arrived. He took one look at Appleton farm, the rats scurrying about and the springs spurting from under the walls, shook his head, and arranged for the house to be rebuilt. Such was a welcome step. It was the Germanisation to which exception was taken. A new head-keeper, backed by an organised staff of officials, took possession of the fields and woods. It was as if an occupying force had taken over a conquered territory. Without even a 'by your leave', strips were cut across the fields of tenants and then planted to make game shelters. Strange eyes peered into byres and stackyards. Local peace of mind became disturbed. An old farm hand thus spoke his mind: 'They's always a-spying here and a-prying there and a-watching everythink I du, and at my time o'life it ain't pleasant, and then the head-keeper he goo by and he niver touch his hat and look at me as much as to say, "You're no friend o'mine".'

The greatest change that came to Sandringham was the rebuilding of the house, completed by 1870.

It was at the end of November 1871 that the Prince of Wales developed typhoid fever. There were two theories as to how he had contracted the disease. In August, while staying in Hesse, he had been, incognito, to Sedan, to see for himself the damage caused by the Franco-Prussian war. His equerry had forgotten to take any money with him and the Prince's pockets were empty, as he was not in the habit of coping with such mundane affairs. The Prince did not wish to reveal his identity, for fear of upsetting French feelings. Late in the evening, after the last train had left for Darmstadt, the royal watch was pawned and produced enough cash to allow the two men to spend a night in an hotel in the plague-ridden town. The Prince had been unwell ever since that date. A more likely source, however, was Londesborough Lodge, at Scarborough, where he had stayed on his way from Scotland to Norfolk. The Earl of Chesterfield, also a guest there, had contracted typhoid and since died.

The Queen, who had herself been seriously ill in September with gout, neuralgia, and an abscess on her arm, was summoned on 29th November. She travelled at once from Windsor, a change of engines being made at Victoria Park station.

Sandringham, November 29.—I was nervous and agitated at the thought of this sad journey, weak as I still am. At eleven I left with the Duchess of Roxburghe and Colonel Ponsonby. Reached Wolferton after three. Affie, Sir William Knollys, and Colonel Ellis met me there, and a quarter of an hour's drive brought us to Sandringham.

The road lay between commons, and plantations of fir trees, rather wild-looking, flat, bleak country. The house, rather near the high-road, a handsome, quite newly built Elizabethan building, was only completed last autumn. Dear Alix and Alice met me at the door, the former looking thin and anxious, and with tears in her eyes. She took me at once through the great hall upstairs to my rooms, three in number.

I took off my things and went over to Bertie's room, and was allowed to step in from behind a screen to see him sleeping or dozing. The room was dark and only one lamp burning, so that I could not see him well. He was lying rather flat on his back, breathing very rapidly and loudly. Of course the watching is constant, and dear Alix does a great deal herself. Two nurses and Gillet, the valet, take turns in the nursing. How all reminded me so vividly and sadly of my dearest Albert's illness! Went over to take tea in Alix's pretty room, with her, Alice, and Affie. Saw Sir William Jenner, who said that the breathing had all along been the one thing that caused anxiety. It was a far more violent attack than my beloved husband's was, and we could not now look for any improvement till after the 21st day.

On the following day the Prince appeared stronger and the Queen returned to Windsor, leaving him in the hands of his wife and sister, Alice, who had learned nursing the hard way when she tended the wounded in the wars of 1866 and 1870.

The Queen's visit had the effect of turning the eyes of the whole country upon the sickroom at Sandringham. Reporters flocked to the area, every room was taken and every gig and fly was hired. It was the first big news story to break at the Prince's country home, and the remote estate was unknown to many members of the Press. Some received a surprise, and some unwonted exercise. One magazine artist thus described his arrival:

The name of Wolferton has recently been brought so prominently before the public that we mentally picture it as a centre of considerable traffic. In reality it is a most primitive little stopping-place. There are no conveyances to be obtained nearer than Lynn, which is eight miles off, and the decayed little village contains neither inn or public-house, so that our artist, before trudging over to Sandringham along a road five inches deep in snow, was fain to warm his inner man with the contents of a bottle of ginger beer. Fortunately the walk is very pretty.

The Queen had not long to wait for another call.

Sandringham, December 8. – Was dreadfully alarmed, though, I own, hardly unprepared for a less good report. The telegram I received at quarter past eight said: "The Prince passed a very unquiet night. Not so well. Temperature risen to 104. Respirations more rapid. Dr Gull and I are both very anxious." This from Sir William Jenner. Felt greatly agitated. When I got up saw Dr Marshall, who said it was very grave, occurring at this stage of the illness, and he thought, if I wanted to go to Sandringham, I should do so to-day.

At three (Louise) and I started on our melancholy journey, the Duchess of Roxburghe and Colonel Ponsonby going with us. At the Victoria Park station Affie joined us. Reached Wolferton at half past seven, Sir William Knollys meeting us and handing me a note from Sir William Jenner, saying condition no worse, but that was all he could say. Got into a brougham with Louise and Affie, and drove in deep snow and hard frost up to Sandringham. Nobody at the door but Lady Macclesfield, who said dear Bertie was *very bad.* Went up at once to the room. The doctors were there, Alix and Alice on either side of the bed, and poor dear Bertie breathing rapidly. I naturally only peeped for a moment, and then remained behind the screen. The state was very critical, but not hopeless, the doctors said.

Now that it was obvious to her that she would be at Sandringham for some time the Queen assumed her customary role of being No. 1. Thus did the Norfolk people learn the true meaning of the expression 'one-ness' which was so well understood at Windsor and Osborne. The first edict concerned time. It was the practice of the Prince of Wales to keep all the clocks in the house half an hour fast. His reason was twofold. Firstly, it enabled him to get extra time for shooting on dark afternoons and, secondly, he hoped by so doing to offset the habitual unpunctuality of his wife. The Queen denounced the practice as a lie and ordered that all hands be put back to Greenwich.

She inspected the stables, the kennels, the school, the cottages of the tenants and the church, to the discomfort of the local grocer who was also the organist. She organised expeditions to Hunstanton, Castle Rising and other places of interest. When it was not judged wise to stray far from the sickroom, she trudged round the gardens in the melting snow. Although Sandringham and surrounding houses were bulging at the seams with royalties, somehow the gardens were empty whenever she appeared.

One afternoon Sir Henry Ponsonby, the Queen's Private Secretary, sought some fresh air and emerged from a side door. He was almost knocked down by a stampede of these royalties, with the Duke of Cambridge at their head and haemophilic Leopold bringing up the rear. 'The Queen, the Queen', they cried in warning, and disappeared from sight behind a potting shed.

The Prince of Wales now passed into a thirty-six hour period of delirium. He talked incessantly, wildly, in all the languages that he knew. He whistled and sang. He used words which one can only hope that the Queen did not understand. He threw pillows and handy objects about the room, and the Princess made her entrances and exits on all fours.

Outside the gates the reporters, in their hired conveyances, waited for the bulletins and then raced away to be first at the telegraph. A coincidental interest had now been added to the Prince's illness. Would the crisis come ten years to the day after the death of the Prince Consort?

Sandringham, December 13. – This really has been the worst day of all, and coming as it has so close to the sad 14th, filled us and, I believe, the whole country with anxious forebodings and the greatest alarm. The first report early in the morning was that dear Bertie seemed very weak, and the breathing very imperfect and feeble. The strength, however, rallied again. There had been no rest all night, from the constant delirium. The pulse varied in quality of strength at intervals, from hour to hour. Got up and dressed quickly, taking a mouthful of breakfast before hurrying to Bertie's room. Sat near by on the sofa, but so that he could not see me. Remained a long time. It was very distressing to hear him calling out and talking incessantly quite incoherently. Strolled round the house and pleasure grounds for a short while. It was raw and damp, and thawing all day.

Returned to Bertie's room, and, whilst there, he had a most frightful fit of coughing, which seemed at one moment to threaten his life! Only Alix and one of the nurses were there, and the doctors were at once hastily summoned. But the dreadful moment had passed. Poor dear Alix was in the greatest alarm and despair, and I supported her as best I could. Alice and I said to one another in tears, "There can be no hope." I hardly left the room, as I was so terribly anxious, and wanted to be of any little use I could. I went up to the bed and took hold of his poor hand, kissing it and stroking his arm. He turned round and looked wildly at me saying, "Who are you?" and then, "It's Mama." "Dear child," I replied. Later he said, "It is so kind of you to come," which shows he knew me, which was most comforting to me. I sat next to the bed holding his hand, as he seemed dozing. Then once more he said, "It's so kind of you to come," and, "Don't sit here for me." Dr Gull and Sir William Jenner were so thankful for this, as was I. I left again when Alix and Alice came in, who had been resting a little.

When I returned I found dear Bertie breathing very heavily and with great difficulty. Another symptom which frightened me dreadfully, was his clutching at his bedclothes and seeming to feel for things which were not there. The gasping between each word was most distressing. We were getting nearer and nearer to the 14th, and it seemed more and more like ten years ago, and yet it was very different too.

The Queen had been quite convinced that the dawn of the dread day would shed its weak light upon a deathbed. Instead she was informed that 'Bertie' was sleeping peacefully. The worst was over. Part claim for the sudden improvement was made by Prince Alfred who had suggested the inclusion of pale ale in the patient's diet.

The Queen returned to Windsor on the 19th. A week later an urgent telegram sent her scurrying back to Norfolk. The Prince had suffered a relapse and this time his mother stayed until he was well on the road to

The royal pew, Sandringham

final recovery. On New Year's Eve she thanked God for having brought her and her family safely through 'the fiery furnace'. She considered that Albert would have lived if he had had similar treatment, but was of the opinion that the chief reason why the son lived and the father died was that the son had more pluck than the father.

The Queen, Princess Beatrice, Prince Leopold and the Duchess of Sutherland in a waggonette with Brown and Bourner on the box, September, 1872

Queen Victoria's half-sister, Feodora, spent the last twelve
years of her life at Baden-Baden. Her husband, Prince Ernest of
Hohenlohe-Langenburg, died there in 1860, and she decided
thereafter to make her home in the German health resort, building
a wooden chalet which she named Villa Hohenlohe. Queen
Victoria visited Baden-Baden, staying at the Villa Delmar, four
months before the death of Princess Feodora. The Villa Hohenlohe
was left to the Queen in her half-sister's will and she made
short stays there in 1873 and 1876. Her last visit was in 1880,
when she spent a fortnight at the villa with Princess Beatrice

Journey Twenty-seven
1873

An Empress in Kent

APRIL in Paris, 1870 . . . The sun shining on a tapestry of colour on the Champs de Mars, sparkling on the breastplates of the Cuirassiers, picking out the scarlet of the Imperial Guard, the green of the Hussars and the sky-blue of the *Cent Gardes*. The bands and the tempo of the trotting hooves proclaimed the glory of France's Second Empire.

By the time that the leaves turned the mob ruled Paris, the cavalry had eaten their horses at Sedan and surrendered to Bismarck, the Emperor was a prisoner in Germany, and the Empress and her son were exiles in England. The sun had gone down on the Napoleons.

Eugénie made her home at Chislehurst in Kent. There, in the following March, she was joined by her husband, a sick and broken man, who was but a shadow of the leader who had arrived, in state, at Windsor in 1855 to visit Victoria and Albert. Crushed as he was, he still had his dreams. He would make a triumphal return to France from the start-point of Elba. His son, learning to be a soldier at the 'Shop', would follow after him. But first, necessarily but reluctantly, he had to see the doctors. They found a mighty stone inside him, and marvelled at the strength and courage of the man who had sat his horse for five hours at Sedan. They tried to break up the stone, fragment by fragment, with rest days in between. But he had done too much, too hard. On the evening of 8th January 1872 Dr Gall prescribed a dose of chloral. The Emperor made his last decision – No. His wife insisted. Sleep came, but there was no waking.

Windsor Castle, February 20, 1873. – A very foggy, raw day. At quarter past ten, left Windsor for Chislehurst, by the South-Western, Beatrice, Jane C., and Colonel Maude accompanying me. We passed through London, which was wrapped in a thick yellow fog. Drove straight from the station in a closed landau, Colonel Maude riding, to the small Roman Catholic Chapel of St. Mary, a pretty, rural little place, quite a village church, a good deal smaller inside than

Whippingham.[1] To the right of the alter, or rather below it, behind a railing, in the smallest space possible, rest the earthly remains of the poor Emperor, the coffin covered with a black velvet pall, embroidered with golden bees, and covered with wreaths and flowers of all kinds, many of which are also piled up outside, to which Beatrice and I each added one. The banner of the French "Ouvriers" was placed near the wreaths. Father Goddard, the priest, a quiet, youngish man, showed us round

Side chapel at St. Mary's Church,
Chislehurst, 1873

and also showed us the plan of the small private chapel, which is to be added on.

From thence drove to Camden House, where at the door, instead of his poor father, who had always received me so kindly, was the Prince Imperial, looking very pale and sad. A few steps further on, in the deepest mourning, looking very ill, very handsome, and the picture of sorrow, was the poor dear Empress, who had insisted on coming down

[1] The Church which the Queen attended when at Osborne.

Camden Place, Chislehurst

to receive me. Silently we embraced each other and she took my arm in hers, but could not speak for emotion. She led me upstairs to her boudoir, which is very small and full of the souvenirs which she had been able to save. She cried a good deal, but quietly and gently, and that sweet face, always a sad one, looked inexpressibly pathetic. She described the poor Emperor's death, and how terribly sudden it had been at the last. She was just going to start for Woolwich to see her son, who wanted to come, but who they thought might agitate the Emperor by going in and out of the room, as he so adored his father. The Emperor had had a better night, but she was told it would be better for her not to go away as "l'Empereur a une petite crise". She therefore took off her hat and went towards his room, which was close by. As she came to the door, Dr Corvisart opened it, calling out "Father Goddard, Father Goddard", and she at once saw that there was danger. When she came into the room and kissed the Emperor's hand, they said to him, "Voilà l'Impératrice", but he no longer was able to see her, though he still moved his lips to kiss her. In five or ten minutes afterwards all was over!

The poor Empress said that he had suffered fearfully, and that already in September, when they were at Cowes, going in a carriage was agony to him. The painful preparations for the funeral, the hammering and knocking in that small house, had been dreadful. Prince Napoleon[2] had behaved very badly, wanting to take the boy, "tout ce que j'ai", away from her and not to leave him in England. But she was firm, having been left, by the Emperor's will, her son's guardian. Prince Napoleon wanted her to take him away from Woolwich (which the boy likes very much, and is only half an hour's drive from Chislehurst), saying that Bertie disapproved of his remaining there, which I assured her was precisely the reverse. Prince Napoleon had wanted to take him away, in order to "faire l'aventure avec lui", and to ruin him, but the boy was quite determined not to yield to his cousin. The Empress showed me the poor Emperor's humble little rooms, which are just as he left them, all his things on the table, so sad to see, as I know but too well!

[2] A cousin of Napoleon III.

The Empress Eugénie

Journey Twenty-eight
1875

Sad Sea Story

August 18.—This has been an eventful day, and one of terrible and undying recollections! At half past five left dear Osborne, with Beatrice and Leopold, and embarked[1] at Trinity Pier. The evening was very fine, so bright, and no wind. The *Victoria and Albert* followed us. When we neared Stokes Bay, Beatrice said, very calmly, "Mama, there is a yacht[2] coming against us", and I saw the tall masts and large sails of a schooner looming over us. In an instant came an awful, most terrifying crash, accompanied by a very severe shake and reel. Horatia (Stopford) and Harriet (Phipps) came running and saying there had been a collision, and at the same time General Ponsonby and Lord Bridport rushed up saying, "There is no danger". Then only a frightful alarm seized me, lest some of our people, who always stand in the bows of the vessel, might get hurt. I was assured, however, they were all safe, and Leopold came round at the same moment, so that I knew nothing had happened to him.

It all took only a few seconds, and, when I enquired to whom the yacht belonged, I was told she had gone down! In great distress I said, "Take everyone, take everyone on board", repeating this several times. I then went forward, to where all the excitement had been going on, and was horrified to find not a single vestige of the yacht, merely a few spars and deck chairs floating about. Two boats were moving round, and we saw one of our men swimming about with a life-belt, and one poor man in the water, who was pulled into the barge, nearly drowned, with his face quite black. I saw no others in the water, but on deck three or four yachtsmen, also a lady, looking anxiously from one side to the other. These had jumped across from the sinking yacht on to the *Alberta*. At first it was hoped that everyone had been saved, and General Ponsonby said the numbers were being counted. Alas! then it became

[1] On board the royal yacht *Alberta*.
[2] The schooner yacht *Mistletoe*, of 120 tons, owned by Mr Heywood, of Manchester.

clear that one lady, whom Leopold had distinctly seen on the deck with the other, was missing, also one man—a dreadful moment.

I was asked to leave the forepart of the ship, as two poor men were being brought up, and the sight was very distressing. However, from near the paddle wheel I could see the poor man being lifted out of the water and lying on the deck, with his coat off and his face perfectly black, Dr McEwan and two sailors bending over him and moving his arms backwards and forwards. But he gave no sign of life. He was the Captain or Master[3] of the *Mistletoe*, as the yacht was called, a big man of at least seventy. The other, whom I had not noticed before, turned out to be Mr Heywood, the owner. He also was insensible, but it was hoped he would do well. The poor Captain had probably been injured by a blow, and it was feared he could not be brought round. We saw one of the yachtsmen holding his arm in great agony. It was broken, and no one could attend to him properly, as the doctor was so occupied with the poor old man. It was now discovered that the poor young lady, who was on board, was the sister of the one who was drowned, and Mr Heywood was the brother-in-law, whose wife was at Ryde, from whence they had been sailing. Commander Fullerton, of the *Victoria and Albert*, had jumped overboard most gallantly, just as he was, only removing his sword, and had hurt his hand in trying to save the poor lady, who had slipped from his grasp! Lieutenant Britten and two sailors had also been in the water. Commander Fullerton and one of our men had actually gone down with the sinking yacht, and had been saved with difficulty. But the poor lady, it is too awful, and I cannot get over it. Harriet had gone off at once to the distraught sister who stood at the end of the vessel, the picture of calm, silent despair, unable to shed a tear. She and the dying man were most harrowing scenes, which as well as the crash, shock, and the complete disappearance of the yacht, will never be forgotten by any of us who were present!

In vain they searched, *no* sign or trace of the poor missing one was to be seen, and so we had to go on finally, having first cut off part of the rigging of the unfortunate *Mistletoe*, which had got entangled on the *Alberta*, whose bowsprit had been carried away. The poor young lady's name was Peel. She was told she might go below to see her brother-in-law, who was recovering, and this was a great comfort to her. The poor old man was dying, in fact I fear already dead. When Miss Peel had come up again I went to say a few words of truest sympathy to her, and pressed her hand. She could only murmur a few words of thanks, and her expression of grief was heart-rending to see.

As soon as we reached Gosport, which we did three-quarters of an

[3] Mr Stokes, who died on reaching land.

hour late, General Ponsonby went on shore and told Admiral Elliot what had occurred. I then sent for him and told him how anxious I was that Mr Heywood and poor Miss Peel should be taken the greatest care of, as well as the poor crew, and he kindly promised everything possible should be done, and he would let us know all. It was a horrid feeling, having to continue our journey and leave these poor people. It was such a lovely evening, and so distressing that it should have been marred in such an awful way!

Removing the wreck of the Mistletoe *after the collision*

Journey Twenty-nine
1877

In a Buckinghamshire Garden

I876 was a year of titles. Queen Victoria became Empress of India and Benjamin Disraeli, her Prime Minister, was created the Earl of Beaconsfield. The year also witnessed the start of a great conflict between the Powers of Europe.

Insurrection broke out in the Balkan areas of the Turkish Empire. Russia, to suit her own ends, planned to back the insurgents. Beaconsfield declared that British interests in India demanded that the Sultan's authority remain inviolate. The Queen backed her Prime Minister, at the same time exerting all her influence with Russia and Germany to prevent an outbreak of hostilities. She failed, and Russia declared war on Turkey in April 1877, winning a decisive victory before the year closed.

In Cabinet meetings on 14th, 17th and 18th December Beaconsfield sought agreement for the early summoning of Parliament, an increase in British forces, and a policy of mediation between the warring nations. He obtained that agreement in the face of considerable opposition. During the crisis the Prime Minister threatened resignation and the Queen talked of abdication. She made her backing of Lord Beaconsfield clear to the world by visiting him at his home at Hughenden. In the New Year British forces sailed for the Mediterranean and it was not until the conclusion of the Congress of Berlin in July that the danger abated. On his return from the Congress the Queen invested Lord Beaconsfield with the Order of the Garter.

Windsor Castle, December 15.–. . . At half past twelve left with Beatrice (who was better), Janie E[1], General Ponsonby, and Colonel du Plat for Hughenden, going by train to High Wycombe, which we reached in about three-quarters of an hour, and where Lord Beaconsfield with the Mayor received us on the platform. There was a great crowd.

---

[1] Marchioness of Ely.

The drawing room, Hughenden Manor, 1877

An Address was handed by the Mayor, in answer to which Lord Beaconsfield said a few words, and the daughter gave me a bouquet. I drove in an open landau with four horses, with Beatrice and Janie E., the two gentlemen riding, and Lord B. and Mr Corry[2] preceding us. The country town was beautifully decorated with flags and festoons and there were several arches with kind inscriptions. We drove down the fine broad High Street. Very large crowds and the people most loyal and orderly. One of the arches was very curious, entirely composed of chairs, which is the staple industry of the town.

It took us hardly quarter of an hour to reach Hughenden, which stands in a park, rather high, and has a fine view. Lord Beaconsfield met me at the door, and led me into the library, which opens on to the terrace and a pretty Italian garden, laid out by himself. We went out at once, and Beatrice and I planted each a tree, then I went back into the library and he gave me an account of yesterday's Cabinet, which had been very stormy. Lord Beaconsfield is determined to bring things to an issue on the 17th, in which I strongly encouraged him.

After my conversation, went in to luncheon, which consisted of Beatrice, myself, Janie E., and Lord B. He showed us several interesting pictures, portraits of friends, and has a very fine head of Lord Byron, whom he knew. He also showed us portraits of his parents. At 3.30 we left as we came, and took leave of Lord Beaconsfield at the station, where I also saw and spoke to Lord Carrington, the Lord-Lieutenant of the County of Bucks.

Did the Czar in far Bucharest shiver?
Did Gortschakoff thrill with a dread?
Did the Sultan in Stamboul feel less of
The storms where he pillows his head?
As from luncheon at Hughenden Manor
The Queen and my radiant Lord B.
Walked out to the lawn and proceeded
To plant a memorial tree![3]

[2] Lord Beaconsfield's secretary, afterwards Lord Rowton.
[3] *Punch.*

Milestone
1878

Alice

December 14.—This terrible day come round again! Slept tolerably, but woke very often, constantly seeing darling Alice before me. When I woke in the morning, was not for a moment aware of all our terrible anxiety. And then it all burst upon me. I asked for news, but nothing had come. Then got up and went, as I always do on this day, to the Blue Room, and prayed there. When dressed, I went into my sitting-room for breakfast, and met Brown coming in with two bad telegrams: I looked first at one from Louis, which I did not at first take in, saying: "Poor Mama, poor me, my happiness gone, dear, dear Alice. God's will be done." (I can hardly write it!) The other from Sir Wm. Jenner, saying: "Grand Duchess became suddenly worse soon after midnight, since then could no longer take any food." Directly after, came another with the dreadful tidings that darling Alice sank gradually and passed away at half past 7 this morning!

Journey Thirty
1879

Introduction to Italy

I878 was a busy year for assassins. In the spring one named Hoedel attempted to kill Emperor William of Germany with shots from a pistol. A few weeks later Dr Nobiling was more successful. Using a heavy fowling-piece he fired from an upper storey window as the Emperor drove down the Unter den Linden. It was at first thought that the aged ruler was dead. More than thirty swan-shot were extracted from his head and during his long convalescence Crown Prince Frederick acted as Regent.

In the autumn a fanatical cook named Passanante, a disciple of the International, attacked King Humbert of Italy with a dagger. The King escaped lightly but his Prime Minister was seriously wounded. Soon afterwards another attempt was made by a member of the International, this time to murder King Alphonso in Madrid.

The outbreak of violence was most upsetting to Queen Victoria. Little perturbed as she was at the thought of attacks on herself, she feared that her Ministers might consider it inadvisable for her to visit the Continent for a while. During that sad Christmas, when the shadow of the death of Princess Alice hung over Osborne, she planned a spring vacation. Germany she could not face now, and Switzerland was too cold. She wanted to find the sun. She had long desired to see Italy, of which 'Vicky', Alice and Arthur had given her such glowing reports. She consulted Lord Beaconsfield and was relieved at his reply:

Italy is probably one of the safest places in Europe. It would appear that there are no British members of the International, and it is said that the Society itself is scrupulous in not permitting foreigners to accomplish (its) behests. Thus, your Majesty will observe that two Germans shot at the Emperor William; a Pole at the Emperor Alexander; Moncasi was a Spaniard; the cook, who tried to stab King Umberto, was a Neapolitan; Vera Sassulitch was a Russian; and though Orsini at Paris was an Italian, the Italians always looked upon the Bonapartes as natives, and especially the last Emperor.

Baveno, Lake Maggiore

On the recommendation of Prince Arthur,[1] the Queen decided to go to Baveno, on the eastern shore of Lake Maggiore, and arrangements were made for her to stay at the Villa Clara. Travelling via Cherbourg on 26th March, she spent the night in Paris. It was while there she received news of the death of her eleven year old grandson, Prince Waldemar of Prussia.

British Embassy, Paris, March 27. – Got up, feeling rested. Received a telegram, which on opening I found, to my unbounded grief and horror, to contain the terrible words: "Have just taken a last look at the beloved child. He expired at half-past three this morning, from paralysis of the heart. Your broken-hearted daughter Victoria." How heart-rending! My poor darling Vicky! Only a week to-day since she returned home, and twelve days since I took leave of her! Our poor family

[1] Created Duke of Connaught, 1874; married, 13th March 1879, Princess Louise Margaret of Prussia.

seems persecuted by this awful disease,[2] the worst I know. I sent and received many telegrams.

After luncheon, received the President, M. Grévy, in the big drawing-room. He was presented by Lord Lyons, and I asked him to sit down. He expressed great satisfaction at my receiving him under the present painful circumstances, and his regret at my not remaining longer, and his not being able to show the friendship and respect entertained for England and me, by France, which he called *la soeur de l'Angleterre*, that France wished and required peace, and that *Chauvinisme* was at an end. He praised Bertie very much, whom they considered *un Parisien*. I shook hands with M. Grévy when he left. Lord Lyons introduced M. Waddington, Prime and Foreign Minister, half an Englishman, who has been at Harrow,[3] and at Oxford with Lord Derby. He was at the Berlin Conference last year, speaks English like an Englishman, and was most civil, expressing much regret for the sad loss of poor dear little Waldie.

M. Grévy, who had just succeeded Marshall MacMahon as President of the Republic, made a most favourable impression on the British Queen. This was in part due to his treatment of John Brown. Far from showing signs of surprise at the confidential position held by the gillie, as had certain people in Belgium and Germany, the President, on this and subsequent occasions, greeted him with a polite bow. The same tactful approach was adopted by Jules Ferry, who succeeded W. H. Waddington. He despatched telegrams along the route which the Queen was to follow, instructing those who were to receive her of the correct treatment to be accorded to the Queen's Personal Servant.

Villa Clara, Baveno, April 1. – In the afternoon drove out with Beatrice and Jane C(hurchill) beyond Gravellona, and back. The mist was low down on the hills, but one could just see that there was much more snow on them. The children on the roads know me quite well, and call out "La Regina d'Inghilterra". There are such dreadful, queer-looking pigs here, as thin as greyhounds, and with quite long legs. Two mounted Carabinieri generally follow the carriage at some little distance, and ones on foot patrol the roads. They look very smart and well turned out.

To the children of the village of Baveno, famed for the red granite of

---

[2] The cause of death was diptheria and not, as has often been stated, haemophilia. The Princess Royal was not a carrier of haemophilia.

[3] The Queen was incorrect about the school. W. H. Waddington was educated at Rugby. In 1883 he accepted the London Embassy, which he held until 1893, dying the following year. He married an American, Mary A. King.

which the pillars of Milan Cathedral are built, the kilt was as much an attraction as the Crown. But Brown was not feeling in holiday mood. Having mastered a few words of French and German and learned how to make himself understood on rudimentary matters (in Germany he had silenced a too noisy band by shouting 'Nix boom boom'), he was now faced with a completely new language. In addition he was feeling unwell, and a few days after arrival developed erysipelas. This disease stems from a wound or abrasion and manifests itself in the spring. Brown had suffered from it before on the legs, but now it spread to his face, entirely spoiling the image of the romantic Highlander. For the first, and only time, during his twenty years with the Queen, he had to stay without her presence. For two weeks the Queen had to learn to become accustomed to take her drives without Brown on the box, and his illness caused her to cancel her plan to visit Venice, where a wealthy Scotsman had offered her the hospitality of his palazzo.

When Brown returned to service, his face still sore, he was adorned with a wide black hat so that the hot sun should not burn his tender skin. Sir Henry Ponsonby commented that he looked 'like an English parson on a holiday tour who is not enjoying himself'. In a letter home to his wife the Private Secretary described the Queen's visit to Milan:

Our expedition to Milan was a failure. The Queen was annoyed two days ago because Paget[4] wanted to telegraph about it. Her idea was that she could go quite incog. (arriving by Special and driving about with a Highlander on the box) and it was only on my pressing it that she allowed him to notify her coming at all. Then it poured. I hinted at a postponement but she said no she would go. So we went. There was a crowd at the station but the people were kept back. At the Cenacola not many and a dozen police, but even here H.M. thought they were too close to the carriage.

We saw the pictures in peace but in haste. At the Cathedral there was a crowd on the steps which increased inside and we had to walk round her. At the tomb of S. Carlo we kept them out—but in the Cathedral itself they thronged round. Not a very great many but still a crowd and this perturbed her and she complained to me that there were not more police. If she had gone as Queen we might have had fifty police there, but she had repeated over and over again that she would go quite privately—so there were only a few police—enough to keep them back—but not to prevent them crowding round. I believe they tumbled Jenner down the steps which has made him wrath with the boys of Milan—but he enjoyed the sights very much.

As it rained the Queen drove in a shut carriage. She wouldn't go to the Brera—so we drove for an hour. And she wouldn't have Paget in her carriage—and didn't ask Lady Paget to come. So with Brown on the box, who never

[4]British Ambassador in Italy.

The Queen in the grounds of the Villa Clara

raised his head to look at anything – she saw nothing. We men opened our carriage as it ceased raining and saw a great deal. I stopped the carriage once and ran back to tell her these were San Lorenzo's columns. But this stopping of the carriage was coldly received and a crowd began to assemble to see the Highlander, so we went on – and I didn't trouble them again.

In the evening the Queen began to reflect that she had seen very little. True. But whose fault? She said she never expected the mob at Milan to crowd as much as they did, seeing how civil the Baveno people are. But Milan is a great city. I admit the people were rather rude and pushing – but unless regular precautions are taken this can't be helped. And Baveno is a little village with very few people in it.

On 23rd April the Queen began her homeward journey, travelling via Milan, Turin and Paris. Despite the recalcitrance and ill health of Brown, she was delighted with Italy and determined to return in the near future.

Journey Thirty-one
1880

Night Train from Scotland

In the Train, November 23.—Finished *Jane Eyre*, which is really a wonderful book, very peculiar in parts, but so powerfully and admirably written, such a fine tone in it, such fine religious feeling, and such beautiful writing. The description of the mysterious maniac's nightly appearances awfully thrilling, Mr Rochester's character a very remarkable one, and Jane Eyre's herself a beautiful one. The end is very touching, when Jane Eyre returns to him and finds him blind, with one hand gone from injuries during the fire in his house, which was caused by his mad wife.

Crossing the Tay Bridge, Dundee

Journey Thirty-two
1881

Edinburgh Review

Holyrood, August 25. – A bright morning, to my joy, on waking. By the time we were at breakfast, the sky clouded over, but there was wind and we all hoped it looked as if it might keep fine. Walked in the garden with Lady Southampton, and showed her the Abbey; looking at the countless thousands of people, who covered Arthur's Seat, and all the heights. On coming in, went to the room beyond the great Gallery, leading to Queen Mary's apartments, to look at the people and volunteers streaming out past the gate. Knighted the Lord Provost – Mr Childers, Lord Thurlow, and Sir John McNeill being in attendance. There was a little rain, but it cleared off again.

Affie and Marie[1] came to luncheon, and by that time the rain increased, and behold, whilst I was dressing, down it came! There was a perfect sea of umbrellas. The sky became white and grey, with mist in the distance, and the ground where the march past was to take place, which could be seen from the windows, and which had partially recovered from yesterday's rain, became like a lake of muddy water, too distressing.

There was nothing for it, but to start with waterproofs and umbrellas; but the gentlemen and servants, and all the poor volunteers, had to remain without any of these protections. We started at quarter to 4, in the open landau and four, Beatrice and Marie sitting opposite to me, Affie, Arthur, George C.[2] and his staff, and my gentlemen, all in uniform, riding with us. As we came out of the courtyard, we first turned to the right and inspected the cavalry, which extended some way up the Queen's Drive, then turned round again, and proceeded right down the line, to the saluting point, behind which was a large stand full of spectators. In the enclosure, below it, stood the unfortunate

[1] Prince Alfred had been created Duke of Edinburgh in 1866. He married Grand Duchess Marie Alexandrovna of Russia in 1874.
[2] Duke of Cambridge.

The Palace of Holyroodhouse, by J. Harding
(reproduced by gracious permission of H.M. The Queen)

Archers' Guard, who were drenched, and looked very cold, the Duke of Abercorn being at their head.

The marching past then began, in a sea of mud, most despairing to witness. There were 40,000 men, and such fine ones. The Highlanders looked splendid, all, with their pipers. The Duke of Sutherland was at the head of his men and Cluny McPherson at the head of his, old Davidson of Tulloch, 80 years of age, looking so handsome with his long white beard, Lord Elcho at the head of the London Scottish, which, as well as some of the other London Scotch volunteer regiments, had come on purpose. Once or twice it seemed as though the rain were going to cease, but only to come down again with renewed force. Pitilessly it came down, drifted by a high wind, on all those poor men, who nevertheless continued marching steadily along, with patient and gallant endurance. How different to the Review, 21 years ago, in bright sunshine, when dearest Mama went with me, and dearest Albert rode by my side!

At 6 we got back, coming in through the garden, and scrambled into the house by a lower passage, close to the kitchen, everyone soaked, but I only partially so, down the side from which the wind came, and while I sat in a pool of water. I had to change many under-garments. After, with great difficulty, getting a fire lit, I ran down to look after Beatrice and Marie, the latter wet through to the skin, the rain having penetrated through her waterproof. She had to have some clothes lent her, till hers could be dried. Beatrice got less wet, but I was more anxious about her, as she had a bad sore throat, and had not felt at all well this morning. I went also to see after Arthur, who had been quite wet through, and his nice new General's uniform quite spoilt by the green of the ribbon of the Thistle coming off on to his tunic. Affie had gone back to the hotel. All the gentlemen were equally wet, but all changed at once, and none seemed to suffer from it.

The Royal Company of Archers marching out of the forecourt of the Palace of Holyroodhouse. From the painting by William Skeoch Cumming, R.S.W., which hangs in the ante-room in Archers' Hall, Edinburgh. (Reproduced by permission of The Royal Company of Archers)

Journey Thirty-three
1882

A Topee in Mentone

ALTHOUGH Queen Victoria's journeys to the south of France are dealt with collectively later, this trip, her first to the Mediterranean, is described individually as it saw the end of another chapter in her travelling life. It was the last time that John Brown was to accompany her abroad. There had been a decade of tours with her mother, twenty halcyon years of exploration with Albert and nearly twenty years of less arduous, but often turbulent, expeditions with Brown. The most peaceful chapter lay before her.

The royal yacht crossed from Portsmouth to Cherbourg on 14th March. Princess Beatrice accompanied her mother, Prince Leopold having gone ahead. He had become engaged to Princess Helen Frederica of Waldeck-Pyrmont.[1] The Queen had some misgivings owing to the delicate health of her son, but considered that the Riviera sun would be beneficial.

Mentone had seen many changes in the nineteenth century. At the time of the First Empire the town belonged to France. In 1815 it reverted to the Prince of Monaco, but severe financial demands caused the inhabitants to declare their independence in 1848, and they moved under the protection of Sardinia. When Sardinia ceded the county of Nice to France in 1860, Napoleon III bought Mentone from the Prince of Monaco and combined them in the Alpes Maritimes. Menton was born, but to the elderly visitors who sought the spring sunshine there it was still 'Mentony'.

The Queen stayed at the Châlet de Rosiers, to the east of the town. A terrace gave her a fine view of the sea and a path led down towards it. But the site was too easily overlooked for the liking of Brown. He was once again suffering from Fenian fever, and this time with good cause. On the afternoon of 2nd March Roderick Maclean had fired a six-chambered revolver at the Queen as her carriage left Windsor station

---

[1] The marriage took place on 27th April 1882. A daughter, Alice Mary Victoria (afterwards Princess Alice, Countess of Athlone) was born the following year.

The coastline at Mentone

for the Castle. The shot had passed uncomfortably close to Brown who was in the rumble.

The rumour now reached him that three prominent Fenians were on their way south from Paris. The local *gendarmerie* made the most of the scare, but the British police accompanying the royal party considered that it was a hoax. Brown was taking no chances and told the Queen. She asked her Private Secretary for a report. He put her fears at rest, and she answered:

> . . . she trusts Sir Henry will also reassure Brown who was in such a state heightened by his increasing *hatred* of being "abroad" which blinds his admiration for the country even. The Queen thinks that one principal cause of all this is that he can communicate with *no* one when out, nor keep anyone off the carriage . . .

She went on to ask about how long it would take to visit Bordighera and Monaco, and whether it would be possible to see over a china factory and a monastery. 'In short,' she ended curtly, 'find out about any excursions within reach.'

So it was arranged. She went to Magnat's famous pottery works, explored Monaco and drove along the Corniche roads to Villefranche.

The excursions caused more than usual interest as Brown insisted upon wearing a topee to keep the sun from his face.

His fears about the exposed grounds of the Châlet de Rosiers were solved when Dr Bennet, author of *Spring on the Shores of the Mediterranean*, put his eight acre garden at the disposal of the Queen. Three hundred feet above the sea, and only ten minutes drive away, here the Queen and her daughter were able to stroll and sketch in absolute seclusion.

Princess Beatrice was now nearly twenty-five. The long mourning for Albert, the ritual of the sad anniversaries, the eternal surveillance, had turned a mischievous and precocious child into a serious and introvert young woman, sheltered to a degree that was almost beyond belief. She had never been alone in a room with a man, even a brother. The word 'engagement' was never allowed to be mentioned in her presence. When this had happened during dinner table conversation at Balmoral, the Queen had relapsed into one of her well known icy silences and the Princess concentrated on her soup. It was clear to those around the Court that the Queen was about to follow a custom, common at this time, of a widow taking her youngest daughter for her own. The names of only two men had been coupled with that of Princess Beatrice. One was the Grand Duke Louis of Hesse and the Rhine, and in this case the Queen knew full well that it would be against the law for her to marry her dead sister's husband. The other was the Prince Imperial, only son of Napoleon and Eugénie, who was beyond possibility on both political and religious grounds.

When it came to affairs of the heart Queen Victoria regarded officers of the British Navy with suspicion, bearing in mind several aberrations of past years. When Prince Louis of Battenberg, a very promising young officer, had dined at Osborne, his behaviour towards the Princess had been considered too 'fresh', and he had been despatched to the China seas. But now, anchored off Mentone, and in full view from the Châlet de Rosiers, were units of the British Fleet.

The spring sunshine would appear to have melted the heart of the Queen somewhat. The Princess wished to explore the shops of Nice and she was given permission to use the gunboat *Cygnet* as transport. She was received with full honours when she boarded *Inflexible*. It is more than likely that it was at Mentone that she came to the conclusion that there was more to life than being secretary and companion to her mother.

Journey Thirty-four
1882

A Great Day for Essex

ONCE upon a time the Forest of Waltham covered the land between Colchester and London. As the population grew in numbers, so did the oaks dwindle. In the seventeenth century a royal commission was set up to determine its extent and decide its future, and that part in the south, known as Epping Forest, was estimated to be of an area of 60,000 acres. It was reserved for hunting. By the beginning of the nineteenth century encroachments threatened the obliteration of the forest, and in 1871 the Corporation of the City of London took action under the Epping Forest Act. 5,600 acres were purchased, for the use of the public in perpetuity. The old time Court of Verderers was revived and rangers, keepers, verderers and reeves appointed. Thus it was that, on a spring day in 1882, Queen Victoria travelled to Epping for the opening.

Windsor Castle, May 6. – At quarter to 3 left with Beatrice for Epping Forest, which we reached at 4. Great crowds all along the railroad and a very great one on getting out. Arthur, Louischen, Louise, and the Lord Mayor met us. Volunteers and troops were out, and everything extremely well arranged. A great stand, full of people, and a very pretty arch had been erected. Arthur rode next my carriage, and Louise, Beatrice, and Louischen drove with me. The Lord Mayor and my two Equerries rode behind the carriage. Drove through enormous crowds, who lined the whole way, nearly 3 miles, to High Beech, where an Address was received, and read, and I declared the Park open.

The sight was very brilliant. There was a temporary building in which the Lord Mayor had entertained 10,000 people at luncheon. He hurriedly dismounted, and put on his robes, before presenting the Address, which was read by the Recorder, and I read a short answer, which caused great cheering. An album with views of this fine and picturesque Park, reminding one of Burnham Beeches and Richmond Park, was presented to me, and a little girl, daughter of Sir Fowell and Victoria Buxton (herself my god-daughter), was held up to the carriage,

to give me a bouquet. I shook hands with the Lady Mayoress and Mrs
Gladstone. Arthur got off and stood near the carriage till the ceremony
was over, and then remounted, as did the Lord Mayor.

Returned the same way. The enthusiasm was very great, and many
quite poor people were out. The Park has been given to the poor of the
East End, as a sort of recreation ground. Nothing but loyal expressions
and kind faces did I hear and see; it was most gratifying.

*The fly-leaf from John Brown's personal photo-
graph album presented to him by Queen Victoria*

Milestone
1883

The Death of John Brown

Windsor Castle, March 28.—Leopold came to my dressing-room, and broke the dreadful news to me that my good, faithful Brown had passed away early this morning. Am terribly upset by this loss, which removes one who was so devoted and attached to my service and who did so much for my personal comfort. It is the loss not only of a servant, but of a real friend.

The portrait of John Brown by Kenneth MacLeay is reproduced by gracious permission of H. M. The Queen.

Journey Thirty-five
1884

To Hesse for a Wedding

T HIS spring excursion of Queen Victoria to Germany became the
subject of a play. On the stage it was satirical; in real life it was
tragi-comedy. The theme was marriage. The setting was a ruritanian
palace set about with narrow winding, streets. The sad clown was a Grand
Duke. The cast was picked exclusively from the Almanach de Gotha,
with Princes and Princesses two a penny.

On 30th April Prince Louis of Battenberg, on leave from the British
Navy, was to marry Princess Victoria of Hesse and by the Rhine, eldest
daughter of Grand Duke Louis IV. She was born at Windsor in 1863 and
was the first granddaughter to be named after the Queen, of whom she
was a particular favourite.

The wedding was to take place at the Grand-ducal palace at Darmstadt,
a sleepy little town lying in the shelter of the hills which rise from the
flat lands to the east of the Rhine. As the decorations went up in the streets,
royal trains converged upon it, guests coming from as far afield as Sofia
and St. Petersburg. It was to be a great occasion–the quintessence of
Grand Dukery.

Yet to Victoria the monotonous clang of the wheels below her saloon
carriage came like the tolling of a bell. To her, the funereal outweighed the
hymeneal. She was sixty-five, and very lonely. There were no longer
posies of primroses from the Buckinghamshire woods now that Beaconsfield had gone. The loss of John Brown had left her as helpless as a cripple
without a stick. She had relied on him too much each and every day for
twenty years, and as long as nine months afterwards it was formally
announced that she could not stand for more than a few minutes. And
then, on 27th March, exactly a year since Leopold had come to her room
to tell her that the gillie was dead, news came from Cannes that Leopold
had hurt his knee. During that night his frail light went out. Another
dread anniversary was to be marked on the calendar.

A few days after the funeral at Windsor, the Queen set off for Darmstadt.
Beside her, in the gloom, was Princess Beatrice, for whom there now

The Grand Ducal Palace at Darmstadt

seemed little chance of escaping into a life of her own. It was a journey of duty, and duty for Victoria took preference over feelings. Since Princess Alice's death six years before she had played an admixture of mother and Jehovah to the Grand Duke's children.

Louis IV was an amiable man, not of the pioneering mould. He wore a Norfolk jacket and added quite a splash of English to his German. He liked Paris and sherry, horses and shooting, and talked of military affairs. He read little and wrote nothing. His people loved him. He was very partial to a joke, and liked lovely women. His wife had tried to carry a lamp which shed the fused light of Florence Nightingale and Albert upon the Hessian scene. Like her father, she had tried too hard, and died even younger than he.

The Grand Duke, in his top hat, was waiting to greet the royal trains as they steamed into Darmstadt station. Around him were his brood— Victoria, the bride; Elizabeth the beautiful, who had just become engaged to the Grand Duke Serge of Russia, spurning the advances of her cousin, William of Prussia, and the chance of becoming Empress of Germany, much to the annoyance of Berlin; Irene, the domestic one, in whom Henry, William's brother, was showing more than a cousinly interest; Ernest Louis, the only surviving son, talented and sensitive; and little 'Alicky', who was only twelve.

Louis always made a great fuss of his mother-in-law. Now he jumped into her carriage before it had come to a stop and smothered her with the extrovert and flattering welcome in which, secretly, she revelled. Thereafter he did everything in his power to mitigate the sadness under which she laboured. Yet he made one strange exception. He omitted to tell her of the plans that he had made for his own future happiness.

The Grand Duke had become the close friend of a charming lady named Madame Alexandrine de Kolémine. Her husband had, for two years, been Russian Charge d'Affaires at Darmstadt. A son, George, had been born in 1876, but the marriage ended in divorce.

Alexandrine was born on 15th November 1852 at Warsaw. Her parents were Count Adam Hutten Czapska and Countess Marianne Rzewuska, and on both sides she was related to the great houses of Poland, including the Radziwills. Her grandfather's sister was Eveline Countess Hanska, the love of Balzac's life. He courted her from 1833, but only succeeded in marrying her in the spring of 1850, three months before his death.

Faced now with the probability that, within the course of a few years, his daughters would depart to join husbands in distant capitals, the Grand Duke decided that he would be wise to remarry, a plan with which Alexandrine was strongly in accord. His elder daughters were also relieved to know that he would be cared for after they had flown.

Now the Grand Dukes of Hesse, with their sovereign powers, had been accustomed to do as they wished on the domestic side. The previous ruler had married his housemaid, who referred to him as 'Der gute Herr'. She was kept in the background, and nobody made a fuss about it. But that was before Prussia put an iron hand over Hesse and before the Grand-ducal house was allied directly to the British Queen by marriage. While Alexandrine's family background would pass muster, the fact that she had been divorced certainly would not.

Whether the Grand Duke just chose to ignore the winds of change, or his hand was forced by his lady friend, or he was plain scared to beard his mother-in-law, is hard to say, but he now did a very silly thing. On the evening of the day upon which H.S.H. Prince Louis of Battenberg married H.G.D.H. Princess Victoria of Hesse, Louis IV married Alexandrine de Kolémine in secret.

On 2nd May the news leaked out and was telegraphed to Berlin. In fury, the old Empress Augusta ordered the Crown Princess and her party to return immediately from that 'contaminated Court'. Queen Victoria told Prince Alexander of Hesse that her son-in-law's action was 'simply beyond expression'. She sent for the Prince of Wales and ordered him to arrange that the marriage be annulled without delay. He, poor man, had the task of interviewing Alexandrine, a session which ended in sobbing and hysterics. The lawyers set about the problem of taking apart those whom God had put together. Fortunately for them, the marriage had not been consummated. But there were many at Darmstadt who considered the Grand Duke a weak character to allow Queen Victoria to dictate to him in his own palace.

Although she had swatted this problem as if it was a troublesome fly, another problem arose with which she could not so easily deal, and one which concerned more closely her personal comfort. Now her cold and calculating eyes followed the movements of two young people – twenty-five year old Prince Henry of Battenberg, the bridegroom's brother, and her own daughter, Beatrice.

Prince Henry was serving with the Prussian Household Cavalry at Potsdam. He was gay, polished, and cut a dashing figure in his white uniform. While his brother had been rebuffed by Beatrice, now the Queen noted the complete reverse. Entirely inexperienced in the sphere of love, the Princess gave away, by the look in her eyes, by the way she walked and talked, every emotion in her heart.

The Queen said nothing. Refusing to allow an unfortunate marriage to upset her arrangements, she left for home, on schedule, on 5th May. Many of those who would otherwise have been at the station to wave her goodbye, now developed tactful illnesses. The decorations were down and Hessians heads were bowed. It was as if a thunderstorm had washed out a gay fiesta. Yet the Darmstadt occasion was to leave its mark on history. Its end-products were to include Queens for Spain and Sweden, a Viceroy for India and a husband for the British Queen.

Back at Windsor the strain told on Princess Beatrice. She blurted out that she wished to marry Prince Henry. There followed one of the outstanding examples of the calculated ruthlessness of Queen Victoria. From May to December, she never addressed a word to the daughter with whom she lived. All communication between them was channelled through notes pushed across the breakfast table. It is difficult to understand how such conditions could have been tolerated for eight months. Part of the answer came in the words of the Princess's daughter, Queen Victoria Eugenia of Spain, some sixty years later: 'She (Princess Beatrice) had to be in perpetual attendance on her formidable mother. Her devotion and submission were complete . . .'

It was not the marriage that worried the Queen, but the fear that Prince Henry would insist upon continuing with his military career and take the Princess away to Potsdam. She had tried the same trick with Alice, attempting to make her and Louis live with her in England. That clever Princess had escaped the net by planting John Brown at Osborne. There was no such alternative for Beatrice.

In the autumn Prince and Princess Louis of Battenberg decided that action must be taken to break the impasse. They invited Prince Henry to stay with them at their home not far distant from Osborne. Prince Henry agreed to give up his military career. The Queen did a sharp about turn. The marriage was on. So another man entered the life of Queen Victoria. It was a gay and laughing relationship, unruffled by the emotional squalls which had blown up for Prince Albert and John Brown. For ten years Henry of Battenberg was, to use her own words, 'the sunshine of her household'.

And what of the fate of poor Alexandrine? By the summer a Court of Law, convened at Darmstadt, pronounced the formal severance of the two who had married in secret. When the divorce was complete, Alexandrine was created Countess von Romrod. After a time she married Basile de Bacheracht, Russian Minister at Berne until his death in 1916. She then moved to Vevey, where she died on 8th May 1941. She had lived for half a century longer than the Grand Duke whom she had loved so much.

Louis IV never fully recovered from the ordeal through which he had passed in 1884. His relations with Prussia could only be strained and it was but family occasions which brought him to England. He developed heart trouble and died in 1892. He was only fifty-five. Poor man, he had made the mistake of doing the right thing on the wrong day.

Alexandrine, with her son Georg

Journey Thirty-six
1886

The Merseyside Roar

IT was raining again when the Queen went back to Liverpool. Yet it washed away nothing of the excitement and the acclamation. When it was all over she said: 'It was certainly a never to be forgotten reception and one impossible to describe.' And a moment of history came while she was on Merseyside. She made use of the telephone to listen to a public occasion for the first time.[1]

The Queen had consented to open the Exhibition of Navigation, Commerce and Industry, and for two days she stayed at Newsham House, on the outskirts of Liverpool, provided for her by the Corporation. With her were the Duke of Connaught, and Prince and Princess Henry of Battenberg.

The Exhibition was opened on 11th May and some 30,000 people came to see the Queen take her place on the throne which had been specially built for the occasion. Seldom did she consent to speak in public, but on this day she replied to the Mayor's address. Many of her listeners were surprised by the clarity and charm of her voice. The Queen then turned a gold key in a model lock, Lord Granville declared the Exhibition open and guns were fired from the North Fort. Before leaving, the Queen knighted the Mayor, Mr David Ratcliffe.

That evening Liverpool was transformed by a network of illuminations and the Duke of Connaught and Prince Henry were guests at a grand banquet at the Town Hall. The Queen and her daughter remained at Newsham House, but they were not out of touch with the happenings. Engineers had laid a wire from the Town Hall to their sitting room and, taking turns, they were able to hear the speeches and applause on a telephone. The Queen recorded that they 'listened through a telephone to the speeches at the banquet. We heard Arthur's quite distinctly, and the cheering had a very curious effect'.

[1] The Queen first spoke on the telephone in 1878, when Professor Andrew Bell demonstrated his invention at Osborne.

At three o'clock next afternoon the Queen drove out through the crowded, decorated streets:

Newsham House, Liverpool, May 12.–Alas! the weather had not cleared by luncheon time, and it blew and rained hopelessly. But there was nothing for it but resolutely to brave the elements, put on waterproofs and hold up umbrellas, as the carriages could not be shut. So we four started in an open landau like yesterday. The whole way from Newsham we drove through lines of the Trades Processions, with all their banners and devices of their guilds, which extended over three-quarters of a mile in length, and they cheered vehemently. The streets along which we drove were beautifully decorated, and there was not a house which had not some motto or flags up. Some of these mottoes were very touching.

The crowds were enormous, and every shop window was full of people. There were several arches, and one large one on the very fine place, on which St. George's Hall stands. I well remember this magnificent building. Here a platform had been erected with a canopy under which we drove and stopped, and a large number of people were gathered there. The Mayor stepped forward and presented me with an Address, enclosed in a beautiful casket. I handed him my Answer, but neither were read.

Then we moved on again, the rain coming down worse than ever. But it did not seem to reduce the numbers of people or mar their enthusiasm. I never saw anything like it. We made the round of the place, where, since we were here in '51, equestrian statues of beloved Albert and myself (by Thornycroft) have been placed. We drove through several more streets to the Prince's pierhead, where we embarked on board the Claughton ferry steamer,–belonging to the Birkenhead Corporation. There was a covered way to it, and everything was beautifully arranged, though we had rather trouble getting on board, as the bridge was so slanting and the cloth which covered it so wet and slippery. We hurried into a little deck cabin, in which there was only room for Beatrice and me, but we could see everything through the windows, though the distance was not very visible, owing to the torrents of rain and furious wind. Everyone had to seek for shelter, as best they could.

We passed close to the enormous liners, which go between Liverpool and America; one was just starting. The Mersey looked so rough and angry. We steamed past New Brighton,[2] a little way on, and then back along the Cheshire coast in between the enormous ships. We took tea somewhat under difficulties in the little deck cabin. The gentlemen

[2] The *Claughton* went as far as the Sloyne, and steamed round the *Great Eastern*, Brunel's 18900 ton giant, which was then lying there.

connected with the docks were presented to me, and then we disembarked at the same place, driving back, more or less, the same way. The illuminations had already started and were beautiful. In spite of the weather, the whole thing was a great success, and the wonderful loyalty and enthusiasm displayed, most touching and gratifying. We got home at seven, quite bewildered and my head aching from the incessant perfect roar of cheering.

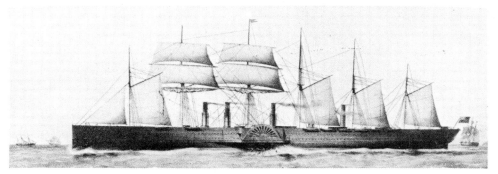

The Great Eastern

In the Monastery of La Grande Chartreuse

IN the Place du Revard at Aix-les-Bains, above a flower-bed shaped like a crown, is a bronze bust of Queen Victoria. In 1943 members of the Resistance took it away and hid it, to avoid it being melted down by the Germans. Back it went with the Liberation, and Aix resumed its unique tradition of celebrating Empire (now Commonwealth) Day, troops parading and bands playing the national anthems of Britain and France.

The origin of the royal connection with the spa was Princess Beatrice's rheumatism. Twinges had plagued her since she was a girl and by 1883 she was finding difficulty in writing and playing the piano. The doctors decided that she must have a three week cure at Aix and off she went, leaving her mother moping over the death of John Brown. It was one of the few occasions that the Queen and her youngest daughter were separated for any length of time.

The Princess returned with her rheumatism so improved, and so delighted with the town and the surrounding countryside, that the Queen decided to accompany her on subsequent occasions. Thereafter it became a habit. While the Princess took her course of thermal treatment, her mother was content with the attentions of a *masseuse*.

While the advantages to the town of having such royal clients were obvious, the Queen and her daughter were very popular in Aix and the memory of them lives on. There is the Avenue Victoria, the Villa Beatrice and the Hotel Windsor, and the royal arms stand above the *epicerie* which provided the royal orders for coffee and groceries. And there are still scones for tea. They were introduced by the Queen, to whom they were served each afternoon when she drove out to La Chambotte. The fashion caught on and today Victoria and scones are indelibly coupled together.

At first the royal party stayed at the old Hotel Bristol, but its numbers demanded the move to more spacious quarters and the Villa Mottet was taken over. It was renamed Villa Victoria and is now the annexe of an hotel. The Queen's bedroom is preserved much as it was when she occupied it. On Princess Beatrice's birthday, which fell during her visits to Aix, a band played in the garden below her window.

In the spring of 1887, before the excitement and exhaustive programme of the Jubilee, the Queen's cortège again set out for the white town under the mountains. First there was a call to make. At Cannes the Church of St. George had been built as a memorial to Prince Leopold, Duke of Albany, and a memorial service was to be held. The Queen stayed at the Villa Eidelweiss, loaned to her by Mr Augustus Savile. The Duke of Edinburgh arrived with a squadron consisting of the dreadnoughts *Thunderer, Agamemnon* and *Colossus*. He got into trouble with the authorities for not saluting the French flag and soil when arriving off Cannes. He extricated himself by explaining that his squadron was not provided with a saluting battery.

On 5th April the Queen and Princess left for Aix, travelling via Valence and Grenoble. As a result of the earthquake of 23rd February 1887, which had brought disaster to the French and Italian coast from Nice to Genoa, there had been discussion about such upheavals. As the Queen lay in bed on the night of her arrival she heard a strange, subdued rumbling. At midnight she rang her bell for the footman in waiting, and despatched him to discover the cause. He returned with the information that the rumbling was not an earthquake but the snoring of her Private Secretary, who was in the room below. When the story was recounted at table next day, Sir Henry Ponsonby, noted for his sense of humour, was for once not amused.

It was during this visit to Aix that the Queen and Princess became the first women of Protestant faith to be conducted over the monastery of La Grande Chartreuse, the mother house of the order of Carthusian monks. The Empress Eugénie was the first Roman Catholic woman to have the privilege. She was enthusiastic about the wonders of the monastery and now used her influence to obtain permission for Queen Victoria to enter. The Pope gave his consent.

In the previous quarter of a century the Queen's attitude towards the Church of Rome had undergone considerable change. On her husband's death she had inherited from him, in exaggerated form, all his likes and dislikes, and on matters religious Prince Albert was bigoted indeed. He had brought with him from Germany a horror of Catholicism, and throughout his life this was apparent in his talk. He spoke of the Reformation as the time when 'our ancestors shook off the yoke of a domineering priesthood'; he volunteered that he would never put much faith in a man who had been educated by the Jesuits; and he described the secretary of the Society for the Propagation of the Gospel as 'an unctuous priest'. Having attended a Roman Catholic wedding he informed his heir that the rites followed were 'perfectly ludicrous' and that when one got among the believers 'all the nonsense becomes apparent'. While the Queen believed that her people should have freedom of belief, she could not abide 'the bowings, scrapings and confessions'.

Her dislike was at its zenith when she returned from Germany through Brussels in the autumn of 1862. Held up by storms, it was suggested that she visit a convent to while away the time. No occupation could have been worse conceived. Hearing singing in the Chapel, the Queen opened the door and peered inside. The Priest stopped the service until she had left. In a cubicle beside a long corridor she noticed a little girl having a music lesson from a male teacher. A nun sat chaperone beside them. That such a precaution was considered necessary filled the Queen with revulsion. She wrote to her eldest daughter that, in her terrible grief, the Catholic religion was hateful to her, recalling that 'dear Papa had such a horror of the priestly dominion'.

The sexual problems of the men and women who hid themselves away from the world behind high walls, intrigued her. When, during those dark mourning days at Balmoral the Queen would disappear to her room, her eyes were not wet with tears, but clearly focussed upon the pages of a book entitled *The Female Jesuit; or the Spy in the Family*. Fascinated, she was absorbing the details of the supposed sexual enormities of the Roman Catholic priesthood.

It was the Empress Eugénie who wrought the change. Just as she titillated

La Grande Chartreuse

the Queen with the mysterious powers of Daniel Dunglas Home, so did she introduce her friend to the brighter, stronger side of Rome. The journeys to Switzerland and Italy helped. But it was the illness and death of Napoleon III, the church at Chislehurst, Princess Beatrice's liking for the Prince Imperial, his tragic death in Africa and his mother's lonely vigil by the Ityatosi river which made the faiths of the two women seem as one.

The monastery of La Grande Chartreuse lies some twelve miles north of Grenoble, 3,200 feet up in the limestone mountains. The religious origins date from the eleventh century, but the existing buildings were erected in 1676. In 1793 the monks were expelled, not returning until after the fall of Napoleon I. They were again expelled in 1903 and the monastery was not reoccupied until 1940.

Aix-les-Bains, April 23.–This was the day for our long-planned and wished-for expedition to the Grande Chartreuse. It was a splendid day. The scenery of the Gorge frequently reminded me of the St. Gothard, and is very grand. We passed the distillery of the celebrated and excellent liqueur, called Chartreuse, made by the monks, who alone possess the secret. It is made of herbs and flowers gathered by them in the country round.

The Monastery nestles in among the high mountains. As we approached, we could see a monk standing under the doorway, who approached our carriage in his white habit and cowl and bare shaven head, a fine-looking man, the Procureur, who wished us *la bienvenue.* Just inside the Monastery the Grand Prieur Général received us, a stout, burly, rosy-cheeked man, wearing spectacles. The interior struck one as very cold. We were led along the Cloisters, which are immensely long, into a room in which were assembled several of the other principal monks, who were introduced to us. Amongst them was a Russian General Nikolai, who had served in the Caucasus, and had also been attached to the Embassy in London. He has been a monk at the Grande Chartreuse for nineteen years. Pictures of St. Bruno and other heads of the Monastery hung on the walls. The we proceeded down another very long Cloister, and went into the Gallery, which overlooks the Chapel, where Vespers were going on.

From there, to the Chapter Room, a large room full of pictures depicting events in the life of St. Bruno and the portraits of the various Généraux. We were also shown a very pretty small Chapel of St. Louis, with mosaics, and a fine large newly finished Library. One part contains small rooms for male visitors who come to the Monastery, and they may spend two nights there and attend Mass, etc. The Grand Prieur showed us the burial-ground, most dreary-looking and small, with flowers, and little low stone crosses, only for the Généraux. The other poor monks had nothing but flowers over them. Some snow was lying there, in the garden, which was quite hard frozen, and yet the sun was burning hot.

We were shown where the cells were, and told I should see a young *compatriote*, an Englishman who had been there for some time. The Grand Prieur unlocked the cell, which is composed of two small rooms, and the young inmate immediately appeared, kneeling down and kissing my hand, and saying, "I am proud to be a subject of your Majesty". The first little room looked comfortable enough, and he had flowers in it. The other contained his bed and two little recesses, in one of which stood a small altar, where he said he performed his devotions and said his prayers. In the other deeper recess, with a small window, is the study, containing his books. I remarked how young he looked, and he answered, "I am 23", and that he had been five years in the Grande Chartreuse, having entered at 18!! I asked if he was contented, and he replied without hesitation, "I am very happy". He is very good-looking and tall, with rather a delicate complexion and a beautiful, saintly,

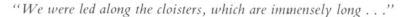

"We were led along the cloisters, which are immensely long . . ."

almost rapt expression. When we left the cell and were going along the corridor, the Général said I had seen that the young man was quite content, to which I replied that it was a pleasure to see people contented, as it was so often not the case.

As I felt very tired, I asked not to go up any more stairs, and we turned back and went down again. The Général expressed his regret at our visit being so short, but excepting the Refectory and kitchen we had seen everything of real interest. He walked across with us to the Hôtellerie des Dames, only a few hundred yards, where the ladies who wish to see the fine scenery and position often come up to spend a night or two. Here two very friendly Sisters, sort of Soeurs de Charité, welcomed us.

Refreshments were prepared in a big room, and here the Général took leave of us, but the Procureur remained. He offered me wine, but I asked for some of their liqueur, and by mistake he gave me some of the strongest.

Queen Victoria was nearing her sixty-eight birthday when she made this long day's expedition from Aix. No better example of her determination, endurance and hardiness could be found. St. Pierre de Chartreuse (formerly Cartusia, after which the monastery was named) is guarded to the south by the Col de Porte (1325 metres) and to the north by the Col du Granier (1164 metres), and the road running between them is narrow, twisting and flanked by sheer drops. Even today it is enough to deter the inexperienced motorist, especially when the snow is melting. When the Queen made the climb by carriage, the rough state of the road made the journey even more arduous.

Bust of Queen Victoria at Aix-les-Bains

Milestone
1887

Golden Jubilee

Buckingham Palace, June 21.—At half-past eleven we left the Palace, I driving in a handsomely gilt landau drawn by six of the Creams, with dear Vicky and Alix, who sat on the back seat. Just in front of my carriage rode the 12 Indian officers, and in front of them my 3 sons, 5 sons-in-law, 9 grandsons, and grandsons-in-law. Then came the carriages containing my 3 other daughters, 3 daughters-in-law, granddaughters, one granddaughter-in-law, and some of the suite. All the other Royalties went in a separate procession. George Cambridge rode the whole way next to my carriage, and the Master of the Horse, Equerries, etc., behind it with of course a Sovereign's escort. It was a really magnificent sight. Dear Fritz[1] looked so handsome and well, and Liko[2] had an English uniform for the first time. The route was up Constitution Hill, through the Arch, down Piccadilly, past Trafalgar Square, along the new Northumberland Avenue, the Embankment, and then turned to the right to the Abbey.

[1] Crown Prince of Germany, afterwards Emperor Frederick.
[2] The family name for Prince Henry of Battenberg.

Journey Thirty–eight
1888

Fireworks in Florence and the Power Game in Berlin

QUEEN Victoria and Prince Otto von Bismarck did not meet until she had been on the Throne for fifty-one years and he had held power in Germany for twenty-six. When at length they faced one another in the ring, without witnesses, she was sixty-nine and he was seventy-three. It was a contest which Europe had long been awaiting.

The resultant success of his Queen mystified Lord Salisbury, the Prime Minister, who had been convinced that she would lose on points when competing away. Thereafter he attempted to use her skill to solve another European impasse, but was quietly told that, at her age, she could not be expected to journey round foreign lands solving other people's problems. Yet she had proved her capabilities.

There was a triplet of reasons for the Berlin meeting—a girl's love, a son-in-law's fatal illness, and the Queen's determination to enjoy a spring holiday in Italy, whether Europe was in a state of unrest or not.

The cause of the unrest was a Battenberg. He was Alexander, known to his family and friends as 'Sandro', and he was the second eldest of the four handsome Princes. In 1879, at the age of twenty-two, he had been elected Sovereign Prince of Bulgaria, the new state that had emerged from the Treaty of Berlin of the previous year. While the Sultan of Turkey still claimed suzerainty over this autonomous principality, Russia regarded it as tied to her by creed and race. 'Sandro's' appointment had been backed by both Bismarck and Emperor Alexander II of Russia. The Emperor wished to keep his fingers in the Bulgarian pie, and Empress Marie was the Battenberg's aunt.

At this time it was not realised, nor could it have been, that when sons of this new House were given an important task to perform, they would do so with dynamism, singleness of purpose, courage and, if the need came, ruthlessness. Nor could Bismarck have foreseen that, within a few years, one Battenberg Prince would be married to Princess Victoria of Hesse and another to Princess Beatrice.

'Sandro' soon showed that he was not content to be a tool of Russia. He assumed the virtual powers of dictatorship and took up the cry of 'Bulgaria for the Bulgarians'. But in 1880 Empress Marie died and the following year Emperor Alexander II was assassinated. Alexander III did not share his father's views. He was anti-German and pro-France and he disapproved of 'Sandro's' policy in Bulgaria. The disapproval developed into a deep personal hatred. Bismarck, fully aware of the new Emperor's animosity towards Germany, was determined that 'Sandro' should not further exacerbate matters.

But the Sovereign Prince went on full steam ahead. He added new territory to the state and in 1885 defeated, brilliantly, an invasion by Serbian forces. He concentrated on developing the country's resources and its military strength, and this was precisely in opposition to the wishes of Alexander III. The Russians wanted a vassal state, without ties to the West, a weak people dependent on the crumbs which fell from the Moscow table.

Having gained the support of a small and discontented section of the Bulgarian army, the Emperor began the process of undermining 'Sandro'. The Prince was bombarded with threats of kidnapping and violence, all of which he ignored. But on the night of 21st August 1886 a gang of one hundred and fifty broke into the palace, dragged him away at pistol point and took him to the Austrian frontier. To further the ignominy, the rumour was put out that he had been found in bed with the sister of one of his kidnappers.

The people of Bulgaria rose against the conspirators, silenced them, and 'Sandro' returned to Sofia on the 29th, receiving a hero's welcome. He tried to make terms with Alexander but the Emperor would have none of it, announcing that only the abdication of the Sovereign Prince would satisfy the Russians. With the threat of murder hanging over him, 'Sandro' abdicated on 7th September. Tired and broken-hearted, he went back to Hesse.

Thus would have ended the sad story of 'Sandro' of Bulgaria but for the trifling matter of an affair of the heart. In 1883, in Berlin, he had met Princess Victoria, seventeen year old daughter of the Crown Princess. She was tall, with blue eyes, golden hair, and she was an incurable romantic. Her nickname was 'Moretta', and the Queen called her 'young Vicky'. She fell in love with 'Sandro' as swiftly and irrevocably as had her aunt Beatrice with his brother Henry. With her parents' consent, they became unofficially engaged.

The 'fors' and 'againsts' began to take sides. The Crown Prince and Princess backed the marriage as they thought solely of their daughter's

Princess Victoria of Prussia, the Kaiser's sister, whose proposed marriage to Prince Alexander of Battenberg led to the duel between Queen Victoria and Bismarck in Berlin

happiness. Queen Victoria was only too pleased to welcome another Battenberg into her family circle. The old Empress Augusta was against as she had other plans for her granddaughter. Prince William was against as he looked down at the morganatic element in the Battenbergs and, on principle, adopted the opposing view to that of his parents. Bismarck was against for three reasons. He feared that the marriage would anger Emperor Alexander; he had a Portugese husband in mind for the Princess; and he had no intention of allowing another Battenberg into the family network of Queen Victoria. And the last was the main reason. In the event, after 'Sandro's' abdication, Emperor Alexander did not care whom he married.

Gradually the matter devolved into a dual personal contest—Prince William versus his mother and Bismarck versus Queen Victoria. All the tricks of espionage were adopted—letters were opened, telegrams intercepted, messages delivered by unsuspecting hand. To some involved, only winning counted and the feelings of a young couple were of small account.

Bismarck saw one possibility of defeat, and that was if the Crown Prince became Emperor. In 1887 Emperor William was ninety and tiring fast. The Crown Prince was suffering from cancer in its advanced stages and could not long survive. But if he was in power long enough, it would be a simple matter for him to allow the marriage to take place.

Emperor William died on 9th March 1888. His dying son became Emperor Frederick III, and he gave his daughter permission to marry. Bismarck's only chance was to employ delaying tactics until such time as Prince William became Emperor, when the marriage would be finally squashed. Then came the bombshell—Queen Victoria announced her intention to visit Berlin.

Bismarck roared into the presence of the ill Emperor, demanding that no honour or military appointment should be given to the deposed Prince of Bulgaria and that the marriage should not take place for fear of upsetting relations with Russia. So determined was the Chancellor that the Emperor agreed to a postponement until a full report had been prepared. Bismarck had won his time. 'Sandro's' invitation to visit Potsdam was cancelled, and Crown Prince William sent him the following message: 'If you marry my sister I shall consider you the enemy of my family and my country.'

Bismarck's next move was to let loose a virulent campaign against Queen Victoria in the German Press. He threatened to resign if the marriage took place, describing it as but a British trick to set Russia and Germany at loggerheads. Count Hatzfeldt, the German Ambassador in London, warned against the dangers of the Queen talking to Crown Prince William in Berlin, as the latter was in such a fury and his head so turned by events that he might say something which would jeopardise the relations between the two countries. The British Ambassador in Berlin warned that the Queen might meet hostile demonstrations in the streets if she ventured there. Lord Salisbury advised, almost pleaded, that she should not go, saying that the German Chancellor was in a state of intense exasperation. The British Press was wholeheartedly behind 'Sandro' and his Princess, and, in the prevailing sense of temper, it appeared as if a spark might set off a mighty fire.

Yet Queen Victoria remained calm—annoyed, but calm. She had every intention of taking her spring holiday as scheduled and quite determined that no one was going to stop her saying goodbye to her beloved son-in-

THE INHARMONIOUS BISMARCK.

Empress (sings). What shall we do with our daughter?
Bismarck. Don't know. If the wedding's to be,
When over you hand her
To Prince ALEXANDER,
You'll then have to do without *me!*

Ensemble.

Empress. } What shall we do with our daughter?
Bismarck. } What will they do with their daughter?

(Spoken.)

Bismarck. I think your Majesty is singing a little out of tune.
Empress. Pardon me, Prince; but it is you who are a great deal too sharp.
Bismarck. Um—well—we'll take two bars' rest, and then sing together——
Both (in unison). Vaterland! mein Vaterland!
La Li-e-ty! La Li-e-ty!
[*Left jödelling.*

THE INHARMONIOUS BISMARCK
A cartoon from Punch *of 21st April, 1888*

law. As for the marriage, she had behaved circumspectly throughout. She had warned Princess Victoria of the dangers of marrying against the wishes of her brother, and recent information had caused her to change her ideas somewhat. She was doubtful if the experience through which 'Sandro' had passed fitted him to be a husband to her inexperienced grand-daughter, and she had heard in secrecy that 'Sandro' had fallen in love with Johanna Loisinger, of the Darmstadt Court Theatre. Yet a battle was apparently desired and so a battle there should be. But first the sunshine and the flowers.

On 21st March the Queen, with Prince and Princess Henry of Batten-berg, left Windsor for Portsmouth, where the royal yacht was waiting to carry them to Cherbourg. Thereafter their train followed the Mont Cenis route via Turin to Florence.

The Villa Palmieri had been lent to the Queen by the Countess of Crawford and Balcarres, and for weeks past it had been the scene of great activity. Not only had the house been painted without, and decorated within, but a special water supply had been connected and even a tele-phone. The road which led to it was named Boccaccio, after the four-teenth century author of *Decameron*, but it was narrow and unlit. Now it had been widened to allow of carriages proceeding to and fro to pass, and street lamps had been put up so that members of the royal party could return from night occasions without fear of molestation.

An outstanding experience for the Queen came when she watched the ceremony of the *Scoppio del Carro* on Saturday in Passion Week. The cart, garlanded, laden with fireworks and drawn by white oxen, entered the Piazza del Duomo. The rocket, in the model of a dove, was lit by a candle from the altar of the Duomo, and thus the holy fire was carried along a wire from church to cart. The fireworks went off, their explosions punctuating the voices of the choir singing *Gloria in excelsis*. Then the bells pealed out.

The only incident that marred the occasion was that the Italian authorities took umbrage that the Queen's dressers and Indian servants were allowed to watch from the loggia next to that of the Queen of Servia.

Royalties were numerous in Florence that spring and the Queen had many callers to receive and return visits to make. Unfortunately the feminine predominated, Kings and Emperors being in short supply. Thus, at a lunch given at the Pitti, the King of Italy entered the dining room with Queen Victoria on one arm and the old Empress of Brazil on the other. Progress was slow.

Villa Palmieri, Florence, April 5.—At eleven received the King and Queen of Italy, who arrived at Florence yesterday evening. The King is aged and grown grey, the Queen is as charming as ever. To my

Florence—a contempory view

astonishment Signor Crispi, the present very Radical Prime Minister, came into the room, and remained there, which was very embarrassing. After the usual presentations of ladies and gentlemen, the King and Queen left. I then went out into the garden for a little. At four, drove with Beatrice, accompanied by the ladies and gentlemen, to the Palazzo Pitti, to pay my visit to the King and Queen, who received me at the private entrance and took me to their own rooms. They were most kind and amiable, making excuses for Crispi's behaviour this morning— the King saying that he was a very clever man, but had no manners.

April 6.—Did not go out, as I had to receive the Emperor[1] and Empress of Brazil at twelve. They brought their nice young grandson Pedro, Gusty Coburg's son. They both looked aged and very ill. After, I drove to the Palazzo Pitti to pay my return visit to the Emperor and Empress and lunch with the King and Queen. The King talked very pleasantly and sensibly. Signor Crispi came in, with whom I had some conversation. He has no *savoir faire* whatever.

There was a terrible report and fuss in the papers, that Bismarck intended resigning, as Vicky and Fritz wanted to insist on young Vicky marrying Sandro.

[1] Pedro II (1825–91). Abdicated 1889.

April 7. – Went down to the Drawing-room with Beatrice to receive the Archbishop of Florence, who came purposely with a message of welcome from the Pope. His two Chaplains were with him.

April 8. – Received a distressing letter from poor Vicky, showing how wickedly and disloyally advantage is being taken of poor Fritz's anxious, uncertain state of health, in order to prevent his doing what he thinks right. Bismarck is behaving disgracefully.

Very much perturbed at a cypher from Lord Salisbury, saying that Sir E. Malet[2] had cyphered to the effect that the proposed bethrothal of young Vicky and Sandro had put Prince Bismarck in a perfect fury; that, as I was supposed to be favourable to it, he might vent his fury on me and England, and that my journey to Berlin might have to be prevented. I was very angry, as I had nothing to do with it; on the contrary, had only warned Vicky against moving in the matter. I let Lord Salisbury know this, and that I would not give up going to see my poor sick son-in-law.

April 12. – Young Vicky's birthday, for whom it must have been a very sad one, poor child! It is a most distressing business, and almost worse for Sandro than for her.

In the train, April 23. – Passed through Pistoja, Bologna, Modena, Mantua, and Verona during the night. At Ala we crossed the frontier into Austria, and had already passed Botzen, when I was ready for breakfast. Splendid scenery amongst the Alps and crossing the Brenner.

At half-past one, we reached Innsbruck, the position of which is magnificent, surrounded by high mountains. The day had become very fine and hot. At the station, on the platform, stood the Emperor Francis Joseph, in full uniform. We got out at once, and the Emperor led me into a room, where luncheon was prepared. I had not seen him since 1863 at Coburg. We lunched *à quatre*[3] in a room full of flowers. I unfortunately had a very bad sick headache and could eat next to nothing. The Emperor was most kind, and talked very pleasantly on many subjects. He said how happy he was at the good relations existing between our two countries, which he hoped would continue, as in case of war we could act together. Russia was incomprehensible, and he thought Bismarck much too weak and yielding to Russia, which was a great mistake. After a very affectionate leave-taking, we went on. The Emperor had travelled seventeen hours from Vienna, on purpose to see me.

The scenery continued most beautiful. Dined at Regensburg, having stopped at Munich at six, where there were many people at the station. The Queen Mother (of Bavaria), in deep mourning, still looking very

[2] Ambassador in Berlin.
[3] The other two were Princess Beatrice and her husband.

pretty, and the Prince Regent (Prince Luitpold) got into my carriage. The Queen, who is the mother of the unfortunate King Ludwig, drowned two years ago, and of the present mad King Otto, is the only and younger sister of dear Princess Charles of Hesse, and reminded me much of her, only much better-looking. She brought me a bouquet of roses, and asked me to write my name in her book . . . Munich looks to be a fine town, with many churches. The Alps were distinctly visible, lit up by the *Alpenglühen*, which lasted for some time. Read and worked, and was full of anxiety for the next day.

The Queen's continental railway carriage

Charlottenburg, April 24. — A fair night, and got up in good time. Very soon after we were up we found we were going quite close round the outskirts of Berlin, and saw soldiers drilling; the country flat beyond belief. The morning was rather grey, but quite warm. Reached the smallish station of Charlottenburg at quarter to nine, where dear Vicky and all her children were waiting to meet me. She stepped into the carriage for a moment, and I clasped her in my arms and kissed her warmly. She looked careworn and thinner, but not ill. William led me along the platform to a barouche with four horses, into which I got with him, dear Vicky, and Beatrice. In about ten minutes we reached the Palace, the entrance to which I remembered. From the entrance up to the door, the Gardes du Corps (Liko's old regiment) lined the road on foot. At the door, two huge men stood sentry, with drawn swords, which is only done for a Sovereign. Prince Radolin (former Count Radolinsky) met us and preceded us. We went up a flight of steps, at the head of which stood sentries of the 4th Infantry Regiment. Here we entered a fine large room, opening into a splendid long gallery which leads to my rooms, charmingly arranged and done up by dear Vicky. They were the rooms of Frederick the Great, and have never been lived in since: a sitting-room, bed-room, dressing-room and bathroom, all *en suite*.

After I had tidied myself up a bit, dear Vicky came and asked me to go and see dear Fritz. He was lying in bed, his dear face unaltered; and he raised up both his hands with pleasure at seeing me and gave me a nosegay. It was very touching and sad to see him thus in bed. Vicky then took me through his rooms, into a very pretty little green one with rococo decorations in silver. Here I breakfasted with her, her three girls, Beatrice and Liko. Afterwards saw Sir M. Mackenzie[4] with Vicky. He seemed to think Fritz was better. Before luncheon, which we took downstairs, went again for a short while to dear Fritz, and afterwards Vicky sat talking with me for some time in my room. She is very sad, and cried a good deal, poor dear. Besides her cruel anxiety about dear Fritz, she has so many worries and unpleasantnesses. The whole dreadful bother about poor young Vicky had been purposely got up, and they had never had a quarrel with Prince Bismarck . . .

At half-past three, drove with Vicky, Beatrice and Liko, with the girls following, and went into Berlin.[5] The afternoon was threatening and oppressively warm. Drove through the straggling little town of Charlottenburg, through the Thiergarten, where hardly a leaf is yet out, through the Brandenburger Thor, which I remembered so well, to Unter den Linden, the principal street, where the great monumental equestrian statue of Frederick the Great stands, just opposite one of the late Emperor. We visited the Empress Augusta at the Schloss, going in at a side entrance, where Fritz and Louise[6] of Baden met us at the door. I went up in a lift alone, and there was the Empress, in deep mourning, with a long veil, seated in a chair, quite crumpled up and deathly pale, really rather a ghastly sight. Her voice was so weak, it was hardly audible. One hand is paralysed, and the other shakes very much. She seemed much pleased at seeing me again, after nine years. I sat some little time talking with the Empress alone, after which the others came in, and I walked downstairs on Fritz of Baden's arm.

From the Schloss drove to Vicky's Palace a short way farther. It was not finished, when we were in Berlin in 1858. The house, as well as the hall, are fine, but there are no really large or good rooms in it. They are beautifully furnished and full of works of art.

[4] The British surgeon who was attending Emperor Frederick.
[5] The thin crowds stood sullen and silent.
[6] Emperor Frederick's sister, married to the Grand Duke of Baden.

April 25.–A little after twelve, Vicky brought Prince Bismarck[7] to my room and left him there. I had a most interesting conversation with him, and was agreeably surprised to find him so amiable and gentle. I shook hands with him and asked him to sit down. He alluded to having seen me at Versailles thirty-three years ago, and again later at a distance. We spoke of beloved Fritz's illness, that I thought him not looking so ill, etc. He spoke a great deal of the German Army, and the immense number of men who could be put under arms if necessary, and of their fitness for defence; of his great object being to prevent war, which I remarked was ours also; of Russia not being dependable. If Austria should be attacked, Germany was bound by treaty to defend her; the danger would then arise lest France should join Russia. In that case England, he said, could be of great use with her fleet. He was also delighted when I told him that Lord Salisbury's Government was much stronger. I said, France did not wish for war, in which he agreed, but her Government was so weak and powerless she might be forced into anything. He thought Austria showed too much fear of Russia, which is strange, the (Austrian) Emperor having made the same remark to me of Prince Bismarck.

I expressed my satisfaction that there was no idea of a Regency, as I knew it would upset dear Fritz dreadfully, and he assured me there would be none. Even if he thought it necessary, which he did not, he would not have the heart to propose it. I appealed to Prince Bismarck to stand by poor Vicky, and he assured me he would, that hers was a hard fate. I spoke of William's inexperience and his not having travelled at all. Prince Bismarck replied that (William) knew nothing at all about civil affairs, that he could however say "should he be thrown into the water, he would be able to swim", for that he was certainly clever. We talked of other personal affairs, and I asked the Prince to tell Princess Bismarck to come to the English Embassy, where I was going in the afternoon, and this seemed to give him much pleasure. He remained with me over half an hour.[8]

Luncheon as yesterday. Soon after saw the Duke of Rutland,[9] who had come to Berlin as Minister, and who was much interested in hearing about my interview with Prince Bismarck. At three came the Empress

[7] Major Bigge (afterwards Lord Stamfordham), who assisted Sir Henry Ponsonby in receiving Prince Bismarck, wrote: 'He was unmistakably nervous and ill at ease; asked whereabouts in the room the Queen would be, would she be seated or standing, etc. We both felt proud that this great man evidently realised he was about to be received by an equally great, or even a greater, woman.'

[8] When Prince Bismarck emerged at the end of the interview he was smiling and admiration was writ clear on his face. Wiping the perspiration from his brow, he exclaimed: 'What a woman! One could do business with her!'

[9] Lord John Manners, who had succeeded his brother in March of this year.

Augusta, whom I met half-way down the gallery. Louise of Baden was with her. They came to my room and remained about twenty minutes. The Empress gave me a fine photograph of the late Emperor, taken after his death.

At half-past four drove with Vicky in a phaeton, the others following as yesterday. Almost the whole way we passed through double lines of carriages, and when we got into the town there were great crowds, who were most enthusiastic, cheering and throwing flowers into the carriage,[10] continually calling out "es hoch die Kaiserin", etc. We went first to the British Embassy in the Wilhelmstrasse, which is a pretty house. Sir Edward Malet and Lady Ermyntrude received me at the door, and he led me into the drawing-room, where we found Princess Bismarck, an elderly, rather masculine and not very *sympathique* lady, and her son Count Herbert, both very civil. Prince Radolin and his daughter were also there. We took tea, and I was shown afterwards the ball-room, a fine room, and the diningroom. Then we took our departure and drove to Mon Bijou, a Schlösschen of the Emperor's, in the grounds of which stands the very pretty English church Vicky helped to get built. The chaplain and church wardens met us there. The crowd was still great when we left, and the people were very friendly.

Got home at seven, and I went directly with Vicky to see dear Fritz, bringing him a bouquet which had been given me at the church. Vicky took me back to my room and talked some time very sadly about the future, breaking down completely. Her despair at what she seems to look on as the certain end is terrible. I saw Sir M. Mackenzie, and he said he thought the fever, which was less, though always increasing at night, would never leave dear Fritz, and that he would not live above a few weeks, possibly two months, but hardly three!! We talked so long that I forgot the time, and had a terrible scramble to get ready for dinner.

It was the same as last night, with the exception of different guests. My people, Prince Bismarck, Enrich Leiningen, Ernest Hohenloe (Hermann's son), the Duke and Duchess of Rutland, Gen. Pape, Gen. Winterfeld, Minister von Putkamer, Minister Dr. Aschenbach, Count Herbert Bismarck, Count Otto Stolberg, Gen. von Albedyl (brother-in-law to the Duchess of Manchester), Count and Countess Eulenburg, Countess Brühl, Sir E. and Lady Ermyntrude Malet and Count Moltke (eighty-seven, looking more like sixty-seven), dined.[11] Went afterwards into the rather small room in which we lunch, and I talked to most of the people.

[10] The change in the reception had been organised by Prince Bismarck.

[11] Prince Bismarck sat opposite Queen Victoria. He was in gay mood. Noticing a bon-bon that bore upon it the picture of the Empress, he seized it and pressed it to his heart.

Prince Bismarck, whom I told of the enthusiastic reception we had met with in Berlin, said it was quite spontaneous, and that, in spite of the disagreeable words used sometimes both in and out of the Press, on both sides, the Germans liked the English and preferred them to any other foreign nation. I shook hands with him in taking leave. Count Moltke looks unaltered, is not deaf, and has hardly a wrinkle in his face. I was very tired by the time I got upstairs.

In the train, April 26.–At three, drove with Vicky in the phaeton, followed by Beatrice and Sophy,[12] young Vicky and Mossy[13] riding with Liko, to a very sandy dusty exercising ground, about quarter of an hour from Charlottenburg, where were drawn up the Gardes du Corps (mounted) and the 4th Regiment of Infantry. We drove down the line, Willy[14] being in command, and then remained stationary for the march past, the Cavalry coming first, and looking extremely well. The marching on foot must have been most trying in the almost ankle-deep sand. The commanding officers were called up to the carriage and presented to me. William rode at the head. We drove straight home. It was bitterly cold with a high wind, but bright. It was too sad to have seen this parade without beloved Fritz.

Went over to dear Fritz with Vicky, before our early dinner, and gave him my photograph, which he kissed, but, a fit of coughing coming on, we left him. Went back to him after dinner, and, after a few minutes' talk, took leave of him, which fortunately passed off without either of us being upset. I kissed him as I did every day, and said I hoped he would come to us when he was stronger. Then I dressed and drove with dear Vicky, Beatrice and Mossy to the station, where all were assembled, as on our arrival, and I took leave of them. Dear Vicky came into the railway carriage, and I kissed her again and again. She struggled hard not to give way, but finally broke down, and it was terrible to see her standing there in tears, while the train moved slowly off, and to think of all she was suffering and might have to go through. My poor poor child, what would I not do to help her in her hard lot!

Six weeks later Emperor Frederick died. His son, who succeeded him as William II, immediately announced that, according to the wishes of his late father, the marriage between Prince Alexander and Princess Victoria would not take place. He had soon proved himself an expert in the terminological inexactitude.

'Sandro' applied to the Grand Duke of Hesse and the Rhine for a non-royal title and in January 1889 became Count Hartenau. A few weeks

[12] Emperor Frederick's third daughter, afterwards Queen of Greece.
[13] Princess Margaret, the Emperor's youngest daughter.
[14] Crown Prince William.

Johanna Loisinger, Countess Hartenau

later he married Johanna Loisinger. When the news reached Queen Victoria she restricted herself to the comment: 'Perhaps they love one another.'

The former Ruler of Bulgaria now joined the Austrian army with the rank of Lieutenant-Colonel, but the strain of the past years had told on him and he died at Graz in 1893. There were two children of the marriage, a son and a daughter. Countess Hartenau died in Vienna in July 1951.

As for 'young Vicky', we shall meet her again.

Journey Thirty-nine
1889

La Reina in Spain

THE Queen's spring holiday at Biarritz was dominated by the sublime on the one hand and the ridiculous on the other. By her visit to San Sebastian she became the first British Sovereign to enter Spain. Although Charles I and Charles II had journeyed there, they were but princes at the time. The Queen was travelling incognito as Countess of Balmoral in France, but at the Spanish frontier she again became Queen Victoria.

The ridiculous (or, as the Queen described it, 'intolerable') aspect of the holiday was made up of the expostulations and entreaties of a divorced Countess whom the Queen refused to receive. Those who accompanied the Queen on her drives and excursions had to be constantly on their guard unless this outraged lady should attempt to fling herself bodily upon the person of Her Imperial Majesty.

Once again, it was on the recommendation of Empress Eugénie that the Queen decided to visit the Pyrenean resort. It was at first announced in the Press that she would stay at the Villa Eugénie, which Napoleon had built for his wife, but there was a change of plan and the final destination proved to be the Villa Rochefoucauld–le Pavillon. This appeared to be a most suitable choice. The Pavillon was picturesque and afforded fine views. The Comte de La Rochefoucauld, a member of an old French family, was delighted and made elaborate arrangements. His library of fine-art books and his folios of French water-colours were available to his guests and a gold key was made so that the Queen's entry to the house should be truly regal. Only one dark cloud appeared on the horizon. The information emerged that the Comtesse was a divorced woman.

Queen Victoria was dead set against divorced ladies. Guilty or innocent, they were never received at Court or by any of her Ambassadors abroad. When she had made up her mind on a point of propriety there was no question of considering a particular case. Only personal convenience could make her change her mind. And, of course, dear Albert's mother had been divorced. So here was a predicament. It was further complicated when, after making enquiries of the Foreign Office, Sir Henry Ponsonby learned that details of this particular divorce were 'more than ordinarily unfit for publication'.

A letter was sent to Madame la Comtesse informing her of the position and that she would not be received by the Queen. Being a perfect Private Secretary, he followed this with further instruction, making it quite clear that she was not to appear at the welcoming ceremony. But, out of instinct or experience, the suspicion remained with him, through the crossing to Cherbourg and the long train journey south, that in the event matters would not be conducted as he had ordered that they should be. So it was that when the royal party arrived at Biarritz station on 7th March, and the Queen was occupied by the attentions of the civil and military authorities, Sir Henry jumped into a cab and hurried to the home of the La Rochefoucaulds.

His suspicions proved very right. On the steps of the Pavillon stood the whole family, Madame la Comtesse jubilant among them. She ran towards the flabbergasted courtier, shaking him by both hands.

Firmly, Sir Henry explained that only the Count should receive the Queen and that the rest of the family should retreat from the immediate area. Whereat Madame la Comtesse became tearful, pleading, begging that she might hide behind a door and watch the arrival through the crack. Not yet knowing his adversary, Sir Henry gave in, on condition that she was not seen.

Up came the carriages. The Count stood on the steps, the gold key in his hand. The Queen approached him. Then back swung a door, out jumped the Comtesse and, before there was time to stop her, she had thrust a bouquet of flowers at the astonished Queen, and proceeded to clasp Lady Churchill, who was in attendance, in a warm embrace.

Eyes-front, Victoria made for her room. From its seclusion she fired a series of rockets which found their mark on her travel-weary staff. Further attempts were made to clarify the position and from them an interesting view point emerged. Madame la Comtesse's first husband had died a month earlier, from an excessive intake of alcohol, and his widow was under the impression that, with his passing, she was virginal white once more. The Queen did not see it that way.

Realising that this line of approach was getting her nowhere, Madame la Comtesse threw her reserves, in the form of husband No. 2, into the fray. He began the action with a heavy bombardment, designed to obliterate all opposition. For ammunition he used supplications, threats and tears, but Sir Henry sat as steady as the squares at Waterloo. Sweet reason followed, the sad tale of how his wife had been beaten by her first husband being unfolded. On learning that guilt or innocence did not affect the Queen's view, an enflanking movement was attempted. The

Count announced that, as his wife was not British, her behaviour fell without the boundaries of the British Queen. The assumption that Queen Victoria should condemn a night of sin in Dover and overlook a similar affair twenty miles away in Calais met with little support. So he risked all his forces in one charge. He went back to the days of the seventeenth century moralists, when Francois, Duc de La Rochefoucauld, wrote *Sentences et Maximes Morales*, and was the most eminent and intimate associate of Madame de Sévigné. In brief, the Count's point was that, with a distinguished and ancient family such as that to which he belonged, the rules of common usage did not apply. This brought from the Private Secretary the comment that, up to the present, he had always thought the story, '*Le bon Dieu pensera deux fois avant de condamner un La Rochefoucauld*', was a fiction, but suddenly he had learned that it was true.

On 30th March the Queen issued her final judgment, penned on black-edged writing paper. She said that the La Rochefoucaulds were quite intolerable and that on no account would the Queen receive *her*.

There remained but one danger–that Madame la Comtesse would emerge from behind a tree as the Queen went about her occasions and attempt a *fait accompli*. But such a step would call for considerable courage and the Queen was experienced in repulsing such attacks. On the occasion when a disgruntled male subject of Berkshire clung to her passing carriage, she quietly leaned forward, tapped the knee of her elderly lady-in-waiting, and ordered her to hit the man with her umbrella. Nothing happened. In thunderous voice she repeated: 'I said, hit him with your umbrella.' Hypnotised into the resurrection of long lost strength, the elderly lady obliged, with such efficiency that the assailant was knocked clear and lay sprawling on the road. Perhaps, at Biarritz, discretion proved the better part of valour, for, though the equerries and ladies-in-waiting kept constant surveillance, no indigenous aristocrat popped out to mar the royal excursions.

And there were many excursions. The Queen explored Fontarabia, Hendaye and Bayonne. She visited the Bernadine Convent at Anglet, and at St. Jean de Luz the Mayor conducted her over the house occupied by Wellington in 1813. At a fête given by the Municipality of Biarritz she watched a match of *pélote au rebot*, the national game of the Basques. Of particular interest to her was the English cemetery at St. Etienne, the burial place of the officers and men of the 2nd Life Guards and of the Coldstream Guards killed during the siege of Bayonne by the Duke of Wellington's army in April 1814, at the end of the Peninsular War. The ground had been purchased by the Guards in the same year. The Queen ordered that wreaths of immortelles be placed on the graves. On each wreath was a card inscribed–'V.R.I. 1889'.

The great excitement of the holiday was the visit to the Queen Regent

The Queen visits the Virgin's Rocks at Biarritz

of Spain at San Sebastian. It was to be even more historic than she realised, for not only was she the first British Sovereign to cross the frontier, but also she was to meet the small boy who, seventeen years later, was to marry her granddaughter, Princess Ena of Battenberg, who thus became Queen Victoria Eugenia of Spain.

Queen Maria Christina Désirée Henrietta Félicité Renier was born in 1858 and was a Habsburg. She was the widow of King Alphonso XII and was called 'the Austrian'. Being a foreigner, her life was not easy. She did not like bull-fighting, but welcomed excitement. She had been up in a balloon, the first Queen to become airborne.

Alphonso XII became King in 1874. At nineteen he fell violently in love with his seventeen year old cousin, Maria de las Mercedes, and married her in January 1878. Six months later she died. The shock upset the balance of Alphonso's life. He developed consumption and took a professional singer as his mistress. Determined to provide an heir for Spain, he asked for a list of suitable candidates for mother. From among these he chose Maria Christina, with whom he had played in Vienna as a child. He knew that his life was running out, and he prayed for a son. To his exasperation, it was a daughter that was born in 1880. Two years later a second daughter followed. It looked as if the race was lost when Alphonso died in November 1885. Six months later the miracle happened. In May 1886 a posthumous son was born—a son born a King.

Biarritz, March 27.—We reached San Sebastian, the position of which is beautiful, just before one (Spanish time) and saw the Queen Regent standing on the platform, surrounded by her Court. There was of course a Guard of Honour. We got out at once, and I embraced the young Queen, kissing her on both cheeks. Then I presented Beatrice and Liko to her. She spoke German to us, with the pleasant Viennese accent. She is an Archduchess, daughter of the late Archduke Frederick and the Archduchess Elisabeth, Marie of Belgium's elder sister. Her grandfather was the celebrated Archduke Charles, whose wife was a Princess of Nassau, and she is second cousin to Helen, also second cousin to Lily, on her mother's side. The Queen has a very charming face and manner, brown eyes, a good nose, and a slight graceful figure.

We entered a carriage alone together, drawn by four horses with postillions, who wore caps and wigs very like what ours have in the Ascot livery, the horses (English, very like mine) with very handsome harness; and two footmen sat behind. We drove slowly along through the streets, which were crowded. The Governor of the place rode next to me, an enormous fat man, seventy years old, mounted on a grey typical Spanish horse, but he only rode a short way with us. There was an escort composed of cavalry, very like the Blues with us, wearing cuirasses, but with white feathers in their helmets, instead of horse-hair plumes. They looked extremely well. The black horses were Spanish, with the peculiar Roman nose one sees always depicted in the pictures of Velasquez. We drove along a wide open *place* or *boulevard*, across the bridge, through two triumphal arches, most kindly erected in my honour, and up a long winding road to the Duchess of Baileu's villa. The noise was great, people calling out "Viva la Reina", bands playing, and incessant firing off of squibs, rockets, etc., quite close to the horses, who were wonderfully quiet. It seems this is a peculiar Spanish custom . . .

Half an hour brought us to the charmingly situated villa, in which the Queen spent some time last year. It stands in a beautiful small park. The pillars on the outside of the house, which is not large, were entwined with green leaves and flowers. The Villa Ayete is comfortably and nicely arranged, with English comforts. The Queen kindly took us upstairs to her room, where I tidied myself up and put on my cap. The Queen showed us about everywhere herself, in the simplest and most unaffected manner. Went downstairs again, where, in a billiard-room near the drawing-room, she presented some more people and I presented my suite. Then we went to luncheon, taking it alone with the Queen. The Queen was quite delightful, talking so pleasantly about everything. A military band played outside during luncheon. Afterwards went upstairs again to put on our things and left, driving the same way as before.

The road was lined for a short way by the National Guard of Guipuzcoa, called Michelistes, who wore red tunics and trousers and the red *boina* on their heads. They distinguished themselves so much in the war that they always form the Sovereign's guard at San Sebastian, and did so to-day at Ayete. Various troops lined the whole route, which, descending the hill, passed first through the new part of the town and the Alameda, crossing the river into the narrow and very picturesque streets of the old town. At the end of a narrow street, which led up to the Square, was a fine old church. This Square or Plaza was most striking, and the effect beautiful. On one side was the Hôtel de l'Ayuntamiente, where we got out, and the other three sides were composed of houses with arcades below and many balconies, all being crammed full of people, and being hung with draperies, while on coloured cloths, some red, some white, were repeated in large letters the word "Welcome". The blue sky appearing above all the great noise, cheering, and clapping of hands, made a wonderful effect.

We went upstairs, the stairs being lined with flowers, the Queen leading me and the Authorities preceding us. A choir in the hall sang *God Save the Queen* in Basque. Here we were received by the Municipality, who were presented, and gave me an album with photographs. We then went on a balcony and sat there with the Queen, the principal gentlemen standing behind us, and witnessed a Basque dance. It was very like what we had seen the other day at Biarritz, and the same quaint music. The men were dressed in white, and first danced singly and then in couples. We got up afterwards for a moment, and some tea was handed round, but it was quite undrinkable, and I only touched it.

We then left, the Queen asking Liko to lead me downstairs. Drove again down the same way to the station, where the Queen most kindly expressed the wish to accompany us as far as the frontier at Irun. She was most charming, full of thanks for my visit, and of hopes of visiting me in England with her children.

A little over half an hour brought us to Irun, and here we all got out, and had to take leave of the dear charming Queen Christine, whom I hope we shall see again, which feeling is very reciprocal on her part. She is deservedly very popular, and does her duty so admirably and has won the esteem and respect of all in Spain, though a foreigner. She remained standing on the platform till our train steamed out.

Journey Forty
1889

Irving and Terry at Sandringham

Sandringham, April 23.–At two left Windsor, with Louise,[1] the Duchess of Roxburghe, Sir H. Ponsonby, Sir H. Ewart, and Dr Reid.[2] Went round London and stopped nowhere, excepting at Lynn, passing Cambridge and Ely, the Cathedral of which is so fine. Soon after it began to pour violently, like a thunder-shower. At Lynn, Bertie and Eddy[3] came in, and the Mayor handed an Address and his daughter a bouquet. A few minutes brought us to Wolferton station. Here there were great crowds. The station was very prettily decorated, and just beyond it there was a triumphal arch. The sun came out, and all looked very bright. I got into Bertie's large landau, open, with four horses and postillions, and dear Alix[4] insisted on sitting backwards with Louise, in order that I might be better seen. Bertie and Eddy rode on either side, Sir D. Probyn[5] in front, preceded by the Hunt,[6] sixty in number, forty of whom were in their red coats. The road was lined with people, and numbers drove and rode. Great enthusiasm. We passed two more arches, and from the last, almost to the gates, there were Venetian masts. It was a very pretty sight. All Bertie's neighbours came out.[7]

Everything came back to my mind, as we drove in at the gates and I again saw the house and stepped out and entered the hall. All was the

[1] Princess Louise, Marchioness of Lorne.
[2] Afterwards Sir James Reid.
[3] Prince Albert Victor, Duke of Clarence.
[4] Princess of Wales.
[5] Comptroller and Treasurer to the Prince of Wales. Keeper of the Privy Purse, 1901–10, and thereafter Comptroller of Queen Alexandra's Household until his death in 1924.
[6] The West Norfolk.
[7] On the Queen's arrival the local children had a celebration tea in one tent, while in another, 'the labourers sat down to a substantial dinner, at which her Majesty's health was drunk with the utmost heartiness'.

Members of the Norfolk Hunt salute Her Majesty at Sandringham

same as at that terrible time,[8] and yet all so different! A happy contrast. Bertie asked me to stand at the door to see the gentlemen of the Hunt, who had escorted me, pass by. There was a Guard of Honour of the Norfolk Artillery with their band, who afterwards marched past. Bertie and Alix then took me upstairs to the well-known old rooms, which have been freshly done up. I had some tea in my room and rested. We dined at quarter to nine, Bertie leading me in, and Eddy sitting on my other side.

April 26. – We went down into the Ballroom, which was converted into a theatre, after talking till ten. There were nearly 300 people in the room, including all the neighbours, tenants, and servants. We sat in the front row, I between Bertie and Alix. The stage was beautifully arranged and with great scenic effects, and the pieces were splendidly mounted and with numbers of people taking part. I believe there were between sixty and seventy, as well as the orchestra. The piece, *The Bells*, is a melodrama, translated from the French *Le Juif Polonais* by

[8] In November and December 1871, when the Prince was dangerously ill with typhoid fever.

Erckmann-Chatrian, and is very thrilling. The hero (Irving),[9] though a
mannerist of the Macready type, acted wonderfully. He is a murderer,
and frequency imagines he hears the bells of the horses in the sledge, in
which sat the Polish Jew, whom he murdered. The way in which
Irving acted his own dream, and describes the way in which he carried
out the murder, is wonderful and ghastly, as well as the scene of his
death. He had carried his secret about with him for thirteen years!

The Bells was followed by the trial scene from *The Merchant of
Venice*, in which Irving played the part of Shylock extremely well,
and Miss Ellen Terry that of Portia beautifully. I often saw her sister
Kate formerly, and as a child in the part of Prince Arthur at Windsor.
It was a most successful performance. I waited a moment in the Drawing-
room to speak to Irving and Ellen Terry. He is very gentleman-like,
and she, very pleasing and handsome. It was one when I got upstairs.

[9] In 1871 Henry Irving's performance of Mathias in *The Bells* saved the fortunes of the
Lyceum theatre. Seven years later Irving opened the Lyceum under his own management, in 1879 Ellen Terry playing Portia in *The Merchant of Venice*. In 1895 he received
the honour of knighthood, the first ever accorded an actor.

*Henry Irving and Ellen Terry performing before the Queen
and the Prince and Princess of Wales*

Journey Forty-one
1889

Sleeping Car

A S the years advanced Queen Victoria became increasingly sympathetic towards the love-lorn, and more understanding of their problems. So it was that in June 1889 she invited her granddaughter 'Moretta' – Princess Victoria of Prussia – to stay with her at Windsor and later accompany her to Balmoral.

It was the first time that the twenty-three year old Princess had been parted from her mother, the Empress Frederick. Her father's death, and the marriage of her beloved 'Sandro' of Battenberg to Johanna Loisinger, had taken the zest for living right out of her. A change of scene, and a chance to meet other young men, were imperative.

It was a blazing June and the grass was very green at Frogmore. 'No one', wrote the Princess, 'knows what grass is until they come to England.' The gardens were full of the scent of flowers and the voices of the birds, and the Eton boys rowed on the river.[1] Grandmama fed her on strawberries and melons and there were picnic teas under the tall trees.

The Princess had a dread of becoming fat and, to the despair of her mother, dieted rigorously. But those teas proved irresistible, and soon she was complaining that she would look like a tub and that her belts were becoming tight. To counteract the tendency, she took to lawn tennis with enthusiasm, her instructor being none other than 'Sandro's' brother, Prince Henry. She ordered a net to be sent to Germany, so that she could continue playing when she got home. Life, she found, was so much easier and more relaxed in England than under the strict Court discipline of Germany. Her great delight was to be able to visit the Windsor shops and choose presents for her family without fuss or favour.

On 6th June the Queen departed for Balmoral. This journey was a rite and the time table, and list of places to be occupied, were published well in advance. On this occasion the special train of the London and

---

[1] The procession up the river on the Fourth of June was watched by the Queen for the first time since the death of the Prince Consort.

North-Western Railway consisted of fourteen carriages 'fitted with electrical communication and all the most modern improvements'.

On these journeys to and from Scotland a curious, and highly prized, privilege had been created since the death of the Prince Consort. It was the honour of sharing the sleeping saloon with the Queen. The first holder of the honour was Princess Helena, from 1862 until her marriage in 1866. She was succeeded by Princess Louise until she also became a bride. For

The Queen's saloon coach

the past eighteen years it had been the perquisite of Princess Beatrice, even after her marriage. This Princess now stayed behind at Windsor, convalescing after the birth of her third child, Leopold.[2] So Princess Victoria was chosen to take her place.

The night of the journey was much too hot for the liking of the Queen. She went to bed with very little on and had only a thin sheet over her. Although both windows were open, the ice in the buckets failed in its cooling purpose, melted and had to be thrown away. It was nearly four in the morning before she dozed off.

[2] The elder children were Alexander, afterwards Marquess of Carisbrooke; and Ena, afterwards Queen Victoria Eugenia of Spain.

On arrival at Balmoral the Princess reported the events of the journey to her mother:

Balmoral, June 7.—Having just had a nice wash, in Auntie B.'s bath, the first thing to do after it is to send you a line to tell you of our safe arrival here! It was a longish journey, but all went off well. We left Windsor last night at 8.30 about & reached this, after 3 o'clock this afternoon. The day had been frightfully hot at Windsor, & when we left the heat was still very oppressive. Poor Grandmama felt very uncomfortable & dreaded the night. After Leamington, where we had some tea, I 'turned in', & a lovely soft bed it was too—one quite forgot that one was really in the train. I never saw anything so perfect in arrangement & comfort. Of course you know the carriage well—I *do* wish you had one like it. I was just dozing off, when Grandmama came to bed—& *how* it reminded me of you, my Mother. She looked so clean & dear—all in white—& it took some time before she was settled—the shawls, & cushions—then the lamps to put out—then again, it felt too hot—then not warm enough, & in the night—Annie was called many a time—to bring her something to drink etc. Oh! it did remind me so of our travels. Well finally we had some sleep, & in the morning I dressed first, so as to make room—& then we soon reached Perth, where the same breakfast awaited us, as you & I enjoyed, some years ago.

The country looked lovely as we travelled on—everything quite springlike—the lilac just coming out & the hills bathed in richest tints. The drive from the station to the castle, is also long, but so pretty. We found a delicious luncheon awaiting us on our arrival & then I took a walk with Ethel, before washing, as the things had not come, & went to the 'Merchants' & bought some nice trifles. Mrs Simon asked directly after you—& remembered me going there with you, which we did together. By next Messenger I shall send some 'oat-cake' which she has made herself & some oatmeal, for porridge.[3]

[3] *Queen Victoria at Windsor and Balmoral*. Edited by James Pope-Hennessy.

Journey Forty-two
1889

Welsh Album

FIFTY-SEVEN years had passed since Princess Victoria toured North Wales with her mother and began to record daily events in her diary. Although the tracks of the journeys of 1832 and 1889 crossed, the full years between had dimmed the Queen's memory and now she could not recall hotels at which she had spent the night so long before.

The visit attracted great attention both from the public and the Press. A journey which deviated from the established itinerary of Osborne–Balmoral was always news, Her Majesty being known in certain parts of the country as 'The Great Unseen'. There were sporadic objections from the heart of Wales, but such are not unusual when royal occasions occur there and no incidents marred the tour. To preserve an example of the coverage given to the descent of Queen Victoria upon an area where she was little known, the main report of the *Illustrated London News* is reproduced verbatim.

For the staff of the newspapers and the magazines the approach of the nineties heralded a new technique and way of life. The photographers were waiting in the wings to take over from the illustrative artists, communications were being revolutionised, and printing processes speeded to cope with fast swelling circulation. The old order was changing fast yielding place to new, and boys then entering journalism were, by middle age, to take for granted cars, electricity, aeroplanes and wireless. Even the humble safety cycle was to play its part in the change. But in 1889 the long established routine still reigned. Reporters on provincial assignments stayed in commercial hotels and relied on the hired carriage to take them about their work, undisturbed on the dirt roads which had been deserted since the railways pushed out the coaches at the beginning of the Queen's reign.

The reporters and artists were in position several days before the Queen's arrival in Merionethshire. Although she only stayed at Palé from 23rd–27th August, her visit was covered in three issues and the number of illustrations used exceeded fifty. For the issue of the 24th the artists worked

Princess Beatrice 'firing a shot' in Wynnstay coal mine, Ruabon

on local scenes which would be in the path of the Queen, either at first
hand or from photographic studies. The reporters familiarised themselves
with the programme and looked about for local tit-bits. In this case one
such concerned two ladies, Lady Eleanor Butler and the Hon Miss
Ponsonby, who had spent their long lives together at a rambling museum
of a house at Llangollen, the survivor dying at the age of ninety in 1829.
They were very odd in their behaviour, it was said, wearing hats, neck-
cloths and coats like men.

   The second issue contained the main report, while the artists concentrated on action pictures of the Queen. The hiatus over, the artists
sent in pictures of unscheduled sights which she had seen and the reporters
added stories collected after the dead-line, as, for example, more details of
Princess Beatrice's descent of the Wynnstay coal mine at Ruabon and
how she 'fired a shot'. With white sheets draped over their shoulders and
bustles, the Princess and her ladies appeared, in the accompanying drawing,
like the witches in Macbeth with immense behinds.

   Her Majesty the Queen, accompanied by Princess Beatrice and her husband
Prince Henry of Battenberg, and by Princess Alice of Hesse, arrived at Lland-
derfel, near Bala, Merionethshire, at eight o'clock in the morning, on Friday,
Aug. 23, to stay a few days in the mansion of Palé,[1] lent by its owner, Mr

[1] Now unoccupied.

H. B. Robertson, for the accommodation of the Royal party. Our last publication contained many views of the beautiful and romantic scenery of Bala Lake and the river Dee, as far as Llangollen, which her Majesty had not seen for many years past, and which she has now had an opportunity of revisiting.

The special train by which the Royal party travelled on a branch of the Great Western Railway, via Chirk, Ruabon, Llangollen, and Corwen, up the Dee Valley, was met at the Llandderfel Station, by Captain R. D. Pryce, the Lord Lieutenant of Merionethshire, and Mrs Pryce, Colonel Evans Lloyd, Mr R. H. Wood, the High Sheriff, Mr R. J. Pryce, of Rhiwlas, and other gentlemen, with some ladies. The platform was gaily decorated, and a covered entrance, adorned with flags and plants, had been erected. When the Queen alighted, Mrs Pryce presented her with a magnificent bouquet, composed of stephanotis, camellias, and gardenias, in the form of a Welsh lyre. The Lord Lieutenant was presented by Sir H. Ponsonby, and in his turn presented the High Sheriff, Mr J. Lloyd Price, Chairman of the Reception Committee. The rain ceased as the Queen entered her carriage, and the sun shone out brightly. The Queen did not appear fatigued by her long journey, but leaned heavily on her stick as she walked to the carriage. The people raised a hearty cheer, which the Royal lady smilingly acknowledged, and the carriage at once drove off to Palé, a few hundred yards from the station. The half-dozen Indian retainers who accompanied the Royal party were regarded with special curiosity. At the Hall the visitors were received by Mr Robertson and the Right Hon Cecil Raikes, the Postmaster-General, the Minister in attendance. Across the stone bridge an arch of evergreen and heather had been erected, bearing the legend "Duw gadwo ein Brenhines". The Welsh version of "God save our Queen". As the carriages entered the gates of Palé, the Royal Standard was run up the flagstaff.

The road to Bala, along which the Royal party drove in the afternoon, is very beautiful. By its side the dark waters of the Dee hurry over their rocky bed, and larch and copperbeech, retaining their freshness in this land of rain, form natural archways of verdure. To the left the valley rises by sloping meadows and heather-covered hills into the long range of Berwyn. Farther on, the heights of Castell Carndochan and Gwynfynydd are discernible, and on a clear day the Arans, with Cader Idris standing like a sentinel over the whole. To the right are low hills stretching away into the distance in graceful curves; and Arenig rises in front. A few little cottages along the road were modestly decorated in honour of the Royal visit. The village was very smart with flags and streamers, and the inhabitants turned out to receive the procession. As Bala was approached the decorations became more profuse, and at Rhiwlas, the old mansion of Mr R. Lloyd Price, was a triumphal arch with the motto "Llangyfarchiadau Rhiwlas", which is said to mean "Congratulations of Rhiwlas". Crossing the quaint bridge over the Tryweryn, that joins the Dee close by Bala, the carriages passed under another arch, which gave a welcome to Merioneth; at the other end of the street was a similar structure, with the sentiment in Welsh, "On a throne unshaken, long live Victoria". The effect of these arches, composed of evergreen and heather, was charming, and the town street was an avenue of flags and streamers.

Opposite the County Hall stands had been erected, and a wooden roofing was built across the road. Here the guard of honour of the 2nd Volunteer Battalion Royal Welsh Fusiliers was drawn up, under the command of Major Rees, and the painting of Bala Lake by Mr Edwin A. Pettitt, to be presented to the Queen from the ladies of Bala and the neighbourhood, was placed. The Volunteer band and the Oakeley Silver Band contributed patriotic and national music. Among those in the reserved seats were Mr Greaves, Lord Lieutenant of Carnarvonshire; Sir John Puleston, M.P.; Mr Pope, Q.C., in the uniform of a Deputy Lieutenant; Sir R. Wyatt, Mr Osmond Williams, and Mr H Ellis Nanney.

Then came the Queen's carriage, drawn by four greys ridden by postillions, with the Scotch gillies behind. Sir J. M'Neill rode by side of her Majesty. The second carriage contained Sir H. Ponsonby and Mr Raikes, and the third the ladies in attendance. The carriage stopped at the platform, the band of the volunteers playing the National Anthem, while the guard of honour presented arms. A bouquet was presented to the Queen by Miss S. M. Clark, of Moel-y-Garnedd. Miss E. K. Williams, of Gwernhefin, presented one to Princess Beatrice. A third was given to Princess Alice by Miss J. A. Jones, of Mount Place. A "buttonhole" was presented to Prince Henry of Battenberg by Miss Catherine Jones, of Plasdeon. The Lord Lieutenant handed to Mr Raikes, who handed to the Queen, the address of welcome from the county of Merioneth, to which her Majesty graciously replied.

The following gentlemen were presented: Mr W. E. Jones, Chairman of the Quarter Sessions; Dr E. Jones, Chairman of the County Council; Mr O. S. Wynne, Mr H. J. Reveley, Mr W. E. Oakley, Mr John Vaughan, Major Amoye Passingham, Mr E. Gilliat Jones, Captain A. R. Pryce, Mr Edward Watkin, County Councillor for Bala, and Mr W. Durant Gibbings, secretary to the Reception Committee. The curtain in front of the painting of Bala Lake was drawn aside, and Mrs Price, of Rhiwlas, asked her Majesty's acceptance of it in the name of the subscribers. The Queen inspected the picture, and expressed her gratification at the gift. This, with the present of the parishioners of Llandderfel, which took the form of a hazel stick grown in the district, mounted with a gold band bearing the inscription "Llandderfel to H.M. Victoria, R.I., 1889", will be to the Queen a pleasant memento of this part of her kingdom. The carriages drove off, while the united choirs of the Bala district began to sing the National Anthem.

The Royal visitors proceeded along the north shore of Bala Lake, in view of Cader Idris and the Arans, to Glanyllyn, the pretty little shooting box of Sir Watkin W. Wynn. Here they were received by Sir Watkin and Lady Williams Wynn, and took tea, staying for half an hour. The house party included the Earl of Stradbroke. Lady Rous, the Hon C. Russell, Mr Robert Ethelston, Mr Lucas, Mr R. W. Williams Wynn, Miss Williams Wynn, of Cefn, Miss Constance Williams Wynn, Captain Rowley Conwy, and Mr O. Slaney Wynne. The return journey to Palé was then commenced, the procession passing again through Bala, where the Queen was heartily cheered. The roads during the day were kept by drafts of the Flint, Denbigh, and Merionethshire Police, under Major Best, Chief Constable of Merionethshire. In the evening Sir Watkin gave a dinner to his tenantry.

Palé Mansion, Llandderfel

On Saturday, Aug 24, her Majesty and the Princesses, with Prince Henry of Battenberg, went to Ruabon and Wrexham, places in Denbighshire near the English Border, which are of some industrial importance, possessing valuable collieries. The town of Wrexham is the busiest and most thriving in North Wales; it has a very fine old parish church, with beautiful monuments; is the headquarters of a military district, and carries on large ironworks, breweries, and the manufacture of mineral waters. In the neighbourhood are the noble wooded parks of Erddig Hall, and other fine mansions, and the site of a famous ancient monastery, Bangor Iscoed, on the Dee. Ruabon, from which Wrexham is distant five miles to the north-east, is the Great Western Railway Junction for the branch line to Llangollen and Barmouth. It is twenty-four miles from Shrewsbury, and sixteen miles from Chester. The collieries, ironworks, brick and terracotta works, support a rather scattered population of 15,000. Close to the village is Wynnstay Park, the seat of Sir Watkin Williams Wynn, Bart., with one of the grandest avenues of oaks and elms in the kingdom. A few miles to the south, on the line to Oswestry, is Chirk Castle, in the Valley of the Ceiriog, which affords a beautiful view. The railway viaduct over the Dee, constructed by the late Mr Robertson, father of the present owner of the Palé, and Telford's aqueduct, erected between 1795 and 1803, are great engineering works, and of imposing aspect.

The Royal party leaving Palé at half-past three in the afternoon, travelled

by train to Ruabon, where the railway-station had been decorated with flags
and carpets and exotic flowers. Colonel Cornwallis West, M.P., Lord Lieutenant of Denbighshire, in military uniform, met the Queen here. Her Majesty
and the party entered carriages, in which they drove by the high road to
Wrexham. There was a beautiful triumphal arch at Ruabon, formed of laurels
and heather, with bosses of marigolds, dahlias, and other flowers, and many
festive decorations, arranged by Mr Owen Stanley Wynne and a local committee. The town of Wrexham gave her Majesty a splendid reception. The
streets from end to end were adorned with Venetian masts and flags and floral
festoons. The Mayor of Wrexham, Mr Evan Morris, had invited to his house,
Rosenath, a large party of ladies and gentlemen, among whom were the Lords
Lieutenant of Merionethshire, Carnarvonshire, and Anglesea, the High Sheriffs,
the Marquis of Anglesey, the Bishops of Bangor, Shrewsbury, and St. Asaph,
Lord and Lady Trevor, Lord Mostyn, Lord Kenyon, several members of
Parliament, and the Chairmen of County Councils and Mayors of towns in
North Wales. After luncheon, they went to Acton Park, the seat of Sir Robert
Cunliffe, Bart., in whose delightful grounds the Queen was to be met. The
Welsh Fusiliers, with their white goat having gilt horns, formed a guard of
honour, and an escort was furnished by the Denbighshire Hussars. Her Majesty
entered the park in a carriage-and-four. "God Save the Queen" was sung, and
the Lord Lieutenant of the county presented an address; to which were added
one from the clergy of the diocese of St. Asaph, presented by the Bishop, with
Dean Owen and Canon Howell; and one from the Nonconformist ministers,
presented by the Rev Dr David Roberts. The address of the Mayor and
Corporation of Wrexham was then read by the Town Clerk. The Mayor
presented a gold medal, specially manufactured by Mr Edwin Owens, jeweller
and medallist, of Wrexham; and Mrs Morris presented a loyal ode, written
by the poet Mr Lewis Morris. Many ladies and gentlemen had the honour of
being presented to the Queen. The assembled choirs sang "The Men of Harlech"
and other Welsh national songs. The Mayor of Wrexham has been knighted.

Her Majesty, on Monday afternoon, Aug 26, went by railway to Llangollen,
and visited Bryntisilio, the residence of Sir Theodore and Lady Martin, with
whom she took tea. At Llangollen, and also at Corwen, the local authorities
and chief residents offered the customary tokens of homage and welcome.
Princess Beatrice, with her husband, in the morning visited a colliery at Ruabon,
descending into the pit and "firing a shot" to blast the coal. Her Royal Highness
went next day to Barmouth, to lay the foundation-stone of a new church;
and in the evening the Royal visitors left for Balmoral.

In her journal the Queen thus described the visit to her husband's
biographer:

Palè-Llanderfel, August 26.—After luncheon we all started for Llangollen, going by rail, and had a beautiful afternoon. In three-quarters
of an hour we reached Llangollen, where it seems I had passed the night
with Mama in a small inn, overlooking the river, which is still standing.

The Roberts family of harpists playing to the Queen at Palé

The station was very prettily decorated. We at once entered our carriages, Beatrice, Alicky, and Liko driving with me. We turned sharp to the left above the station, where there was a Guard of Honour of the Volunteer Battalion of the Welsh Fusiliers, with their band and goat, with its gilt horns (my gift), and drove up the beautiful, wooded, mountain-girt, deep valley, dotted with villas and cottages, to Bryntysilio, the well-known residence of Sir Theodore Martin, who with Lady Martin received us at the door. The place is beautifully situated, and the house is furnished and arranged with the greatest taste. They showed us all their rooms and his study, with the table at which he wrote dearest Albert's life. Had tea in the Drawing-room, during which a selected number of Llangollen choirs sang Welsh songs, in the pretty sloping garden. It is wonderful how well these choirs sing, being composed merely of shopkeepers and flannel weavers.

The following day the Queen, through her Private Secretary, sent the following reprimand to her eldest son:

. . . Would Sir Henry write fully to the Prince of Wales of the excellent and enthusiastic reception we have all met with here and to Sir F. Knollys[2] to tell him *how* much this naturally *sensitive* and warmhearted people *feel* the neglect shown them by the Prince of Wales and his family, and that really it is very wrong of him not to come here. It is only five hours from London, and as the Prince of Wales takes his title from this country, which is so beautiful, it does seem very wrong that neither he nor his children have come here often, and indeed, the Princess and the children not at all . . .

Although the criticism was justified, it was, to some measure, a case of the pot calling the kettle black. In a full page drawing, under the title 'Come Back to Erin!', *Punch* made the point that the Queen had not visited Ireland since 1861. *Truth*, in a vitriolic outpouring against the Queen's addiction to Scotland and the Scottish, included these lines:

> When one looks into the question it appears
>   exceeding funny
> That a Queen so highly civilised, so amorous
>   of money,
> Courtly manners, low lip-service, and high
>   Constitutional style,
> Should select for special patronage that
>   portion of her isle
> Least susceptible to culture, which they say
>   *emollit mores*,
> And where millionaires and manners were almost
>   as rare as Tories.
> Yet it seemed that there was nothing could
>   their Mighty Queen so please,
> As to dwell in the "North Countrie" and among
>   the great Bor-Bees . . .

[2] Private Secretary to the Prince of Wales.

Journey Forty-three
1890

Of a Bishop, a Donkey and an Emperor

O N 18th March Prince Bismarck offered his resignation, which was immediately accepted, and Europe buzzed with excitement.
Young Emperor William hastened to tell his grandmother that health reasons necessitated this step being taken. Such was the state of mental excitement of the Chancellor that the All Highest was likely to be floored with an inkpot if he dared to contradict. Queen Victoria received a somewhat different version from the Empress Frederick. 'William fancies he can do everything for himself,' she wrote, adding that he was 'a thorough despot and not the Frederick the Great he imagines'. The thirty-one year old ruler had not taken long to prove the aptness of his nickname–'The Only'.

One of his first actions after taking over the helm from the aged pilot was to smile benignly towards London and Windsor. He was most polite to his Uncle 'Bertie', which was a marked change, and he arranged to meet his grandmother at Darmstadt in April.

On 24th March the Queen, accompanied by Princess Beatrice and her husband, left for a holiday at Aix-les-Bains. While there she received a most interesting visitor.

Aix-les-Bains, April 9.–Received the Archbishop of Chambéry, who was accompanied by his Vicaire-Général. The Archbishop is a dignified, portly old man, with white hair. He wore a purple cloak and soutane[1] and a red skull cap, a very fine cross hanging from a chain, and episcopal ring of a single amethyst surrounded with diamonds. He kissed my hand, and then, at once, took a large paper out of a cover and read a beautiful address. I could only say how pleased and touched I was. The Curé of Aix, a pleasing man, but not the same one as before,

[1] Cassock.

came with the Archbiship as well. After luncheon received the Pasteur Evangélique, an insignificant-looking, very nervous little man, who also spoke very kindly.

The address was both complimentary and friendly, and when later the Queen sent it to Dr Davidson, Dean of Windsor, he commented:

> I doubt whether any parallel could readily be found in history for an Address couched in these particular terms, emanating from a Roman Catholic dignitary, and addressed to a Protestant Sovereign, to whom he himself owes no direct allegiance. It is no small matter that the excellence and advantage of the principles, not merely of *tolerance*, but of liberality and comprehension, should be thus officially recognised in such a quarter, and it makes one hopeful that some at least of the estrangements and the recriminations which even in modern days have sometimes characterised the mutual relation of Christian Churches may be giving way to a more really 'Christian' tone and temper. That your Majesty has done something at least to promote such a spirit, both in our own land and elsewhere, must be hereafter recognised as a great fact of English history.

Another interesting experience was with a donkey. By 1887 the Queen had begun to find trouble in walking and wished to find some easy means of locomotion by which she could perambulate around garden paths and take small expeditions. One April afternoon at Aix, when she was friving in her carriage by the Lae du Bourget, she had seen the answer to her wish jogging towards her. It was a small and young donkey with a kind face, and it was harnessed to a cart in which sat a peasant. The donkey was thin and it was dirty, but the Queen must have spotted some hidden worth. She stopped her carriage and opened proceedings by enquiring if the owner wished to sell.

'All depends', came the answer—an obvious time saver while the situation was summed up.

The Queen adopted the approach direct. 'How much did you pay for him?'

On learning—true or false—that the man had paid 100 francs, the Queen doubled it.

The owner now indulged in a period of deliberation and hesitation, in the obvious hope that the bid would be raised. But when the French detective accompanying the Queen cut in with the information that two donkeys could be bought for that sum, the bargain was sealed. That evening the donkey joined the Queen's horses, entering a state of comfort to which he was entirely unaccustomed and, shortly afterwards, began his duties of pulling a small carriage. The Queen christened him Jacquot and at the end of the holiday he was boxed and despatched to Windsor.

His Imperial Majesty, William II, the German Emperor

Jacquot became an important part of the Queen's life and on this
occasion when she went to Aix, he went with her. But on arrival at
his birthplace, indigenous excitement overcame him. He broke out of
his waggon and trotted smartly to the stable where he had been so kindly
treated at the time of his purchase. The Queen remarked that the French
maxim, 'As silly as a donkey', should be changed.

At the end of April the Queen journeyed on to Darmstadt, where
other guests of Grand Duke Louis of Hesse and the Rhine were Emperor
William, Empress Augusta Victoria and the Grand Duke of Baden.
Occupations were military, luncheons large, and conversation centred
around the resignation of Bismarck.

Darmstadt, April 25.—After tea, Louis and Liko went to the station
to meet William, who arrived at seven. He came up to see me at once,
and was very kind and friendly. There was a large dinner in uniform,
downstairs in the dining-room. Sat between Louis and William. The
latter was very cheerful and gay.

April 26.—At a quarter to eleven we started for a review of the
troops of the Darmstadt garrison. At the door I met Dona, whom I had
not seen since she was Empress, and who had just arrived from Berlin.
Drove with her in a phaeton with four horses. We were received with
royal honours. The troops were formed up in two lines; General
Bülow, who commands the Hessian Division, was in supreme command.
After driving along the ranks our carriage halted at the saluting point,
and the troops marched past. At the conclusion of the parade we
returned to the Neues Palais. The streets were crowded, and the people
were very excited, shouting, "Lebe hoch!" Had a large luncheon in
the dining-room, to which Fritz and Louis of Baden and the Land-
gravine of Hesse came.

I had a good deal of conversation with William and Fritz of Baden,
between whom I sat. The former spoke of Prince Bismarck and his
resignation. He said it would have been impossible to go on with him,
and that his violence in language and gesture had become such, that he
had to put a stop to it. He was sorry to say that Bismarck was intriguing
with Russia behind his back, telling the Emperor that William was
entirely changing his policy. Fritz of Baden spoke in still stronger
terms about Bismarck's conduct.

Journey Forty-four
1891

Naval Occasion at Portsmouth

BEFORE Queen Victoria left Windsor by special South-Western train for Portsmouth on the morning of 26th February, a telegram arrived from the German Emperor in Berlin:

May it please your Majesty to accept my warmest wishes for the success of the ceremony your Majesty is in the act of performing. May the two fine new ships built by British hands prove a powerful addition to the Royal Navy, and may they always in their future career uphold the honour of the British Navy . . .

As she drove to the station, people in the streets were whistling the Great MacDermott's song:

We don't want to fight, but, by Jingo, if we do,
We've got the ships, we've got the men, we've
    got the money too . . .

The Queen was going to christen and float the *Royal Sovereign*, the largest ironclad in her Fleet and, on completion, to be the heaviest ship in the world, and to christen and launch the *Royal Arthur*, an armour-protected cruiser of new design.

The *Royal Sovereign* was 380 feet in length and of 14150 tons displacement. Four great guns, weighing 67 tons apiece, were perched high on barbette towers, and for secondary armament she had ten rapid-firing guns, each weighing five tons. Her armour was eighteen inches thick and her decks of three inch steel. Of 13,000 horse power, she was capable of travelling from Plymouth to New York and back without replenishing her bunkers.

The *Royal Arthur* was 360 feet long, with a displacement of 7350 tons, and intended for commerce protection anywhere in the world.

Windsor Castle, February 26.—At ten minutes to eleven left with Beatrice, Liko, the Duchess of Roxburghe, Ethel C(adogan), Sir H.

Ponsonby, General Gardiner, Sir H. Ewart, Sir J. Cowell, and Colonel
Clerk. The fog continued very thick till close to Portsmouth. Our
train went into the dockyard, and here dear Arthur,[1] Sir E. Commerell,[2]
etc., met us, and we three got into an open landau and four, the suite
following. Proceeded to the place where the *Royal Arthur* was to be
launched. The whole way was lined with troops and marines, the whole
garrison, 4,000 men, being out. I walked up two longish flights of
steps to a platform immediately in front of the enormous vessel's stern.
Louischen[3] with her three children, Affie,[4] the Lords of the Admiralty,
and the German Admiral von der Goltz, whom William had sent over
on purpose, in a German man-of-war, the *Oldenburg*, were there.
Lord George Hamilton[5] presented the Admiral. Then began the short
service, then I pressed an electric button which broke a bottle of wine,
while I said, "Success to the *Royal Arthur*", and she glided down splendidly, amongst the booming of guns, of bands, playing *God Save the
Queen* and *Rule Britannia*. It was a very fine and moving sight. The
sun shone out brightly and the sea was very blue. The ship turned and
went a little way across the harbour. The space where she had been was
filled up by innumerable boats. Before leaving, Mr White[6] (Director
of Naval Constructions) and Mr Deadman, the Chief Constructor of
the *Royal Arthur*, were presented.

We re-entered our carriages and drove to another platform to
christen the *Royal Sovereign*, but as she was still bigger there was no
launching, otherwise the ceremony and religious service were the same.
We then drove to Admiralty House, where I had been before on different occasions, and where the Admiral, Lady, and Miss Commerell
received us. We had luncheon, during which the Admiral's string band
played, and afterwards went into the ballroom, where I received the
Mayor, the German officers, the Board of Admiralty, and the colonels
of the regiments.

The last time I lunched at Admiralty House was in '60, and once
before when I christened the *Marlborough*, which was rather an unfortunate occasion, as she stuck, would not slide down, and almost
heeled over!

In 1833, Mama and I went over from Norris Castle and visited the
Queen of Portugal, who was only fourteen, and her stepmother the
Duchess of Braganza. They were returning to Portugal to take pos-
session of the kingdom, after the war. I remember it all so well.

[1] The Duke of Connaught then held the Portsmouth Command.
[2] Admiral of the Fleet; C.-in-C. at Portsmouth, 1888–91.
[3] Duchess of Connaught.
[4] Duke of Edinburgh.
[5] First Lord of the Admiralty.
[6] Afterwards Sir William White.

At 5.35 p.m. on Whit Thursday, 21st May 1891, Queen Victoria arrived at Derby to lay the foundation stone of a new hospital, to be known, by her desire, as the Royal Derbyshire Infirmary. It was the first State visit that she had paid to Derby, but she had stayed there in 1832 and 1843 on her visits to Chatsworth and on several occasions she, her husband and children had spent the night at the Midland Hotel when en route from Windsor to Balmoral.

The decorations were described as 'making the festive streets avenues of triumph'. Shops were closed at noon and soon afterwards the processional route was closed to vehicular traffic. The Sherwood Foresters took up their positions. The crowd was so great that its number was left unassessed.

The Queen, escorted by a squadron of the 6th Dragoons, was greeted by the peel of church bells, the competition of numerous bands and the singing of 10,000 children. In front of the Town Hall she received the address of the Corporation, to which was added a superb gold casket.

At the infirmary grounds the Lord Bishop of Southwell said two prayers, the Queen did her duty at the foundation stone and accepted the beautifully worked trowel. Then, with Princess Beatrice and Prince Henry, she returned to the station and continued her journey to Scotland. The train was, fittingly, drawn by 'The Beatrice', an express passenger locomotive built at the Derby works.

Journeys Forty-five and Forty-six
1893 and 1894

Villas in Florence

IN the spring of these years the Queen spent four week holidays at Florence. In 1893 she travelled via Cherbourg, Aix-les-Bains, Mont Cenis and Turin; in 1894 the route was changed to Port Victoria (Queenborough), Flushing, Brussels, Luxembourg, Basle and the St. Gothard tunnel, which had been opened in 1882. Her bed, couch, arm-chair and green topped desk left Windsor in advance.

The Queen was accompanied by a caravan of eighty persons. When her Private Secretary pointed out that such a large entourage strained sleeping accommodation to the limit, she went patiently through the list and assured him that she could not do without a single soul of them. As a result Sir Henry found that he had been allocated a disused drawing-room. On opening his eyes in the morning he saw Pauline Borghesi, near naked, on the ceiling.

The Italians had by now come to accept Highlanders as part of the Victorian scene. It was the Indian servants and Jacquot who aroused their interest. The Indians, they were convinced, were all royalties, which was partly understandable since the Munshi behaved as if he was. But that a Queen and Empress should be towed about by a small donkey, with whom she was obviously on most friendly terms, was beyond their comprehension.

In 1893 the Queen stayed at the Villa Palmieri, as she had done on her previous visit. In 1894 her destination was the Villa Fabbricotti. From the viewpoints of historical connections and interior decoration, the former was the more interesting. The latter was selected because of the superb views which it commanded.

In 1348 the Villa Palmieri was described as 'a rich and beautiful palace' and was then called Tre Visi. Boccaccio chose it as the scene for romance, and he describes his ten careless young people strolling casually there on the third morning of story-telling, after they had fled from the plague

Villa Fabricotti

rife in Florence. Manni, in his *Illustrazioni* to the *Decameron*, identified the villa. In 1454 it was bought by Matteo di Marco Palmieri. A member of a distinguished Florentine family, he was an author, orator, and classical scholar. During the eighteenth century the Palmieri family died out and in 1764 George Nassau, third Earl Cowper, became the master of the villa. He was twenty-six, eccentric, and on the Grand Tour. He fell in love with Florence and thereafter refused to leave it. He was probably the original of the term, *Inglesi Matti*.

Florence was then the mecca of London's social set and their galas and antics, romances and scandals made the task of the gossip writer easy – 'Among those present were the Earl and Countess of Northampton, the Duchess of Grafton, Lady Orford, Mr Lyttleton, Lady Mary Coke . . .' The British Minister, Sir Horace Mann, complained of 'the *crouds* of English who will be his ruin, as they all expect him to feast them'. Royalty also graced the scene. On Lord Cowper's invitation list were the Dukes of Gloucester and Cumberland, with their morganatic wives, Maria and Anne, the gay bachelor Duke of York, and Prince Charles Edward, – now but an alcoholic cartoon of 'Bonnie Prince Charlie' – with his sad wife, the Countess of Albany. Thus a century later Queen Victoria walked among the ghosts of the Stewarts and the Hanovers. One can only hope that, in life, they were not asked to the same parties.

Florence, 1894

Lord Cowper died at Florence in 1789 and his widow, Anne Gore, in 1826. The Villa Palmieri then passed to a rich Englishwoman, Miss Farhill, and in 1860 was purchased by the Earl of Crawford and Balcarres.

In contrast the Villa Fabbricotti, on the Collina Montughi, had been built in 1864. A woman reporter wrote of it:

> In having the Villa Fabbricotti for her abode in Florence, the Queen has scarcely been as fortunate as when she was last in the City of Flowers. Villa Fabbricotti is a modern structure, though standing on the site of an antique villa, and has been furnished and planned with but scant taste. Everything in the house is new, and somewhat loud in tone, and the eye has nothing to repose upon with comfort. But outside all is beauty . . .

Vacations for the Queen did not mean a holiday from work. Each morning she attended to State papers and it was usually not until noon that she was free to drive with Jacquot to some garden which she had been invited to visit. There was no saying when the Queen's Messengers would come and how much homework they would bring. On one occasion a Messenger arrived after the Queen and her staff had retired for the night. No lights showed. Not wishing to spend the night in the garden and fearful of raising a commotion which would disturb the royal sleepers, he crept round the villa and selected a window behind which he hoped slept a servant. He tapped gently. His luck was out. A few minutes later he was surrounded by a posse of halfclad footmen. He had chosen the window of Queen Victoria's bedroom.

The Queen filled every afternoon with an engagement. There was a carriage drive with the King and Queen of Italy. There was a Battle of Flowers in the Corso in honour of Princess Beatrice's birthday. With her artist daughter, Louise, as guide, she toured the picture galleries in the Palaces of Uffizi and Pitti. She saw the churches of Santa Maria Novella, Santissima Annunziata, and Santa Croce. Lord Ronald Gower met her at San Marco:

> The Queen arrived at five o'clock; the visit lasted one hour. She was wheeled in her chair through the church and the cloisters, but could not, unluckily, inspect the cells on the first floor; but the Queen saw what is most worth seeing in San Marco, namely, 'The Last Supper', by Ghirlandaio, and Fra Angelico's great 'Crucifixion'–also Sogliani's great fresco, the so-called 'Providenza', before which the Queen remained a long time.

On Good Friday she drove to San Felice to watch the procession of 'Gesù Morto'. The trees and the windows were decorated with coloured lamps as the procession wound through the village. At its head was the Cross of Penitence, next a group of girls, then friars, in sackcloth, carrying the image of Christ, and last the married women and the crowned likeness of the Virgin Mary, draped in black.

The Queen made trips along the Siena line, travelling as far as Poggibonsi. Then she would take her sketchbook with her, storing memories of Certaldo and Maiano. In 1893 it had been planned that she would return via Venice, staying at the Palazzo Rezzonico, the house where Browning

A Baldwin Compound Locomotive photographed by Princess Beatrice in Italy

died. But now in her mid-seventies, mobility was her problem, and the idea did not materialise. In 1894 she travelled home via Coburg, as we shall see.

Victoria was very much liked in Florence. She mingled remoteness with the common touch. When she was nice, she was very, very nice, and the happy smile which lit her face when she stepped from the train on arrival was noted and appreciated. At the end of her holidays she received the Sindaco and the Giunta Municipale and thanked them sweetly for all the attentions which she had received.

April 26, 1893.—Our last morning here. I am very sorry. Breakfast out. The heat intense. We are just going. I am very grateful for this stay, and hope much to come here again.

She took home with her some palm trees, and planted them in the garden at Frogmore.

Journey Forty-seven
1894

To Coburg for a Wedding

QUEEN VICTORIA had her own set of rules governing love, marriage and sex. No one ever really understood them. They were based on the frailest of foundations. An only child, brought up in a sheltered schoolroom, she had not known her father. She parted from her mother's control at the age of eighteen, and in any event would have regarded as suspect any information coming from that quarter. As Queen, she had made the early mistake of confusing a tumour on the liver of Lady Flora Hastings with an advanced state of pregnancy. She had aroused the ire of the Cambridges by making accusations against her cousin George. Marriage to an academic German, with no desire to philander with women, did not greatly increase her horizon—except in the field of child-birth, in which she became so experienced that at length she was advising the doctors and midwives of the next step to be taken.

Without the guiding hand of Albert her rules became even more unpredictable. On points on which she was supposed to be inflexible, she would suddenly adopt an opposite view. She was averse to the remarriage of widows, but was all smiles when her friend, the Duchess of Manchester, became the Duchess of Devonshire. It began to dawn on her advisers that she had two sets of rules, one applying when her own convenience was not involved, and the other when it was. The marriage of Princess Beatrice was an example.

She was a great planner of marriages, on occasion picking brides and grooms for her children and grandchildren soon after they were born. To some extent her interest waned with the marriage ceremony and she was not addicted to drooling into prams. To immortalise Albert by spreading his seed around the courts of Europe was an obvious aim. The marital bed was her accepted cure for young men who showed signs of friskiness, and she was convinced that the problems of young people who raised points about compatability, would be solved once the bedroom door was closed behind them. The resultant happenings would, she considered, bind them irrevocably together. Suspicious as she always was, it was fortunate indeed that her lack of experience and communication downwards saved her from discovering certain *affaires* which went on not far from her nose.

In conflict with her eldest daughter, she not only approved of marriages between cousins and between grandchildren, but encouraged them. She told the Empress Frederick that 'the same blood only adds to the strength' and was a much preferable course to allowing Princes to wander around Europe selecting for themselves some unhealthy Princess who might be suffering from goodness knew what. She seemed to leave out of her reckoning the mental illness of George III, the porphyria which plagued both him and his son, Edward, Duke of Kent, and that she herself was a carrier of haemophilia.

Through the night of 16th–17th April 1894 she travelled from Florence to Coburg to attend a wedding which was soon to prove the most disastrous of those to which she had given her backing. Five years later, when the union disintegrated, she declared that she would never arrange another marriage. The decision was somewhat late.

The bridegroom was Grand Duke Ernest Louis of Hesse and the Rhine, aged twenty-five, and the only surviving son of Princess Alice. The bride was seventeen year old Princess Victoria Melita of Saxe-Coburg and Gotha, daughter of Prince Alfred.

'Young Ernie', as his grandmother called him, had succeeded to the Grand Dukedom on the death of his father in 1892. He was handsome, gay and artistic. He was fond of the theatre, floral decoration and china. He was a heart-flutter for the Hessian girls and he fitted exactly into the old world way of life that still reigned in Darmstadt. He was in need of an understanding woman who would give a lead among the many organisations, covering the fields of welfare, housing, hospitals, schools and mental health, which had been originated by his adored mother.

Victoria Melita was known as 'Ducky'. She was tall, dark and farouche and carried herself like an empress. She was a superb horsewoman and at an age when equine matters dominated her days. She was half Russian. Her domineering mother, Duchess Marie, acclaimed the superiority of St. Petersburg, hated having to give precedence to the Princess of Wales and stamped her feet in temper at the omnipotence and 'oneness' of Queen Victoria. The Duchess was therefore delighted when, on the death of Duke Ernest, the Prince Consort's brother, in 1893, her husband succeeded to the Duchy of Saxe-Coburg and Gotha. Despite the obvious handicaps, everybody seemed to think that 'Ducky' would make an excellent wife for 'Ernie'.

As her train neared Coburg, memories of the long ago crowded the Queen's mind. It was all but fifty years since she had first seen her husband's birth-place. Then he had been sitting beside her in the carriage, excitedly pointing out familiar landmarks as they came into view. Again he was beside her, as if there had been no years between then and now.

Coburg, April 17.—As we approached Coburg, the weather, which had been very showery, cleared, and many conflicting feelings filled my heart. When the dear old Festung came in sight, I could but think of my beloved Albert's joy when we approached Coburg the first time, and he pointed out everything.

At length we reached the station, stopping a little way beyond to avoid steps. Affie, Marie, the two eldest girls,[1] and young Alfred[2] were there, besides their suite, all the gentlemen in uniform, as Liko and mine were. A squadron of my Prussian regiment of Dragoons was drawn up, William having specially sent them here. I got into Affie's carriage, driving with him, Marie, and young Alfred straight to the Schloss Ehrenburg, through the very gaily decorated streets and houses, and passed under two triumphal arches, which were beautifully designed. On the top of one of them stood young ladies in white, throwing down flowers. The Bürgermeister stood with the Municipality and made a pretty speech of welcome. Stopped outside Affie's "Palais", where he got out and marched past at the head of his battalion, then my Dragoons marched past.

We afterwards drove on to the Schloss under the archway, but I got out, where there were no steps, into a sort of hall Affie had had arranged, as well as a lift, which brought me into one of the saloons, where the endless numbers of Princes and Princesses were assembled, the Cesarewitch, Ernie of Hesse, the Grand Duke Vladimir,[3] Arthur,[4] Serge,[5] Paul,[6] Henry of Prussia,[7] Ferdinand of Roumania, etc. After embracing the Princesses and talking to the Princes, Affie and Marie led me, through the adjoining rooms, to mine. Poor Alexandrine[8] was in my room, in deep mourning, so kind and loving, but very much upset at seeing me again for the first time. However, she soon recovered. Marie and Beatrice soon came in and we had tea together, after which Alexandrine left.

My sitting-room opens into my bedroom, and near by I have a little dressing-room. We dined in the Thronsaal, a very pretty room

[1] Marie, Princess Ferdinand of Roumania, afterwards Queen Marie of Roumania; Alexandra, married, 1896, Prince Ernest of Hohenlohe-Langenburg.
[2] Only son of the Duke of Edinburgh and Saxe-Coburg and Gotha.
[3] Representing the Emperor of Russia.
[4] Duke of Connaught.
[5] Grand Duke Sergius of Russia.
[6] Grand Duke Paul of Russia.
[7] Brother of the German Emperor.
[8] Widow of Duke Ernest of Coburg.

Family group on the occasion of the engagement of Princess Alix to the Cesarevitch. Left to right, front row: *Princess Beatrice of Coburg, Princess Feodora of Saxe-Meiningen.* Second row: *The Emperor of Germany, Queen Victoria, Empress Frederick.* Third row: *Prince Alfred of Coburg, the Cesarevitch, Princess Alix of Hesse, Princess Louis of Battenberg, Princess Henry of Prussia, Grand Duchess Vladimir, Duchess of Coburg.* Fourth row: *Prince of Wales, Princess Henry of Battenberg, Princess Philip of Coburg, Princess Ferdinand of Roumania, Princess Marie Louise, Duchess of Connaught.* Fifth row: *Prince Louis of Battenberg, Prince Henry of Battenberg, Grand Duke Sergius, Prince Ferdinand of Roumania, Grand Duke Vladimir, Duke of Connaught.* Back row: *Grand Duke Paul of Russia, Prince Philip of Coburg, Count Mensdorff, Princess Alexander of Saxe-Coburg, Grand Duchess Sergius, Duke Alfred of Coburg*

(red and white), the party being Affie, Serge, Ella,[9] Beatrice, Liko,
Victoria and Ludwig B.,[10] the Philip Coburgs, and good old Arthur
Mensdorff, who is seventy-seven. Bertie arrived late and came to see me.
The enormous number of Royalties and suites are lodged in the Schloss,
in Affie's house and elsewhere.

It was, in fact, one of the largest royal collections of the nineteenth
century. It covered four generations, for a great-grandchild of the Queen
was present. The multitude had to be divided into two sittings for dinner,
but managed to squeeze close enough together to be photographed by
one camera.

The wedding took place on the 19th, the civil marriage taking place
privately in the Queen's apartments and the religious service following
in the chapel of the Schloss. The Empress Frederick noted that tears
rolled down the cheeks of her mother who, 'looked so nice in her white
cap and veil and diamonds'.

When, ten years earlier, the Queen had travelled to Germany to attend
the wedding of Princess Victoria of Hesse and Prince Louis of Battenberg,
the spotlight had been switched from the bride to another woman – in
that case Madame de Kolémine. Strangely enough, at the Coburg wedding
the same thing happened. This time it was the bridegroom's youngest
sister, 'Alicky', who was bathed in the bright light. Everybody knew
that 'Alicky' was in love with Cesarevitch Nicholas and he with her, and
he was an unexpected guest at the wedding. Would the Princess now
overcome her aversion to the necessary change of religion and accept a
future as Empress of Russia?

'Alicky' was twenty-two. Her mother had died when she was only
six, and thereafter she had been deified by her English nurse and pampered
by Queen Victoria. Her grandmother had plans for her to become the
wife of Prince Albert Victor, eldest son of the Prince of Wales, thus
putting her in line for British Queenship. But the dilatory young cavalry
officer – 'a gleaming goldfish in a crystal bowl' – did not fit in with the
Princess's idea of a life partner and firmly she turned him down. To reject
such prospects gave her the reputation of being a self-determined and
strong character. It may well have given her a false idea of her own
importance.

She was moody and introspective, serious-minded and shy. Often she
would leave her brother's gay parties and seek refuge in her room, where
she would lose herself in some book on religion or the occult. A Hessian
divine gave her religious instruction, and delved deep into the complications of this world and the next, with the result that she groped

[9] Grand Duchess Sergius of Russia.
[10] Prince and Princess Louis of Battenberg.

sightlessly in the mists dividing earth and heaven. David Strauss had done the same for her mother. The result was that the Princess was lacking in that essential of the regal role, being able to 'cerclé' among people of all walks of life, to make people think that she liked them and that they were important, and to hold her own in Court circles.

On the health side, her mother had died at thirty-eight and her father at fifty-five, and she was likely to be a carrier of haemophilia. She suffered from sciatica and had had a nervous breakdown after her father's death. She was described by a German relative as 'a stupid little English girl'.

Yet this was the candidate which the Queen supported to share the Throne of Russia with the weak and evasive Cesarevitch Nicholas, this the Princess who was supposed to take the lead among the intriguers, the scandalmongers and die-hards of the Court at St. Petersburg, this the frail body that was to survive the cold and darkness of the Russian winters. Nobody seemed to remember the tragedy of the Empress Marie, also a Princess of Hesse, whose health and spirit had been crushed in that same land.

Throughout the wedding festivities Nicholas, her sisters and general band of relations did their best to persuade 'Alicky' to agree to a change in her religion, as the Grand Duchess Ella had already done so. The Queen weighed in with her own theory that really there was little difference between the Orthodox and Lutheranism. Signs of weakening began to show. May be diplomacy was at work. May be the thought of returning to Darmstadt to play second fiddle to a farouche tomboy of a Grand Duchess, five years younger than herself, was proving more powerful than the preachings of the Hessian divine. On the morning of 20th April 'Alicky' surrendered.

April 20.–Breakfasted alone with Beatrice. Soon after Ella came in, much agitated, to say that Alicky and Nicky were engaged, and begging they might come in. I was quite thunderstruck, as, though I knew Nicky much wished it, I thought Alicky was not sure of her mind. Saw them both. Alicky had tears in her eyes, but looked very bright, and I kissed them both. Nicky said "She is much too good for me". I told him he must make the religious difficulties as easy as he could for her, which he promised to do. People generally seemed pleased at the engagement, which has the drawback that Russia is so far away, the position a difficult one, as well as the question of religion. But, as her brother is married now, and they are really attached to one another, it is perhaps better so.

April 21.–Alicky and Nicky breakfasted with me and were very dear. He is so natural, simple, and kind. Gave them each a small souvenir. Went over to Affie's Palace, where, in the garden, the whole of our large family party were photographed by English, as well as German,

The Festung

photographers. Many groups were taken, and some of me with Vicky and my three sons and William. Then drove up to the Festung with Vicky and Victoria B. I was so glad to see it again. It was a little hazy for the extensive distant view. Vicky, Beatrice, Serge, Ella, Philip and Louise, Victoria B., and Arthur Mensdorff lunched with me, and William came to take leave. I gave him the Colonelcy-in-Chief of the 1st Royals,[11] which seemed to please him exceedingly.

[11] On 24th April Emperor William wrote to Queen Victoria: 'Deeply and sincerely do I thank you for the great honour which you conferred upon me by naming me Hon. Colonel of the Royals. I am moved, deeply moved, at the idea that I can now too wear beside the Naval uniform the traditional British "Redcoat".'

Journey Forty-eight
1894

Manchester-on-Sea

> Near Oxford Road the dry dock is, to caulk and to
> careen, Sir;
> Our Chief West India Dock is where the pond was at
> Ardwick Green, Sir;
> That is to say, they *might* have been there, had these
> plans been done, Sir,
> And vessels might have anchored there of full five
> hundred tons, Sir.

So ran a song from the Manchester pantomime of 1825. It was a lament that the city had no outlet to the open sea, the idea of a canal having been first mooted at the beginning of the eighteenth century. But nothing had been done about it, and Manchester remained the great workshop of Lancashire, and Liverpool 'the residence of the non-producers who live upon its industry'.

In 1877 a plan was put forward for the construction of a tidal canal right up to Manchester. Five years later this idea was shelved in favour of a canalised channel. There then began one of the most mammoth struggles in the history of Private Bill legislation. Opposition came from Liverpool, the canal companies and the railways. Altogether 175,000 questions were asked, and answered. The Bill received the Royal Assent in 1885 and in 1887 the necessary capital was subscribed. The first turf was cut in November of Golden Jubilee year.

The Manchester Ship Canal was opened by Queen Victoria on 21st May 1894. Thirty-seven years had passed since she had last visited the city. She arrived at London Road station at half-past four. Ahead of her lay eight miles of streets gay with Venetian masts, from which hung festoons of decorations. Triumphal arches guarded the approaches to Albert Square and the grime of years had been cleaned from the stone of Albert himself. Fire brigades made arches of their ladders and took up airy points of observation. But the Town Hall remained bare of

The Queen's yacht passing up the canal

decoration, as the Queen had expressed the wish to be able to enjoy 'the architectural beauties of the edifice'.

On the dais the Lord Mayor presented the Queen with an address and the Lady Mayoress gave her a bouquet. Addresses were also exchanged with Owen's College.

Trafford Wharf was reached at half-past five and the royal standard went up over the pavilion. The royal party boarded the steam yacht *Enchantress* and the swing bridge turned aside. The Queen then knighted the Lord Mayor of Manchester[1] and the Mayor of Salford[2] and was introduced to those who had played a leading part in the construction of the canal.

The central act of the ceremony came at Mode Wheel. *Enchantress* was brought to and the Queen 'put into electrical communication with the hydraulic machinery'. As the huge gates swung back, admitting the white yacht *Norseman* to the higher level, trumpets blared and a salvo was fired by guns on the race-course. Slowly *Enchantress* returned to the splendid pavilion by the quay, the Salford Corporation presented an address, and the Queen made her way to the Exchange station. There a special train was waiting to carry her, Prince and Princess Henry of Battenberg and their children, and the Princess of Leiningen, through the night to Balmoral.

It was estimated that a million people saw the Queen on her last visit to Manchester.

[1] Alderman Anthony Marshall.
[2] Alderman W. H. Bailey.

Journey Forty-nine
1895

Frederick's House

THE Empress Frederick was very lonely after the death of her husband. She was only forty-seven and had been married to him for thirty years. They had been through many troubles together and were very close.

During the mourning period Emperor William indulged in a round of ceremonies and tours and showed an inhumanity which annoyed both his mother and his grandmother. The Empress was convinced that Bismarck desired her to leave Germany. This she was determined not to do. Wishing to be free of the intrigues, hostility and noise of Berlin, she decided to make a home for herself and her daughters somewhere in the country where the climate was mild. In 1889 she bought the Villa Reiss in the Taunus forest, by Kronberg. The small estate had previously belonged to a Manchester business man who had given his name to the house. Woods and hills backed it and, before, the view extended over a wide stretch of countryside. The Empress purchased surrounding land and became the owner of 250 acres. She mapped out her park round the cedars, centuries old chestnuts, Wellingtonias and rare conifers.

The new house was designed by the well-known architect, Herr Ernst Ihne, under the personal supervision of the Empress. She instructed him: '*Rien ne doit altérer le regard, mais tout le retenir.*' Another piece of advice was that he should go to England and examine certain stately structures. The result was that, when the building was completed in 1893, there was criticism that the Empress's home was more of an English country house than a German *schloss*. As her every action since her arrival in Germany had been subject to criticism, she took little account of it.

The castle showed mixed influence. Tudor predominated in the exterior, and in the reception rooms and salons within Italian Renaissance varied with the eighteenth century. The terrace, some of the ceilings and the main staircase were after Haddon Hall. On the suggestion of Princess Victoria, the new home was called Friedrichshof, for her mother looked

The Queen on the castle terrace at Friedrichshof

upon it as a memorial to the Emperor and *Frederici Memoriae* was carved above the main entrance.

The contents of the castle soon rivalled that of a museum. The Empress's deep interest in history, art, archaeology and political economy showed in her fine library. Three hundred portfolios of photographs went back to the time when photography began. Her mother's letters, covering a third of a century, were mounted and bound in volumes of half leather. Other portfolios held her sketches and paintings, for she was a talented artist. Carefully displayed were her collection of autographs and medallions. She had ever been a collector of curios and antiques, which were uncharitably referred to by her daughters as 'dirty, ugly, horrid old rubbish', but now they came into their own at Friedrichshof. It was the harvest of a lifetime.

The Empress moved in early in 1894. The village people turned out to welcome her, there was a triumphal arch and the bells were ringing. It was some consolation for the bitterness which she had endured. Before she was properly settled down, Emperor William decided to descend upon his mother, accompanied by a suite of eighteen. Ever curious, ever determined to make his presence felt, 'Willie' and his noisy troop of A.D.Cs. tramped round the new house, praising this and criticising that, with scant regard for the bruised feelings of the widow.

In April 1895 came a more welcome visitor, none other than Queen Victoria, on her way home after a holiday in the south of France. This was a great day for the little town of Kronberg, and also for the Empress, who admitted that she was 'all in a tremble and flutter'. Not only was she to have a verdict on her dream house, but this was to be the first time, except for the occasion at Charlottenburg in 1888, that the Queen had been under her roof since her marriage.

The Queen, supported by Indian and Highland attendants, drove round the grounds in a donkey carriage, and from that position planted a memorial tree. She inspected the lovely rose garden and the stables. There was, and had to be, something of Balmoral and Osborne about the place. The Queen liked Friedrichshof. She said that she preferred it to Darmstadt and would like to stay there when next in Germany. In the event there was no return, as in 1896 the Queen saw ground in Emperor William's behaviour for grandmotherly reproof and for three years she did not see him, or give him the chance to see her.

Empress Frederick died from cancer at Friedrichshof in August 1901. It was a still afternoon and, as she died, a butterfly flew out of her open window into the park and on towards her rose garden.

Opposite: *Queen Victoria at Osborne with Prince Alexander, Princess Victoria Eugenie (Ena), Prince Leopold and Prince Maurice of Battenberg*

Milestone 1896 · *The End of a Battenberg*

"Prince Henry wanted something to play with,
Something he'd ne'er seen before,
So they gave him a sword and a helmet,
To play on West Africa's shore.'

So ran a popular jingle.

To 'Liko', Prince Henry of Battenberg, life was proving too tame. More and more did the ageing Queen rely on the services of his wife. He dwelt upon the careers of his father and his brothers, and craved for action. At the end of 1895 he volunteered for service in the Ashanti campaign. Against the wishes of his mother-in-law, he went. He contracted fever on the march to Kumasi and died at sea on the journey home.

Osborne, January 22 1896. – A terrible blow has fallen on us all, especially on my poor darling Beatrice. Our dearly loved Liko has been taken from us! Can I write it? What will become of my poor child? All she said in a trembling voice, apparently quite stunned, was, "The life is gone out of me".

Journey Fifty
1897

Jubilation in Sheffield

THE people of Sheffield wrote the prologue to the Diamond Jubilee
story. They had a brand new Town Hall and the Queen had consented to open it. She arrived at five o'clock on the afternoon of
21st May. It was her first visit to the great industrial centre. With her
were two of her children, Princess Christian and the Duke of Connaught,
and two Battenberg grandchildren. She was met at the station by a
distinguished reception committee which included the Mayor and
Mayoress, the Archbishop of York, the Earl of Scarborough as Lord
Lieutenant, and four Members of Parliament.

The Mayor was none other than Henry, 15th Duke of Norfolk, whose
seat was Norfolk Park. The Mayoress was his sister, Lady Mary Howard,
the Duchess having died in 1887. The Duke, who was also Postmaster
General, wore the mayoral robes over his Earl Marshal's uniform. In
the role of Mayor the Duke had varied experience. He was the last to
hold the title in Sheffield, the title of Lord Mayor being conferred on his
successors. He was the first Mayor of Westminster in 1900 and in 1902–
03 he was Mayor of Arundel.

The Chief Constable, with mounted police and a troop of the 17th
Lancers, headed a procession of nine carriages. Then, with an escort of
Life Guards before and behind, came the royal carriage, in semi-state
trappings and drawn by four bays.

That afternoon the Queen received one of the most rousing receptions
of all her reign. Jubilee spirit was one reason for the vast crowds, but
there were others. The great majority of those who lined the streets and
waved from the stands and windows had been born since her accession.
Few indeed could recall her Coronation. Only the fortunate few could
afford the money, and the time, to travel to London to see her on her rare
appearances. She was 'the Great Unseen', in the nature of a minion of
God, and seemingly eternal. Suddenly she popped up in Sheffield for a
few hours. A slice of gilt and gingerbread was mightly welcome.

At the Town Hall the Queen, remaining in her carriage, listened to the

The royal carriage passing from the station to the town hall

address of the Recorder, afterwards receiving from him an ornate and spendid golden casket in which the document of the address had been placed. After other addresses had been read, and answered, the Queen placed a gold key in a detached lock, connected electrically with the main gates. As she inserted it, the gates swung back and Sheffield's Town Hall was open.

Next she went to Norfolk Park, where fifty thousand children were having a jamboree at the invitation of the Duke. Their singing delighted the Queen and was somewhat in contrast with her next assignment. At the Cyclops steel and iron works of Messrs Cammell she watched the rolling of an armour-plate for the new battleship *Ocean*. Her carriage was drawn up in a shed near to the furnace and a glass screen was necessary to shield her from the heat.

At half-past seven her train pulled out of Sheffield on the long haul to Ballater via Carlisle. Three days later came her seventy-eighth birthday.

Milestone
1897

Diamond Jubilee

Buckingham Palace, June 22. – A never-to-be-forgotten day. No one ever, I believe, has met with such an ovation as was given to me, passing through those six miles of streets . . .

The night had been very hot, and I was rather restless. There was such a noise going on the whole time, but it did not keep me from getting some sleep . . . The head of the procession, including the Colonial troops, had unfortunately, already passed the Palace before I got to breakfast, but there were still a great many, chiefly British, passing. I watched them for a little while. At a quarter-past eleven, the others being seated in their carriages long before, and having preceded me a short distance, I started from the State entrance in an open State landau, drawn by eight creams, dear Alix, looking very pretty in lilac, and Lenchen sitting opposite me. I felt a good deal agitated, and had been so all these days, for fear anything might be forgotten or go wrong. Bertie and George C. rode one on each side of the carriage, Arthur (who had charge of the whole military arrangements) a little in the rear. My escort was formed from the 2nd Life Guards and officers of the native Indian regiments, these latter riding immediately in front of my carriage. Guard of Honour of Blue-jackets, the Guards, and the 2nd West Surrey Regiment (Queen's) were mounted in the Quadrangle and outside the Palace.

Before leaving I touched an electric button, by which I started a message which was telegraphed throughout the whole Empire. It was the following: "From my heart I thank my beloved people, May God bless them!" At this time the sun burst out.

THE ROYAL FAMILY, 1897

Back row, left to right: *Alexander Duff, Duke of Fife, Prince Christian of Schleswig-Holstein, Helena, Princess of Schleswig-Holstein, Louise, Duchess of Connaught, Arthur, Duke of Connaught, Victoria, Princess of Wales, Mary, Duchess of York, George, Duke of York, Victoria, Empress of Germany, John Campbell, Marquis of Lorne, Louise, Marchioness of Lorne, Albert, Prince of Wales, Maud, Princess of Denmark, Charles, Prince of Denmark, Marie, Duchess of Coburg-Gotha, Alfred, Duke of Coburg-Gotha, Helen, Duchess of Albany, Christian Victor, Prince of Schleswig-Holstein;* front groups, left: *Lady Maud Duff, Louise, Duchess of Fife, Lady Alexandra Duff, Margaret, Princess of Connaught, Patricia, Princess of Connaught;* centre: *Arthur, Prince of Connaught, Alexandra, Princess of Wales, Edward Albert of York, Queen Victoria;* right: *Leopold, Prince of Battenberg, Alexander Albert, Prince of Battenberg, Beatrice, Princess of Battenberg, Maurice, Prince of Battenberg, Victoria Eugenie, Princess of Battenberg, Charles, Duke of Albany, Alice, Princess of Albany, Helena Victoria, Princess of Schleswig-Holstein*

Journeys Fifty-one–Fifty-seven
1891–1899

The South of France

IN her last ten years Queen Victoria visited the south of France seven times. In 1891 she stayed at the Grand Hotel at Grasse; in 1892 at the Hotel Costebelle, Hyères; in 1895 and 1896 at the Grand Hotel de Cimiez, Nice; and in 1897, 1898 and 1899 at the Hotel Excelsior Regina, Cimiez. She paid 40,000 francs for six weeks at the Grand at Cimiez and 80,000 francs for two months at the Regina. The minimum stay of thirty-five days at the Grand involved an outlay of £1,500. As an indication of the value of money in those days a woman worker at the Grasse scent factory received 1 franc 25 centimes for a ten hour day, but the man from *The Times* earned £50 per week for reporting how royals relaxed on the Riviera.

Except for the outward journey in 1899, when she travelled by the steam packet *Douvres-Calais* from Folkestone to Boulogne, the Queen went in the royal yacht *Victoria and Albert* from Portsmouth to Cherbourg, spending the night in the French port and entraining early next morning. In every case she had an escort of torpedo boats. The crossing in the steam packet proved somewhat of an ordeal for the eighty year old Queen. The crowds on both sides of the Channel were immense and the directors of the British and French railways all thought that it was their duty to accompany her. She hated people to see that she was too infirm to walk down the gang plank and at Boulogne she was carried down in full view of the crowds. When travelling in the royal yacht, the gang plank was covered in and there was much less fuss. However, while such details could be controlled, the mood of the sea could not.

"Victoria and Albert", Cherbourg, March 11 1898. – Arrived here at 4.30 after a rough disagreeable crossing, which tried me a good deal, though I was not sick. We had been told that the sea would be perfectly smooth, but it began rolling soon after I went below, and in the middle of the Channel there was one lurch just as if the ship had had a blow, the port hole burst half open, the sea came in, and the chairs were sent

spinning. The maids, steward, and footmen all rushed in, in a great state, and found part of the cabin full of water. I was taken in the rolling chair across to my bedroom, where I got on to the sofa, feeling much upset. Was very thankful when we got into Cherbourg at last. We had been quite misinformed about the weather.

The royal train consisted of seven coaches, two of which were the Queen's private property. These, her drawing-room and sleeping cars, were kept at the Gare du Nord at Brussels, as they had been built and furnished in Belgium. They had special springing and no brakes, thus eliminating the grind of the shoes when the train slowed for signal or station. The day car consisted of a small compartment for the Scottish servant, who always travelled with the Queen, and the drawing-room. A short corridor led to the sleeping car which was divided into dressing-room, bedroom and a compartment for light luggage, and here the maids slept on sofas.

The walls of the drawing-room were hung with silk *capitonnée*, blue for the dado and pearl grey above, brocaded, in pale yellow, with the shamrock, rose and thistle. Four lights were let into the padded ceiling. The curtains were blue and white and a dark Indian carpet fully covered the floor. A beech wood table stood between the windows. A sofa, two armchairs and foot-stools, all in the style of Louis XVI, were covered in blue silk, with yellow fringes and tassels.

The motif in the dressing-room was Japanese, with protective bamboo hung round the walls. Dark red morocco leather covered the wash-stand, and the basin, as were all the items in the toilet service, was made of white

The Grand Hotel Costabelle, 1892

The drawing room car on the Queen's continental train

metal. There were two beds in the sleeping compartment, the larger for the Queen and the smaller for Princess Beatrice.

The speed of the royal train was limited to thirty-five miles an hour by day and twenty-five by night. It was halted between eight and nine in the morning so that the Queen could dress in comfort, and stops were made for meals. Gentlemen requiring hot water for shaving sent word ahead and a jug awaited them at a convenient station. French menus were preferred to the stew which, packed in special containers, accompanied the travellers from Windsor.

In her comings and goings the Queen was set of habit. She left Windsor in the second week in March and returned in the last week of April. Under no circumstances would she cross the Channel on a Friday. She travelled under the title of Madame la Comtesse de Balmoral, but this made no difference.

In the train, March 11 1897. – At a little before six stopped at the junction of Noisy-le-Sec on the Ceinture railway outside Paris. Here the President of the Republic, M. Félix Faure, came into my saloon, and was presented by Sir E. Monson. I received the President alone, and asked him to sit down. We had some conversation, and he began by compliments about my coming again to France, saying the pleasure it gave the people to have me in their country. Then I remarked that the present was a very anxious time, that political affairs seemed very difficult, in which he

The Queen being greeted by President Faure

agreed . . . M. Faure is a tall, good-looking man, elderly, very gentle-
manlike, and pleasing, evidently sensible and quiet.

The royal cavalcade numbered between sixty and one hundred, depend-
ing on how many Princesses and their suites accompanied their mother.
Her personal staff of servants included a first waiting-woman, with six
dressers; a French chef, backed by three cooks and numerous assistants; a
Scottish gillie; and the Indian attendants. There were also a coachman, an
outrider and a dozen grooms, whose task was to care for the donkey and
its attachment and the Queen's own carriages and horses, for she always
used her own equipage, local livery stables fulfilling further requirements.
Half an hour was allowed for loading and unloading the train. While the
indigenous contingent took masses of luggage to cope with every possible
ceremony and change in weather, the needs of the Indians appeared to be
met by the contents of two large pocket handkerchiefs.

As the years passed the Queen's liking for France increased. She welcomed the enthusiasm and spontaneity of the French people, she revelled
in the spring sunshine and never tired of sight-seeing and attending
fêtes and religious festivals. Gone now were both her condemnation of
French morals and her horror of the Catholic domain and each year she
showed childish excitement at the thought of exchanging Windsor for the
Mediterranean. On arrival she behaved more like a girl of seventeen than
a Sovereign in her seventies. At the time of the Fashoda affair, when
relations between Britain and France became most strained, the Queen
feared that she might have to put off her holiday. However Lord Salisbury
was convinced that it was more essential than ever that she should visit
France. Accordingly she went, and her reception was as always. She told
the Empress Eugénie that, if ever it came to a point of war between the
two countries, she hoped that the good God would take her first.

Although the visits of the Queen boosted the tourist trade along the
Riviera, her popularity stretched beyond that. When she arrived at Nice
the whole town turned out to greet her and it took four regiments of
infantry and a battery of artillery to control the crowds along the route
from the station to the hotel. The fishwives brought her a present of
flowers and their corpulent leader kissed the Queen soundly on each
cheek.

A military guard was mounted at the hotel, a task popular with the
soldiers as the Queen was most solicitous for their welfare. But the officers,
accustomed to *café au lait* at six in the morning, *dejeuner* at eleven and
dinner at six found it somewhat disturbing to have to adjust themselves
to the English hours of breakfast at nine-thirty, lunch at one and dinner
at a quarter to nine. The guard turned out to salute the Queen only when
she set out on her afternoon drive, and when she returned. But they had

Breakfast at nine-thirty, luncheon at one and tea at four

to be ready to receive visitors in the appropriate way and the coast was
thronged with royalties, from Hyères to Menton. The Prince of Wales
and the Duke of Cambridge were regulars and the Connaughts came when
military duties permitted. Other callers included Emperor Francis Joseph
of Austria, his daughter-in-law, Archduchess Stephanie (who, to the
annoyance of Empress Elizabeth, refused to wear mourning for her
husband who had died at Mayerling), the Dowager Empress of Russia,
King Leopold of the Belgians, young Queen Wilhelmina of Holland, the
Queen of Hanover, the Duke of Coburg, the Emperor of Brazil and the
Duchesses of York and Albany. A knowledge of the Almanach de Gotha
was therefore an essential.

One afternoon M. Paoli, the detective responsible for the safety of
the Queen, saw a guard of honour mounted outside the hotel. Not being
aware that a distinguished visitor was calling, he hurried over to find the
reason. The officer in charge informed him that an Empress was expected.
In this he was quite correct—an Empress was on her way, but it proved
to be Eugénie, the exile who had fled from the Tuileries in 1870. That the
soldiers of the Republic should turn out to salute the wife of Napoleon III
was a *faux pas* which would have rocked France, and be taken by some as a
sign that the Bonapartes were on their way back. Never was a guard
dismissed more quickly, but it was still in view when the Empress came
round the corner. She guessed what had happened.

Perhaps the people who most welcomed the coming of the Queen
were those most in need of a helping hand—street singers and musicians,
hungry children ever on the watch for a few centimes, deformed and
crippled beggars, and the homeless old. The Carusos of the boulevards,
the string strummers and the bow scrapers, mostly Italian born, quickly
learned that the Queen appreciated their talents and never let them go
unrewarded. At ten in the morning they made their stealthy way into
the hotel gardens and congregated below her balcony. *Funiculi, Funicula,*
was a favourite offering. Back would come the lace curtain, revealing a
regal smile of approbation. A distribution of coins followed.

The needy posted themselves at intervals along the route of the afternoon
drive, the necessary information apparently coming through some grape-
vine. The Queen carried on her lap a bright blue purse full of small change.
As each tragic case came in sight she made quick calculation as to his or
her financial worth, and withdrew the necessary cash. She came to know
some of them well and greeted them like old friends. Outstanding among
these was a one-legged comedian from Marseilles. In 1897 his picture
appeared in the newspapers of the world.

This old man relied for transport on a small go-cart of his own construction, which was pulled by two large dogs. He frequented the Villefranche road. His conveyance and his antics first attracted the attention of

The Queen and the beggar

the Queen in 1895 and thereafter she gave him ten francs whenever she saw him and sent him fifty francs when she left. The royal recognition and patronage gave the beggar some local importance and he was quick to take advantage. He picked up a few English phrases and referred to the Queen as 'Our Majesty'. In Diamond Jubilee year he staged his coup. Having waited for the royal carriage to pass, and received his ten francs, he set off in pursuit. Urging on his dogs, he not only succeeded in catching up with the carriage but he outpaced the trotting greys. It so happened that a newspaper artist had stationed himself on that stretch of road.

The Queen was amused but a line had to be drawn somewhere. When next she saw the go-cart it had been decorated with the inscription, 'By special appointment to Her Majesty'. Orders were given that this be erased, but the payments were continued.

Hyères, 1892

Every morning the Queen worked at her State correspondence from ten to eleven. Then she would exchange her white muslin cap for a large garden hat, put on a silk cloak and, assisted by an Indian attendant, take her seat in the donkey carriage. The hours until lunch were spent inspecting gardens or dealing with unfinished work in the shade of a tree.

As the grounds of the hotels were open to tourists, more secluded retreats were required and of these there was no shortage. Every owner of a villa was eager to have royal patronage, one taking down a piece of wall so that the donkey cart could pass through. At Grasse she had the freedom of the policies of the Villa Victoria, so named in honour of the visit. The owner was Miss Alice de Rothschild. The Queen had great respect for money in large quantities and had a regard for the Rothschilds similar to that held by Emperor William of Germany for the Vanderbilts. Behind her back she referred to Miss de Rothschild as 'the All Powerful'. The respect was returned and the gardens were transformed to meet the Queen's convenience. Mrs Flower, who became Lady Battersea the following year, thus described a morning's outing:

Villa Victoria, Grasse, April 1 1891 . . . We had a delicious morning, with air like crystal; part of it I spent on the mountain side, *panting* after H.M.'s donkey chair. Off goes the donkey at a good firm pace, led by the groom, Randall. H.M. in a grey shawl, with a mushroom hat, a large white sunshade, sits comfortably installed in a donkey chair; then come the two Princesses close behind, walking like troopers; the two Scottish servants not quite so active; beside them romps the collie "Roy", Lady Churchill and I close up the procession, and the little pug belonging to Princess Beatrice toddles last of all. The Queen never stops, but goes steadily on to the end of Alice's delightful mountain drive, and then into the gardens of a villa belonging to a great perfume manufacturer. At the entrance of this garden Alice is continuing her road as a surprise to the Queen; but Her Majesty's keen eyes discovered signs and tokens of the new road and she was informed of Alice's plans. I told Her Majesty that it was a state secret, and begged of her not to appear as if she knew anything about it when Alice will conduct her for the first time on the road, which is being levelled, widened, and straightened by about fifty stalwart Provençal peasants. "It is a secret, a secret," said H.M. with a smile and a twinkle, like a child who thinks that the great fun of a secret is in divulging it.

At Cimiez the Queen was able to enjoy an even wider pleasance. Around her were the Villas Liserb, Coleman, Monterey, Ste. Anne and Val Rose and, through the cooperation of the owners and the local authorities, she was able to drive along six miles of private paths. In the grounds of the Villa Liserb, owned by Mr Cazalet, she did much of her morning's work. However it was soon learned that not even here was she free of prying eyes. She could be observed by passengers travelling on the newly constructed electric tramway. The directors undertook that the service would be discontinued while the Queen was in the gardens.

Cimiez, April 4 1898.—A beautiful day. Very anxious about Spain and the United States. Went to the Liserb garden with Louisa A. and sat in a sheltered spot, whilst she read to me. Leopold Hohenzollern came to luncheon, and was as pleasant as ever. Wrote a letter to the Queen of Spain, who has appealed to me, poor thing.

Took a lovely drive with Beatrice and Marie E., up the Corniche road, beyond the Observatory, turning down a steep narrow road, which passed close to the upper gate of Lord Salisbury's property. On our way down to Villefranche we met Leopold of Belgium walking. He had arrived in Villefranche Harbour on his yacht this morning. It was a most beautiful evening, and the view from the Corniche road was marvellous, on the one side the snow-clad Alps and on the other the sea.

The two hour afternoon drive was the big event of the day and, mistral or no, Victoria drove out. On occasion she returned as white as a miller from the dust. She did not appear to mind the discomfort but her ladies took a very different view. Although she had little regard for the physical strain that she imposed upon those who attended her, she was always mindful of the welfare of her horses. On long drives she would personally supervise the points at which relays would be waiting. On long hills she insisted that her Scottish servant got down from the box and walked to the top. By this time gillie Rankin was growing somewhat fat and short of breath. As he was both unaccustomed to the heat and partial to a large lunch, he was soon left behind, panting, lame, scarlet of face. Following carriages soon caught him up. The sight was too much for the French detective, whose sympathies lay more with the human than equine. He therefore opened his door and invited the Highlander to take refuge within. At first fear of the wrath ahead kept him going, but at last physical prostration forced him to accept. Crouching low, he was able to regain his breath and trot back to his post when the crest was reached. Although this subterfuge was practised on many occasions, Rankin always went in fear that he would be rumbled.

Once away from the hotel, detective Paoli never let the Queen out of his sight. He was not only guardian, but guide as well. He wrote of her:

> . . . My royal client was interested in the old legends . . . She also liked to go to the local festivals, particularly those which recalled the ancient customs of the country, such as the *festin des reproches* and the *festin des cougourdons*. The *festin des reproches* is held at Cimiez, on the first Sunday in Lent. In the old days, young couples came to make mutual admissions to each other of faults committed during the excesses of the carnival. They confessed their misdeeds ingenuously, scolded each other for form's sake, attended a religious service; then they all spread over the market-square, shaded by magnificent olive-trees, over the sands and along the neighbouring paths, where the couples became reconciled, kissed and broke the traditional *pan bagnat* together. The *festin des cougourdons* also takes place at Cimiez, on the 25th of March, the feast of the Annunciation or Lady Day. It is the most important of all the fairs; and it is attended by over twenty-five thousand visitors every year. There is one great sea of booths and rustic stalls. The Queen was very fond of this quaint exhibition. Almost every year, she went there with the Princesses to make purchases . . . On her second visit, she was not a little surprised to find that a large number of gourds or *cougourdes* (whence the name of the fair) were adorned with her coat of arms . . .

The Battles of Flowers provided the greatest fun of the holidays. The exhortations of her Battenberg grandchildren gave the Queen legitimate excuse to make spirited attacks on French officers and participants on the floats. So fast did she use up her supply of ammunition that even the Rothschild resources were strained, and a nimble footman had to be employed in collecting flowers, which had already been thrown, from the street and hurrying back with them to replenish the arsenal.

The evenings were the time for music. Puccini and Leoncavallo, François Thomé and the choristers of the Russian Imperial Chapel

Returning from a drive by the Villefranche road; in the background H.M.S. Cambrian

alternated with local quartettes and quintettes, violinists and harpists. When the supply of international and local talent ran out, Princess Beatrice and a lady-in-waiting would play duets on the piano, the Queen conducting with a knitting needle. Stars of the stage also came to the hotel:

April 22 1897. – At half-past six the celebrated and famous actress Sarah Bernhardt, who has been acting at Nice and is staying in this hotel, performed a little piece for me in the drawing-room at her own request. The play was called *Jean Marie*, by Adrien Fleuriet, quite short, only lasting half an hour. It is extremely touching, and Sarah Bernhardt's acting was quite marvellous, so pathetic and full of feeling. She appeared much affected herself, tears rolling down her cheeks. She has a most beautiful voice, and is very graceful in all her movements. The story is much the same as that of "Auld Robin Gray". The two who acted with her were also excellent, particularly the one who took the part of Jean Marie. When the play was over, Edith L. presented Sarah Bernhardt to me, and I spoke to her for a few moments. Her manner was most pleasing and gentle. She said it had been such a pleasure and honour to act for me. When I expressed the hope that she was not tired, she answered, "Cela m'a reposée."

Before the Queen retired to bed there came a short interlude when one of her daughters or ladies read out to her items from the newspapers. This was not as simple a task as it might seem, as the items selected had to be of a happy, humorous or optimistic nature. This ensured that the Queen went to bed content that all was well with the world and that its inhabitants were kindly and well-wishing. Serenity, tranquillity and the image of Albert passed with her into the dark hours. Princess Louise was of the opinion that this shielding from the more lurid and real life items which appeared in the Press gave her mother a false idea of everyday life, but she overlooked the fact that in her morning correspondence Queen Victoria dealt with more than enough of this world's major tragedies and ills to last an old woman for one day.

On occasion the sobriquet was dropped and Madame la Comtesse de Balmoral became Queen for a day.

Cimiez, April 25 1898.—Drove down to the Promenade des Anglais a little before eleven, with Beatrice, Marie E., and Drino to see a parade of the troops of the garrison. They were anyhow to have been inspected by the Governor, General Gebhardt, this morning, but he asked that the salute should be given to me. He met us on horseback before we got to the Promenade, and with his staff preceded us. Our carriage was drawn up near the pier, facing the Jardin Public. The troops, numbering about 2,000 marched past, General Caze, commanding the brigade, riding by at their head. It was a very pretty sight and the marching very fast, as is always the custom of the French. I complimented General Gebhardt on the appearance of the troops, in return for his expression of thanks for the *grand honneur* I had done them by being present. The Préfet also came up to the carriage, and in a very flowing speech expressed the same. The day was splendid, but the glare of the white road very trying to the eyes.

Cimiez, April 27 1899.—At a quarter to four started with Lenchen, Beatrice, Thora, Leopold, and the two ladies following, the gentlemen and Sir E. Monson having preceded us, for the new bridge at the end of the Boulevard Carabacel, which I was asked to open. The bridge was beautifully decorated with flags and garlands. The Maire and his

Adjunct met us on arrival, the band playing *God Save the Queen*, and he addressed a few words to me, thanking me for the honour I had conferred upon the town, also presenting a most enormous and lovely bouquet. I answered in flattering words, "Je suis bien touchée que vous m'avez demandé d'inaugurer votre nouveau pont, et je fais des voeux bien sincères pour la prospérité de la ville de Nice et des ses environs." Flowers were given to the Princesses. We then drove over the bridge, the band playing the *Marseillaise*. There were great crowds, who were all most enthusiastic.

Hotel Cimiez

During the last days of her holiday the Queen was fully occupied in deciding on the Orders, donations and presents that she should bestow. While monetary gifts to charities, churches and her pet beggars were simply arranged, Orders led to complications and jealousies. They were much sought after by the French who, as Lord Sysonby described it, regarded them 'like a rare stamp or an unknown egg to a collector'. A line had to be drawn, officials in the Préfet being included but hotel managers excluded. This much upset one manager who considered himself in the van of those contributing to the success of the visit. He had to be content with a bust of his royal client, when he had dearly hoped to be able to add the letters M.V.O. to his name.

The Queen's chief joy was in the distribution of presents. Stationmasters and hotel porters, receptionists and officials' wives—none were forgotten. With her from Windsor she brought a huge trunk, with the contents of which she could have opened a jeweller's shop. In it were watches and chains, pins, rings and bracelets, framed photographs and statuettes, pens and inkstands, cigarette holders and boxes. She kept a ledger, which she called her 'gift book', and into this each year she entered full details of the presents which she had given. She was never known to make a mistake, either by giving a cigarette holder to a non smoker, or presenting the same present twice.

In 1899 she tarried at Nice into the month of May. It seemed as if she knew that she would not see France again.

May 1 1899.—Drove to Beaulieu. Had our tea at St. Jean, where Lenchen and Beatrice joined us. Alas! my last charming drive in this paradise of nature, which I grieve to leave, as I get more attached to it every year. I shall mind returning to the sunless north, but I am so grateful for all I have enjoyed here.

Opposite: *a silk handkerchief of the time of the Boer War*

Milestone
1899
War

The Queen was at Balmoral. On 10th October she received from Mr Joseph Chamberlain copies of a telegram from the South African Republic and the British Government's reply, which led to the outbreak of the Boer War.

'When you've shouted "Rule Britannia"—when you've sung "God save the Queen"—
When you've finished killing Kruger with your mouth—
Will you kindly drop a shilling in my little tambourine
For a gentleman in kharki ordered South?'

Rudyard Kipling, 4th November, 1899.

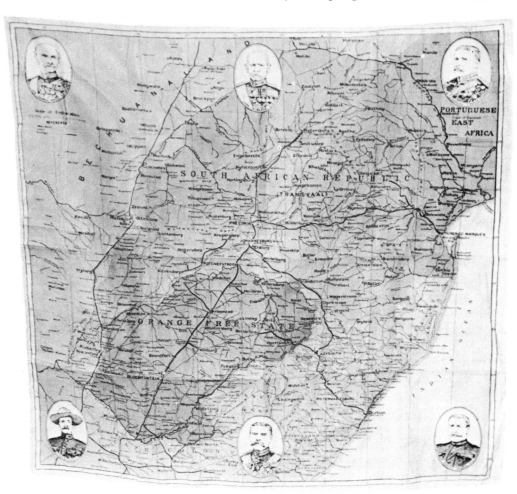

Journey Fifty-eight
1899

Curtain Fall at Bristol

ON Wednesday, 15th November 1899, Queen Victoria performed
her last public duty in the English provinces. She travelled to
Bristol to open the new Royal Convalescent Home, built to
commemorate the long span of her reign. She was supported by three of
her children, Arthur, Helena and Beatrice.

Sixty-nine years had passed since the then eleven year old Princess
Victoria of Kent had visited Bristol with her mother. This tour of 1830
was the first of the 'Royal Progresses' which had so annoyed King William
IV. Now, in her reply to the address of welcome, she recalled her first
sight of the 'ancient city, so rich in associations with history and with my
colonies over the seas'. Bristol also became richer by two Knights, Mr
Edward Payson Wills, President of the Home, and the Lord Mayor, Mr
Herbert Ashman knelt down. The Duke of Connaught passed a drawn
sword to his mother, and steadied it as she touched the Mayor's shoulder.
'Good old Sir Herbert', roared the crowd.

At the new Home the Queen's carriage stopped before a splendid
pavilion. There the celebrities awaited her—the Duchess of Beaufort,
Lord and Lady Somerset, the Bishop of Bristol, Sir M. Hicks Beach,
Sir M. White Ridley, the Lord and Lady Mayoress and the Lord Chamberlain. Miss Violet Wills, dressed all in white, stepped forward and presented a bouquet of roses and lilies. Then a plate, with an electric button
in the centre, was handed to the Queen. She pressed the button, the
trumpets blared, and the doors of the Home swung back. So the Queen
came to the end of seventy years of openings.

Queen Victoria always had a soft spot for old soldiers and liked to listen
to their memories. On this day at Bristol she met two. The first old
soldier was the son of the man who had sounded the charge at Waterloo.
The name of the second was Maby. He was small and very old and he
was escorted up to the Queen's carriage by a policeman. In his hand he
held a cornet. He told the Queen that it was the cornet that he had played
in the reception for her at Bristol in 1830.

Journey Fifty-nine
1900

In the Wards of Netley

O N 19th May 1856 Queen Victoria laid the foundation stone of the
Royal Victoria Hospital at Netley, near Southampton. She lavished
much attention on this military hospital. She knitted a woollen
scarf and requested that it should be 'placed round the shoulders of a
dying officer'. This practice was carried out until such time as it was
noticed that the sight of the scarf being carried down the corridors had an
unfortunate effect on the morale of patients, each fearing that the work
of the Queen's hands was about to be presented to himself. So the scarf
was put on view in a glass case, where it became an object of historical
interest rather than a portent of the finale.

Once again Netley was in the forefront of the Queen's thoughts. The
tide in South Africa was turning. Kimberley had been relieved and General
Buller was nearing Ladysmith. The wounded were being brought home,
and the hospital ship *Princess of Wales* had just arrived at Southampton,
to be met by the Princess herself.

Windsor Castle, February 27.—Received during breakfast the following
telegram: "General Cronje and his whole force capitulated at day-
break this morning, unconditionally. He is now a prisoner in my
camp. Hope H.M.'s Government will consider this satisfactory, occurring as it does on the anniversary of Majuba. ROBERTS." We are
all greatly rejoiced, for it is indeed grand news.

At 11.20 left for Netley. Sir Baker Russell received us at the station,
and the principal authorities received us at the door of the hospital.
Went up in the lift to the second floor, where all the wounded were
assembled, almost all, with few exceptions, being able to stand in the
corridors. They looked wonderfully well, considering how badly they
had been wounded. Far the greatest number were from the Highland
Brigade, which suffered so at Magersfontein. I handed flowers to those
in bed. There were a good many Guardsmen, and also men from the
Irish regiments. Then we went to the wards and corridors in which

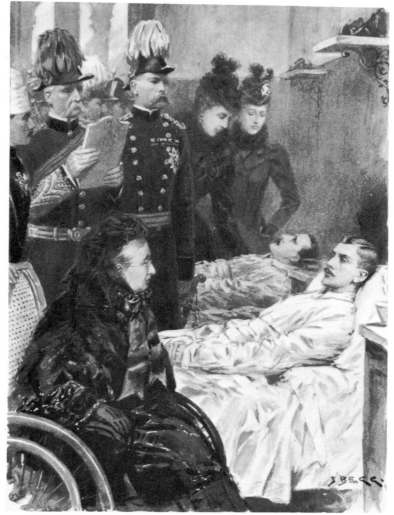

were the sick. It was sad to see so many with heart disease brought on by overmarching and hard work.

Another long telegram arrived from Lord Roberts, saying that the prisoners numbered 4,000, and six guns were taken. Cronje had asked to be kindly treated, and that his wife, grandson, secretary, adjutant, and servants might be with him wherever he was sent. This was granted, and they were all despatched yesterday to Cape Town. Georgie, May, and their children arrived during the evening.[1]

[1] Edward ('David'), afterwards Prince of Wales, Edward VIII and Duke of Windsor, born 1894; Albert ('Bertie'), afterwards Duke of York and George VI, born 1895; and Mary, afterwards Princess Royal and Countess of Harewood, born 1897. Henry, afterwards Duke of Gloucester, was born on 31st March 1900.

Back to Erin

ON 3rd April 1900 two old ladies rocked and rolled out from Holyhead. The sea ran high and the glass was falling. The Queen and her paddle steamer, *Victoria and Albert*, were off on the last of many journeys that they had made together. A new royal yacht had been built and had already been to sea.

It had been the Queen's intention to take her spring holiday at Bordighera, but Continental criticism of Britain's role in the South African war had dimmed the attraction of the Mediterranean sun, while the reports from the front of the gallantry of the Irish troops had lit in her a bright flame which was all consuming. She decided that she must thank the Irish in person.

She had not crossed St. George's Channel since August 1861, at the time when the Prince of Wales was in camp at the Curragh and about to yield to the temptation of Nellie Clifden. While there were many reasons why she had not returned, predominant was the case of Albert's statue. In the dark years of her mourning she had arranged for his likeness to be fashioned, carefully packed and despatched to Dublin. The Mayor and Corporation had refused to accept it. The day of its return unopened, to Windsor, was one of the blackest of her reign.

Now all was forgiven. The threats of the Fenians, the coffins which had greeted the Prince of Wales in the streets of Cork in 1885, the absence of greetings from Ireland on the Jubilee days, all faded clean away. *Sic omnia transeunt*—even Albert.

Courage was to her the greatest attribute of man. She had told Mr Balfour in December, when the news from the Cape was very bad indeed: 'Please understand that there is no one depressed in this house; we are not interested in the possibilities of defeat; they do not exist.' In March she had issued the following instruction: 'Her Majesty the Queen is pleased to order that in future, upon St. Patrick's Day, all ranks in Her Majesty's Irish regiments shall wear, as a distinction, a sprig of shamrock in their head-dress, to commemorate the gallantry of her Irish soldiers during the recent battles in South Africa.' She did more than that. She decided upon the creation of a battalion of Irish Guards and, because she dearly loved a secret, she ordered that the news should be withheld until she reached Dublin.

As the royal yacht wallowed on its south-westerly course, Queen Victoria was a prisoner in her cabin, sickness her lot and her only moral comfort the words of Empress Eugénie—'Queens do not drown'. Others in her party were suffering the same fate, yet not by one iota was the angry sea allowed to interfere with the prescribed rules of the galley. Nine course meals were served on time, regardless of whether they were pushed away untouched or became burnt offerings to the fishes. For poor young Gabriel Tschumi,[1] an apprentice chef from Switzerland, the ordeal was both enlightening and terrifying. His duties had to be done, *mal de mer* or no. His primary task was to fetch supplies from the larder, which was situated below the groaning paddle-wheel. He expected that each journey would be his last and, as he clasped pheasant and pâté, he feared that, when the yacht foundered, no one would think of keeping a place in the boats for an apprentice trapped far below.

As there were signs that the storm would grow worse and the Queen had already suffered enough, the time-table was abandoned and the yacht made the shelter of Kingstown long before she was due. All there was quiet but the guns of the warships brought the people racing into the streets, and the Duke of Connaught, commanding the troops in Ireland, and the Lord Lieutenant made a spectacular dash across the harbour in a pinnace.

Viceregal Lodge, Dublin, April 4.—We landed at the Victoria Wharf at half-past eleven, being received by Lord and Lady Cadogan, Arthur, Louischen and their children, also by Lord Dufferin, and Lord Meath. We three wore bunches of real shamrocks, and my bonnet and parasol were embroidered with silver shamrocks. On entering my carriage, in which I sat alone, Lenchen and Beatrice opposite me, an Address was presented from the Chairman and Councillors of Kingstown, and I said a few words in handing my reply.

The procession, consisting of four carriages, then started, mine coming last. Arthur rode near my carriage all the way, and I had a travelling escort of the King's Dragoon Guards. The whole route from Kingstown to Dublin was much crowded, all the people cheering loudly, and the decorations were beautiful. For some distance the road was kept by bluejackets, but in many parts of the more country roads there was scarcely a policeman or soldier. There were many loyal inscriptions put up, suspended across the road, the following being two of them:

[1] Afterwards chef to Edward VII, George V and Queen Mary.

*Viceregal Lodge, Phoenix Park, showing also the view of the
Wicklow hills in the distance*

"Blest for ever is she who relied
On Erin's honour and Erin's pride,"
and

"In her a thousand virtues closed,
As Mother, Wife and Queen."

At Ballsbridge the travelling escort was replaced by a Sovereign's
escort of Life Guards, and a large number of military and other mounted
officials joined the procession.

At Leeson Bridge an archway was erected, a facsimile of the entrance
to Biggotrath Castle, and according to the ancient custom the gates
were closed till the procession approached, when Athlone Pursuivant-
at-Arms advanced saying, "I demand to be admitted to the presence
of the Lord Mayor". At the same moment the bugler on the top of
the arch blew a blast. Athlone passed in, and the gates were reclosed.
Bowing to the Lord Mayor he said: "My Lord Mayor of Dublin, I
seek admission to the City of Dublin for her Most Gracious Majesty
the Queen"; the Lord Mayor replying, "On behalf of the city, I tender
to her Majesty the most hearty welcome to this ancient city, and on
her arrival the gate shall be thrown open on the instant". This was
done, and I passed in, my carriage stopping opposite the Lord Mayor,
who with the aldermen, councillors, and officials received me and
presented the old city keys, twelve in number, and 600 years old; the
city sword was offered by the Lord Mayor (Mr Devereux Pile). A loyal
address was then read and presented to me in a beautiful gold casket.

I answered, "I thank you for your loyal address and this hearty reception.
I am very glad to find myself again in Ireland". I handed him the written
answer.

The drive lasted two hours and a half. We went all along the quays in
the poorer parts of the town, where thousands had gathered together
and gave me a wildly enthusiastic greeting. At Trinity College the
students sang *God Save the Queen*, and shouted themselves hoarse. The
cheers and often almost screams were quite deafening. Even the Nation-
alists in front of the City Hall seemed to forget their politics and cheered
and waved their hats. It was really a wonderful reception I got and most
gratifying.

Lord and Lady Cadogan received and welcomed me at the door of
the Viceregal Lodge. I recognised the outside of the building, but not
the inside. I was rolled a good way to the staircase, up which I was
carried, as there was no lift. I have very comfortable rooms.

Lenchen came in with some startling news from Bertie, who had been
shot at as their train was leaving Brussels. A man[2] jumped on to the
step of the railway carriage in which he and Alix were sitting, and fired
straight at them.

For the Queen, one of the high-lights of the visit was the great gathering
of children in Phoenix Park. They came from all parts of Ireland. Sadly,
there was a hitch in the travelling arrangements of a schoolmistress and her
squad from distant Mayo. Shortly before the proceedings began a telegram was received from her requesting that the programme be held up
until she and her charges arrived. Later the Queen gave a little show of
her own to the boys and girls from the Atlantic coast.

Viceregal Lodge, April 7.–Drove with Lenchen and Beatrice, the
ladies in a second carriage, to the public part of the Phoenix Park, where
52,000 school-children from all parts of Ireland were assembled with
their masters and mistresses. It was a wonderful sight, and the noise
of the children cheering was quite overpowering. I drove down the
line so that they could all see me, and stopped for a moment to receive
a nose-gay, presented by the twin daughters of Lady Arnott, who,
with the Lady Mayoress, was presented by Lady Denbigh.

Each afternoon the Queen went on drives of twenty miles or so. The
weather was hot and the jog pace eternal. To begin with the posse around
her carriage consisted of six members of the Constabulary, two equerries,
two grooms and an outrider. It was the plan that the same posse should
ride out daily, but after several expeditions there were few intact backsides

[2] Sipido, an Italian.

Children's Day in Phoenix Park

left among them. It was therefore decided the numbers of riders should be decreased. As to date there had been no greater sign of hostility to the Queen than the remark of a husband who, in compliment to his wife's cry of 'God save the Queen', had added 'And down with the Minister-in-Attendance', it was felt that this could be safely done. Posterior skins were therefore given the chance to heal and harden.

Apart from the saddle exercise, the duties of the equerries were not arduous. The Queen slept most of the time. It was only necessary to ensure that the Princess beside her was apprised of the presence of small gatherings by the roadside, so that she might prod her mother into sufficient wakefulness to produce the wave and smile. The afternoon siesta was most essential for the Queen, for there were public engagements most mornings and dinner parties most evenings.

Viceregal Lodge, April 17.—After breakfast saw a quantity of lace and embroideries done by the very poorest people and quite beautiful. Have altogether made many purchases from the various local industries.

After luncheon drove with Lenchen and Ismay S.[3] in a landau with postilions and a travelling escort of the 2nd Life Guards, the equerries riding. We drove into Dublin to the Adelaide Hospital, situated in the very poorest part of the town. The street in which it stands is a very narrow one, and the people literally thronged round the carriage, giving me the most enthusiastic welcome, as indeed I receive everywhere. Lord Denbigh[4] awaited me at the hospital, and presented the Committee of Management, as well as all the doctors and the Lady Superintendent, Miss Fitzpatrick, who gave me a bouquet.

On leaving the hospital we drove by White Friars Place, Stephen's Green, and Leeson Bridge. We passed through the picturesque village of Donnybrook to Sandford Road, where the escort left us, and the Mounted Constabulary replaced them. The road was very pretty, through lanes, everywhere crowds of people, cheering wildly and waving flags. On our arrival at Mount Anville, the Convent of the Sacred Heart, we passed up an avenue decorated with Venetian masts and garlands. Were received by the Rev Mother Stuart, Superior Vicar of the Houses, the Rev Mother Roche, local Superior, the Bishop of Canea (Dr Donnolly), and Canon Matthews, all of whom were presented by Lord Denbigh. The pupils of the Convent and some from the other sister houses, numbering between four or five hundred, were drawn up, as well as about fifty of the nuns. The children were all dressed in white, the boarders carrying arum lilies in their hands,

[3] Lady Southampton.
[4] Lord-in-waiting 1897–1901. The Queen had asked him to be in attendance as he was a Catholic.

whilst the others carried daffodils, and they all sang the National Anthem. Two of the girls gave me a beautiful nosegay, and the Mother Superior kissed my hand. There were great outbursts of cheering as I drove away.

April 19.–Went out with Lenchen and Ismay S(outhampton), and saw all my Jubilee Nurses, who had come from different parts of Ireland on the terrace in front of the house. I had previously given to Lady Cadogan, who had presented the nurses to me, the 3rd class of the Victoria and Albert order. In the afternoon drove with Beatrice and Ismay S. to Clontarf, along by the seashore. A great many people along the road cheering and waving flags. We then drove through St. Anne's, Lord Ardilaun's place, which is beautiful, and has a very pretty approach to it. Stopped a moment at the house, where were Lord and Lady Ardilaun. The latter gave me a large nosegay of primroses, to-day being "Primrose Day".

Viceregal Lodge, April 20.–Very warm. Went with Beatrice and Ismay S., Lord Denbigh, and Sir A. Bigge to the Zoological Gardens, going in by pony chair. It is close by, just across the road, beautifully managed and most interesting. The lions are the great feature, and they have some splendid specimens.

In the afternoon drove with Lenchen and Beatrice in a landau and four, but without an escort, to the Meath Hospital, where Lord Denbigh met us and presented the authorities, doctors, and matron, the latter giving me a lovely nosegay. There were great crowds and much enthusiasm. We then drove over Portobello Bridge through the village of Rathmines, which was gaily decorated, to Rathfarnham, where we drove through the grounds to the Convent of Loretto. Here we were greeted with much cheering by a vast crowd. In front of the Convent were grouped 200 nuns and 600 pupils, these latter all dressed white, which made a charming contrast to the nuns in their dark garb. The National Anthem was played by the orchestra of the Convent. There were six harps, one being played by a nun. I received a beautiful bouquet from one of the pupils, also an embroidered harp, and an illuminated card.

The review in Phoenix Park, with the Duke of Connaught in command, attracted the greatest crowd of the visit and only the drastic efforts of the escort prevented the Queen and her daughters being joined in their carriage by a band of fervent admirers. An unusual attraction for such proceedings was the inclusion of mounted ladies, among them the Duchess of Connaught and Countess Cadogan, riding with the staff, and excitement was added when some deer, roused from their pastures, intermingled with the horses and marching men.

Driving down Sackville Street in semi-state

Viceregal Lodge, April 21. – Very fine and warm. Sat in the garden. Later we were all photographed by Lafayette. In the afternoon at four drove in the large carriage and four, Lenchen and Beatrice sitting backwards, to the Review Ground called the Fifteen Acres. Had a Sovereign's escort of Life Guards. We drove through enormous crowds, who cheered tremendously. I received the royal salute on arrival, then drove slowly down the line, Arthur riding next to my carriage. On returning to the saluting point the march past took place. The Naval

Brigade Field Batteries and Bluejackets with their maxim guns came first, then the Marines, 2,100 from the Channel Fleet, Sir Harry Rawson standing by my carriage as they passed. Next came all the troops, the little boys of the Hibernian School bringing up the rear. At the end of the review, Arthur called for three cheers for me. We then drove home amidst such tremendous cheering as I have never heard. Only the ladies to dinner; afterwards Madame Ella Russell sang to us quite charmingly.

The Queen sailed for Holyhead on the 26th. She gave out her presents, which included £1,000 to the poor of Dublin and the promise of a silver cup to the Corporation. On the deck of *Victoria and Albert* she handed Victorian Order medals to twenty-six policemen who had ridden beside her carriage. Then she opened her 'gift trunk' and distributed souvenirs to all those who had accompanied her.

The sun was shining and the sea as smooth as glass. The Queen slept.

With her donkey at Viceregal
Lodge, 1900

Journey Sixty-one
1900

Mafeking and Wellington

THE Prince Consort did not approve of English boys of the privileged classes. Neither did he like their habits. Judging by the practices then extant in some public schools, there were certain grounds for his prejudice. When, therefore, it was proposed that a college for the education of the sons of officers should be built at Sandhurst 'in memory of the dear old Duke', and named after him, Albert saw the chance to' do some cleaning up with a new broom. He embarked on the planning stage with the same enthusiasm and love of detail that he had previously displayed in the reorganisation of Buckingham Palace and the Windsor farms, the building of Osborne and Balmoral and the staging of the Great Exhibition. He gave much thought to the selection of the site, made suggestions for the design of the buildings and watched over their construction. He was appointed chairman of the governing body. It was on his suggestion that Dr Benson,[1] the first headmaster, spent the summer prior to taking up his appointment in Germany, studying the educational system there.

The Queen opened Wellington College in 1859 and awarded an annual medal for good conduct. The rules for this prize were composed by her husband and any boy complying with them in exactitude would have immediately qualified for the angle choir. Other helpful gestures of the Prince Consort were the presentation of a library and the pattern for a school uniform. Unfortunately, in its finished form, this uniform bore a strong resemblance to that worn by the personnel of the railway company which served the area. Lord Derby, arriving at the station to attend a College occasion, handed his ticket to a senior boy who was waiting to greet his *mater*. The boy was furious.

Among the Queen's human contributions to the College was the eldest son of Prince and Princess Henry of Battenberg. He was Prince Alexander, known as 'Drino', born in 1886. To 'Drino' and his brothers Prince

[1] Afterwards Archbishop of Canterbury.

Henry was rather a frightening figure, seldom seen, who died too soon to be brought into focus. Yet to their sister, Ena he was both confidant and hero. Queen Victoria favoured the boys, as she always did, to the disadvantage of the only girl. With their mother fully occupied in assisting the Queen in state and other duties, and dominated by her, it was to their grandmother that the Princes turned for advice and treats. Thus their childhood was spent in a make believe world of long ago. When 'Drino'

A Plate commemorating the relief of Mafeking

arrived at Wellington, the boys looked upon him as Little Lord Fauntleroy, while he considered them a set of bloodthirsty hooligans.

'Drino' was unaccustomed to handling money and soon spent the allowance which had been doled out to him at the beginning of term. Accordingly, he wrote to his grandmother for replenishment. She replied in the negative, telling him that he must learn to live within his means.

A few days later a further letter arrived from Wellington. In this the Queen was informed by her grandson that she need worry no more about the money, as he had sold her last letter to another boy for thirty shillings. In later life, when Marquess of Carisbrooke, 'Drino' became the first member of the Royal Family to enter business.

The day when Queen Victoria visited him at Wellington was one which he was always to remember.

Windsor Castle, May 19. – The following telegram was received from Major-General Baden-Powell, dated 17th May; "Happy to report Mafeking successfully relieved to-day. Northern and southern columns joined hands on 15th, attacked enemy yesterday, 16th, entirely defeating them with loss. Relieving force marched into Mafeking this morning at nine. Relief and defence force combined, attacked enemy laager, shelled them out, nearly capturing Slyman, and took large amount of ammunition and stores. Townspeople and garrison of Mafeking heartily grateful for their release."

Started at half-past three with Arthur and Jane C. for Wellington College, Beatrice having preceded us. Changed horses at Bracknell. The whole way along people turned out and cheered, especially where there was an immense crowd, who came up quite close to the carriage, cheering loudly, and finally singing *God Save the Queen*. Flags were hung up and pictures of General Baden-Powell exhibited in honour of the relief. The people are quite mad with delight, and London is said to be indescribable. Reached Wellington College at five, Colonel Legge meeting us on horseback outside the gates and Sir F. Edwards outside the college, where he presented the headmaster, Mr Pollock.[2] Beatrice, with Drino, was also there. Went first into the Chapel, where Mr Pollock showed us the memorial to the late Archbishop Benson, who was first headmaster at Wellington. Then was rolled in my chair to the Library and big dining-hall, through the Cloisters, re-entered my carriage, and drove to Mr Pollock's house, where we had tea. Sir Lintorn Simmons was there, who is one of the Governors, and lives close by. Mr Bevir, one of the masters in whose house Drino is, was presented, as well as his wife.

Left again at six. All the boys were drawn up, including the volunteers, and the head boy presented a bouquet in the college colours. There was tremendous cheering as we drove off, Arthur and Beatrice being with me. A very fine arch was put up near Wellington College, on which was inscribed, "Welcome to the Queen of Mafeking". Bracknell was beautifully decorated.

[2] Afterwards Bishop of Norwich.

Finishing Line

2nd of January. The Queen lay dying at Osborne. As morning turned to afternoon she raised herself slightly from her pillows and said:

'Oh, if I were only at Nice, I should recover.'

Bibliography

Letters of Queen Victoria, 1837–1901. 1st series edited by A. C. Benson and Viscount Esher; 2nd and 3rd series by G. E. Buckle (John Murray, 1907–32).

The Life of H.R.H. the Prince Consort (5 vols.). By Sir Theodore Martin (Smith, Elder & Co., 1874).

The Girlhood of Queen Victoria (2 vols.). Edited by Viscount Esher (John Murray, 1912).

Leaves from the Journal of Our Life in the Highlands (1848–1861). Edited by Arthur Helps (Smith, Elder & Co., 1868).

The Early Years of H.R.H. the Prince Consort. Lieut.-General The Hon. C. Grey (Smith, Elder & Co., 1867).

George, Duke of Cambridge (2 vols.). Edited by Edgar Sheppard (Longmans, Green, 1907).

Letters of the Prince Consort, 1831–1861. Edited by Dr Kurt Jagow (John Murray, 1938).

Dearest Child: Letters between Queen Victoria and the Princess Royal, 1858–1861. Edited by Roger Fulford (Evans, 1964).

Dearest Mama: Letters between Queen Victoria and the Crown Princess of Prussia, 1861–1864. Edited by Roger Fulford (Evans, 1968).

Letters of the Empress Frederick. Edited by Sir Frederick Ponsonby (Macmillan, 1928).

Queen Victoria at Windsor and Balmoral: Letters from Princess Victoria of Prussia, 1889. Edited by James Pope-Hennessy (George Allen and Unwin, 1959).

Alice, Grand Duchess of Hesse: Letters to H.M. the Queen (John Murray, 1885).

The Empress Frederick Writes to Sophie. Edited by Arthur Gould Lee (Faber & Faber, 1955).

Correspondence of Sarah Spencer, Lady Lyttleton, 1787–1870. Edited by Mrs Hugh Wyndham (John Murray, 1912).

Letters of Lady Augusta Stanley, 1849–1863. Edited by the Dean of Windsor and Hector Bolitho (Gerald Howe, 1927).

Later Letters of Lady Augusta Stanley, 1864–1876. Edited by the Dean of Windsor and Hector Bolitho (Jonathan Cape, 1929).

Reminiscences of Court and Diplomatic Life (2 vols.). Lady Bloomfield (Kegan Paul, 1883).

Life with Queen Victoria: Marie Mallet's Letters from Court, 1887–1901. Edited by Victor Mallet (John Murray, 1968).

The English Empress. Egon Caesar Conte Corti (Cassell, 1957).

Reminiscences. Lady Constance Battersea (Macmillan, 1922).

My Memoirs. Princess Victoria of Prussia (Eveleigh Nash & Grayson, 1929).

My Memories of Six Reigns. H.H. Princess Marie Louise (Evans, 1956).

The Queen Thanks Sir Howard. Mary Howard McClintock (John Murray, 1946).

Recollections of Three Reigns. Sir Frederick Ponsonby (Lord Sysonby) (Eyre & Spottiswoode, 1951).

Collections and Recollections. George W. E. Russell (Nelson, 1903).

Leaves from a Journal. Queen Victoria (André Deutsch, 1961).

H.R.H. the Duke of Connaught and Strathearn. Major-General Sir George Aston (Harrap, 1929).

King Edward the Seventh. Sir Philip Magnus (John Murray, 1964).

King Edward VII (2 vols.). Sir Sidney Lee (Macmillan, 1927).

The Private Life of Queen Alexandra. Hans Roger Madol (Hutchinson, 1940).

Christian IX. Hans Roger Madol (Collins, 1939).

Prince Consort. Frank B. Chancellor (Philip Allan, 1931).

The Coburgs. Edmund B. D'Auvergne (Stanley Paul, 1911).

Queen Victoria's Sister. Harold A. Albert (Robert Hale, 1967).

The Prince Consort. Roger Fulford (Macmillan, 1949).

On the Queen's Errands. Captain Philip Wynter (Pitman, 1906).

My Royal Clients. Xavier Paoli (Hodder & Stoughton).

The Empress Brown. Tom Cullen (The Bodley Head, 1969).

Old Diaries. Lord Ronald Sutherland Gower (John Murray, 1902).

Lady de Rothschild and her Daughters. Lucy Cohen (John Murray, 1935).

Overture to Victoria. McKenzie Porter (Longmans Green, Toronto, 1961).

Queen Victoria. Richard R. Holmes (Boussod, Valadon, 1897).

Queen Victoria. Sidney Lee (Smith, Elder, 1902).

Queen Victoria's Relations. Meriel Buchanan (Cassell, 1954).

V.R.I.: Her Life and Empire. The Duke of Argyll (Eyre & Spottiswoode, 1902).

Queen Victoria. E. F. Benson (Longmans, Green, 1935).

Victoria R.I. Elizabeth Longford (Weidenfeld & Nicolson, 1964).

Victoria: Her Life and Reign. Alfred E. Knight (Partridge, 1897).

The Mother of Queen Victoria. D. M. Stuart (Macmillan, 1942).

Victoria, Queen and Ruler. Emily Crawford (Simpkin, Marshall, 1903).

Life of Her Majesty Queen Victoria. G. Barnett Smith (Routledge, 1897).

Daughters of Queen Victoria. E. F. Benson (Cassell, 1939).

Concerning Queen Victoria and Her Son. Sir George Arthur (Robert Hale, 1943).

The Private Life of the Queen. By One of Her Majesty's Servants (C. Arthur Pearson, 1897).

Royal Chef. Gabriel Tschumi (William Kimber, 1954).

A Queen at Home. Vera Watson (W. H. Allen, 1954).

A History of the Scottish People. The Rev Thomas Thomson (Blackie & Son, 1889).

The Life and Times of H.R.H. Princess Beatrice. M. E. Sara (Stanley Paul, 1945).

The Life of the Queen (3 vols.). Sarah Tytler (J. S. Virtue & Co.).

"Fritz" of Prussia: Germany's Second Emperor. Lucy Taylor (Nelson, 1891).

King Alfonso. Robert Sencourt (Faber & Faber, 1942).

The Youthful Queen Victoria. Dormer Creston (Macmillan, 1952).

Nicholas and Alexandra. Robert K. Massie (Victor Gollancz, 1968).

Behind the Throne. Paul H. Emden (Hodder & Stoughton, 1934).

The Prince Imperial. Katherine John (Putnam, 1939).

Napoleon the Third. Walter Geer (Jonathan Cape, 1921).

Illustrated London News
Punch
Graphic
Truth

The Times
Morning Post
Daily Telegraph

Index

I. Places

Sub-divided by areas as follows:

Index

II. People